the Art of
LEADERSHIP

CULTIVATING
AN EARLY CHILDHOOD CURRICULUM

Exchange Press
17725 NE 65th Street • B-275
Redmond, WA 98052
(800) 221-2864 • www.ChildCareExchange.com

THE ART of LEADERSHIP

Cultivating an Early Childhood Curriculum

The Art of Leadership series replaces the popular Exchange Press textbook, *The Art of Leadership: Managing Early Childhood Organizations*. The entire series demonstrates the great complexity of an early childhood leader's job. Each volume expresses the importance of one aspect of this role. Each leader will need to prioritize all these roles based on many factors, including the skills that reside within the members of his team.

These articles were originally published in *Exchange Magazine*.
Every attempt has been made to update information on authors and other contributors to these articles. We apologize for any biographical information that is not current. *Exchange* is a bimonthly management magazine for directors, owners, and teachers of early childhood programs. For more information about *Exchange* and other Exchange Press publications for directors and teachers, contact:

Exchange Press
17725 NE 65th Street • B-275
Redmond, WA 98052
(800) 221-2864 • www.ChildCareExchange.com

ISBN 978-0-942702-62-0

Printed in Korea by Four Colour Print Group, Louisville, Kentucky

© Exchange Press, 2017

Cover Design: Scott Bilstad

This book may not be reproduced in whole or in part by any means without written permission of the publisher.
Evaluation forms are an exception — they may be photocopied for your own use.

the Art of LEADERSHIP
CULTIVATING AN EARLY CHILDHOOD CURRICULUM

Introduction

The Leader as Keeper of the Faith *by Roger Neugebauer* 6

Chapter 1: Understanding Child Development

Friendship — Loving: What Early Childhood Education is All About *by Ashley Montagu* 10

What Should Young Children be Learning? *by Lilian G. Katz* 13

The Effects of Culture on Thinking *by Barbara Bowman* 16

Primed for Learning: The Young Child's Mind *by Karen Stephens* 20

Building Brains One Relationship at a Time *by Gina Lebedeva* 27

The Wisdom of Children *by Ruth A. Wilson* 40

Chapter 2: Crafting the Curriculum

Designing a Curriculum for Early Childhood Teachers
and Caregivers *by Lawrence J. Schweinhart* 46

Everyday Differentiation: How Administrators Support Differentiation of
Curriculum and Instruction in Early Childhood Classrooms *by Ann Gadzikowski* 51

The Importance of Order *by Jim Greenman* 58

Taking a Stand on Standards of Experience *by Lilian G. Katz* 61

Responding to Racial and Ethnic Diversity in Early Childhood Programs *by Francis Wardle* 64

Preparing Bicultural, Bilingual Children to Succeed in School *by Hazel Osborn* 69

A Journey towards Inclusion *by Kate Jordan-Downs* 73

The Intangibles in the Early Childhood Classroom *by Carol B. Hillman* 78

Universal Early Childhood Curriculum Principles
by Lawrence J. Schweinhart and Diane Trister Dodge 82

Chapter 3: Designing the Space

The Physical Environment: A Powerful Regulator of Experience *by Elizabeth Prescott* 88

Places to Live: Important Dimensions of Child Care Settings *by Jim Greenman* 92

How to Create an Environment that Counteracts Stereotyping *by Alice Sterling Honig* 97

Places for ALL Children: Building Environments for Differing Needs *by Diane Trister Dodge* ... 104

Children Need to Live in the Real World *by Jim Greenman* 110

Planning Intentionally for Children's Outdoor Environments
The Gift of Change *by Nancy Rosenow* 113

Are Your Children in Times Square?
Moving from Confinement to Engagement *by Sandra Duncan and Michelle Salcedo* 117

Creating Environments that Intrigue and Delight Children and Adults
by Wendy Shepherd and Jennifer Eaton 123

Chapter 4: Evaluating the Program

Looking at the Quality of Early Childhood Programs *by Lilian G. Katz* 132

Measuring the Quality of Early Childhood Organizations
Guidelines for Effective Evaluation Tools *by Ann S. Epstein* 134

Learning to See… Seeing to Learn
The Role of Observation in Early Childhood Development *by Diane C. MacLean* 139

Are We Doing Things Just Because We've Always Done Them this Way?
by Kim Turner 144

Questions to Guide Our Work *by Margie Carter* 147

Conducting a Realistic Self-assessment with the *Environmental Rating Scale*
by Thelma Harms 152

Seeing Children's Lively Minds at Work *by Deb Curtis* 155

Be the Change You Wish to See in Your Program *by Elizabeth Beavers and Donna Kirkwood* 162

The Leader as Keeper of the Faith

by Roger Neugebauer

When I as pursuing my master's degree in Child Care Administration, my advisor, Gwen Morgan, insisted that I study the works of experts from the world of business. Four decades later, I still remember the observation of management guru Peter Drucker that the leader of an organization is "the keeper of the faith." His point was that the leader needs to thoroughly understand, and be committed to, the vision, goals, and values of the organization in order to keep everyone in the organization focused on these fundamentals.

Another business expert, Charles Garfield, put it another way: "Truly effective leaders have a sense of being involved in a creative mission that matters." They have a vision for their organization that gives their work meaning, that inspires them to act.

This vision not only inspires the leader, it also infects all those in the organization. Warren Bennis reports that "leaders' visions are compelling and pull people toward them. Intensity coupled with commitment is magnetic."

One would expect that in a caring profession such as early childhood, that a director would clearly be a keeper of the faith — a person deeply committed to the organization's strategies for making a difference in the lives of children and families. And, of course, that is largely true. However, there are scenarios where this is not so much the case….

The burned-out director. The job of a director is hugely demanding with crises popping up all the time — a lead teacher calling in sick at 7:00 AM, payroll approaching with only a few dollars in the bank, a parent of a bitten child angrily demanding the ouster of the biter, the toilet in the preschool room overflowing again. In such a stressful role, it may be hard for a director to maintain her enthusiasm, to remain fully committed to the lofty goals for the center. Too often worn down directors shift from being keepers of the faith to maintainers of the status quo, just trying to keep the center going from day to day.

The business manager as director. Sometimes when a center is experiencing hard times, the board of directors or owner of the center decides that what is needed is to bring in a skilled business person to shape the operations of the center. While it is often the case that a director well versed in the pedagogical issues of running a high-quality program may lack enough business skills to keep the center afloat, having the person at the top who lacks pedagogical understanding can be just as dangerous. If this person is making decisions primarily based on dollars and cents, she may make decisions that go against the vision and goals of the organization. She may veto the plan to convert the playground into a nature-based classroom because it is 'too expensive,' or fire a teacher who may have a prickly personality in spite of being far and away the best teacher in the center, or come down hard on struggling parents who are late in paying fees.

The ever-changing board. Some non-profit centers have by-laws that call for boards of directors to be reinvented every one or two years. Likewise, centers operating in religious facilities may be answerable to boards of trustees that change periodically. What this requires is that the director, this lonely keeper of the faith, must continually be educating new decision makers about the goals and values of the program. I once helped establish a new center in a church and worked with the director to advocate for operating a high-quality NAEYC-accredited service for members of the church and families in the community. Then once we got the board of trustees excited about and committed to our goals, the trustees were replaced by next year's volunteers who could not understand why we needed to spend so much money on 'babysitting' and why we should serve families who didn't belong to the church.

A cog in the system. When a center is a part of a larger system, the leader at this center may not have complete independence in setting and pursuing goals. This is true whether this system is a large Head Start agency, a social service agency such as a YMCA, a for-profit chain, or a center operated by a business for its employees. If the overall organization allows the leadership of individual centers to participate in setting the goals and defining the curriculum, these leaders will be more likely to buy into the demands of the overall organization. However, if the center leader is simply carrying out the plans developed higher up, this leader may be less motivated to inspire her team to carry out these plans.

The bottom-line is that it's not always easy being the keeper of the faith. But no matter the scenario, the staff in a center are more likely to deliver appropriate outcomes for children and families if the center director…

- is well aware of and fully committed to the goals of the organization.
- inspires team members to work toward the achievement of these goals.
- closely monitors the center's daily adherence to these goals.
- leads the team in periodically reviewing these goals and updating these goals.
- understands and supports the curriculum that has been designed or selected for achieving these goals.
- conveys to parents, regulators, and funders the importance of these goals.

Roger Neugebauer

Roger Neugebauer is founding publisher of *Exchange Magazine* and a co-founder of the World Forum Foundation.

CULTIVATING
AN EARLY CHILDHOOD CURRICULUM

CHAPTER 1
Understanding Child Development

Friendship — Loving: What Early Childhood Education is All About *by Ashley Montagu* 10

What Should Young Children be Learning? *by Lilian G. Katz* 13

The Effects of Culture on Thinking *by Barbara Bowman* 16

Primed for Learning: The Young Child's Mind *by Karen Stephens* 20

Building Brains One Relationship at a Time *by Gina Lebedeva* 27

The Wisdom of Children *by Ruth A. Wilson* 40

Friendship — Loving

What Early Childhood Education is All About

by Ashley Montagu

Love is the supreme form of human communication. In the hierarchy of needs, love stands as the supreme developing agent of the humanity of the person. As such, the teaching of love should be the central core of all early childhood curriculum — with all other subjects growing naturally out of such teaching.

Why is Love so Important?

To appreciate the significance of love, we only need to look at what happens when love is withheld.

As late as the second decade of the 20th century, the death rate for infants under one year in various foundling institutions throughout the United States was nearly 100%, and no one had the least idea why. The mystery was solved, almost accidentally, by Dr. Fritz Talbot of Boston when he was visiting the Children's Clinic in Düsseldorf, Germany. All the wards shown to Dr. Talbot were very neat and tidy, but what piqued his curiosity was the sight of a fat old woman carrying a baby on her hip. "Oh, that is Old Anna," Dr. Talbot was told. "When we have done everything medically we can for a baby, and it is still not doing well, we turn it over to Old Anna. She is always successful."

As hospitals began introducing a regular regimen of mothering in their wards, mortality rates for infants dropped dramatically. At Bellevue hospital in New York, for example, following the institution of mothering, the mortality rates for infants fell from 55% to less than 10% by 1938. In short, it was discovered that infants need something more than the satisfaction of their basic physical needs if they are to survive and grow and develop in physical and mental health. That something came to be recognized as tender, loving care.

The physical, mental, and social price an unloved child pays is devastating. Not only can one detect the impact of lack-love in the arrested social development of children, but also in their bone structure. (We can actually detect the lack of love with x-rays.) When we see a child who is not being loved, we see a child who is undeveloped as a human being behaviorally. But we also see a child who is shorter than average for his age, whose skin is pallid and wrinkled, whose immune system is deficient, and whose entire biochemistry is different from that of a loved child.

The impact of lack-love can most dramatically be observed in some children thought to be suffering from a condition diagnosed as idiopathic hypopituatarism, or dwarfism. These children are stunted in their physical growth, appear to be mentally retarded, and are very incompetent socially. This condition was formerly attributed to some physical or genetic deficiency. However, it has been observed that when these individuals are placed in a loving environment their height shoots up, their mental retardation disappears, and they become virtually normal human beings. Once again, we see that the critical missing ingredient is love.

In a very profound sense, love is the most basic of all human needs, for love is the nutriment from which both physical and mental health draw their strength. Never has this been better said than by George Chapman, the Tudor poet and playwright, who in his play, "All Fools," acted in 1599, writes:

*I tell thee, Love is Nature's second sun
Causing a spring of virtues where he shines;
And as without the Sun, the World's great eye,
All colours, beauties, both of art and Nature,
Are given in vain to men; so without love
All beauties bred in women are in vain,
All virtues born in men lie buried;
For love informs them as the Sun doth colours;
And as the Sun, reflecting his warm beams
Against the earth, begets all fruits and flowers;
So love, fair shining in the inward man,
Brings forth in him the honourable fruits
Of valour, wit, virtue, and haughty thoughts,
Brave resolution, and divine discourse.
Oh, 'tis the Paradise, the Heaven of Earth.*

Love will always remain a matter of such fundamental importance, and will have such far-reaching consequences for humanity and society, that we are urgently called upon to consider what we can best do to restore its birthright to humanity. To bring about the desired changes, we must first understand more fully what love is, and how it is fostered.

What is Love?

Love can be defined as the act of communicating to others one's profound involvement in their welfare, one's devotion to the optimum fulfillment of their potentialities, by giving them all the sustenance, stimulation, support, and encouragement they require for growth and development. Love is the communication that one will never commit the supreme treason of letting others down when they stand in need of you.

Love is not based on self-interest, but on the interest of the other. In loving another, you show with feeling carried by demonstrative acts that you are truly involved in their welfare.

Every baby is born with this profound capacity to love, and an equally profound need to be loved. The infant's need for love is not adequately satisfied unless it receives the necessary stimulations for the development of its capacity to love. It may, indeed, be said that the child's need for love from others is important principally because that love is the most significant developer of its own capacity to love others. The child learns to love others by being loved.

It is now clear that the only way in which one ever learns to love is by being loved. The only way one learns to relate to other people is to be warmly related to during one's infancy and early childhood.

How can Early Childhood Programs Foster Friendship?

If we are to promote the development of mentally, socially, and physically healthy adults, we need to be certain that they, as children, are raised in loving, stimulating environments. The family, of course, must be the principal locus of attention. But many families do not provide loving environments. Many children lead very unhappy lives, because their parents do not realize how important it is to satisfy their children's need for love, for friendship, and for stimulation. Therefore, schools should be reconstituted as agencies, second only to the home — and sometimes superior to it — for the teaching of love.

The principal qualification for an early childhood teacher should be the ability to love. This requirement should stand above all others. A teacher of young children, more than anything else, must be able to love children unconditionally, to be able to communicate to them, without any patronizing and without any strings attached, that she is their friend — for friendship, it must be understood, is just another word for love.

Early childhood educators are the unacknowledged legislators of the world. By befriending children they care for, they teach children how to be friends, how to be deeply involved in the welfare of others. By sharing their commitment to friendship with parents — in a nonthreatening, non-patronizing manner — they can help parents see the value of providing a loving environment in the home.

It is literally what the child absorbs from its teachers, as well as from its parents, that constitutes the most important influence in the making of a personality, in the acquisition of all those skills one requires for functioning well as a member of one's society and of fulfilling to the optimum one's uniquenesses, one's potentialities, for being what one has it in one creatively to be. An early childhood program with friendship as its core curriculum can enable children in its care to reach their full potential.

Ashley Montagu

Montagu studied at the University of London and the University of Florence and received his PhD from Columbia University, New York City, in 1937. He lectured and taught at a number of schools, including Rutgers, The State University of New Jersey, where he chaired the department of anthropology from 1949 to 1955. He first attracted public attention as the author of UNESCO's "Statement on Race" (1950), in which he called for ethnic equality, arguing that race is a social invention with no biological basis. He published this and subsequent versions as "Statement on Race" (1951; revised edition, 1972). Montagu also wrote on such varied topics as human evolution, culture, and child care, and possibly his most influential work is *The Natural Superiority of Women* (1953). In 1999, a heavily revised edition of the book was published. His other works include *Man's Most Dangerous Myth: The Fallacy of Race* (1942; 5th revised edition, 1974), *Touching: The Human Significance of the Skin* (1971; 3rd edition, 1986), *The Nature of Human Aggression* (1976), and *Growing Young* (1981; 2nd edition, 1989).

What Should Young Children be Learning?

by Lilian G. Katz

Recent research on intellectual and social development and learning is rich in implications for curriculum and teaching strategies for early childhood education. Unfortunately, educational practices tend to lag behind what is known about teaching and learning. This digest discusses curriculum and the methods of teaching, which best serve children's long-term development.

The Nature of Development

The concept of development includes two dimensions: the normative dimension, concerning the capabilities and limitations of most children at a given age, and the dynamic dimension, concerning the sequence and changes that occur in all aspects of the child's functioning as he grows. It also addresses the cumulative effects of experience. While the normative dimension indicates what children can and cannot do at a given age, the dynamic dimension raises questions about what children should or should not do at a particular time in their development in light of possible long-term consequences.

In many preschool programs and kindergartens, young children are engaged in filling out worksheets, reading from flash cards, or reciting numbers in rote fashion. But just because young children can do those things, in a normative sense, is not sufficient justification for requiring them to do so.

Young children usually do willingly most things adults ask of them. But their willingness is not a reliable indicator of the value of an activity. The developmental question is not "What can children do?" Rather, it is "What should children do that best serves their development and learning in the long term?".

Learning through Interaction

Contemporary research confirms the view that young children learn most effectively when they are engaged in interaction rather than in merely receptive or passive activities. Young children should be interacting with adults, materials, and their surroundings in ways, which help them make sense of their own experience and environment. They should be investigating and observing aspects of their environment worth learning about, and recording their findings and observations through talk, paintings, and drawings. Interaction that arises in the course of such activities provides a context for much social and cognitive learning.

Four Categories of Learning

The four categories of learning outlined below are especially relevant to the education of young children:

- **Knowledge.** In early childhood, knowledge consists of facts, concepts, ideas, vocabulary, and stories. A child acquires knowledge from someone's answers to his questions, explanations, descriptions, and accounts of events as well as through observation.

- **Skills.** Skills are small units of action that occur in a relatively short period of time and are easily observed or inferred. Physical, social, verbal, counting, and drawing skills are among a few of the almost endless number of skills learned in the early years. Skills can be learned from direct instruction and improved with practice and drill.

- **Feelings.** These are subjective emotional states, many of which are innate. Among those that are learned are feelings of competence, belonging, and security. Feelings about school, teachers, learning, and other children are also learned in the early years.

- **Dispositions.** Dispositions can be thought of as habits of mind or tendencies to respond to certain situations in certain ways. Curiosity, friendliness or unfriendliness, bossiness, and creativity are dispositions or sets of dispositions rather than skills or pieces of knowledge. There is a significant difference between having writing skills and having the disposition to be a writer. Dispositions are not learned through instruction or drill. The dispositions that children need to acquire or to strengthen — curiosity, creativity, cooperation, friendliness — are learned primarily from being around people who exhibit them. It is unfortunate that some dispositions, such as being curious or puzzled, are rarely displayed by adults in front of children.

A child who is to learn a particular disposition must have the opportunity to behave in a manner that is in keeping with the disposition. When that occurs, the child's behavior can be responded to, and thus strengthened. Teachers can strengthen certain dispositions by setting learning goals rather than performance goals. A teacher who says, "I want to see how much you can find out about something," rather than, "I want to see how well you can do," encourages children to focus on what they are learning rather than on their performance, and how others will judge their performance.

Risks of Early Academic Instruction

Research on the long-term effects of various curriculum models suggests that the introduction of academic work into the early childhood curriculum yields good results on standardized tests in the short term, but may be counterproductive in the long term. For example, the risk of early instruction in beginning reading skills is that the amount of drill and practice required for success at an early age will undermine children's dispositions to be readers.

It is clearly not useful for a child to learn skills if, in the process of acquiring them, the disposition to use them is lost. On the other hand, obtaining the disposition without the requisite skills is not desirable either. Results from longitudinal studies suggest that curricula and teaching methods should be designed to optimize the acquisition of knowledge, skills, desirable dispositions, and feelings.

Another risk of introducing young children to academic work prematurely is that those who cannot relate to the tasks required are likely to feel incompetent. Students who repeatedly experience difficulties may come to consider themselves stupid and may bring their behavior into line accordingly.

Variety of Teaching Methods

Academically focused curricula for preschool programs typically adopt a single pedagogical method dominated by workbooks, drill, and practice. It is reasonable to assume that when a single teaching method is used for a diverse group of children, a significant proportion of these children are likely to fail. The younger the children are, the greater the variety of teaching methods there should be, since the younger the group is, the less likely the children are to have been socialized into a standard way of responding to their environment, and the more likely it is that the children's readiness to learn is influenced by background experiences which are idiosyncratic and unique. For practical reasons, there are limits to how varied teaching methods can be. It should be noted, however, that while approaches dominated by workbooks often claim to individualize instruction they really individualize nothing more than the day on which a child completes a routine task. Such programs can weaken the disposition to learn.

As for the learning environment, the younger the children are, the more informal it should be. Informal learning environments encourage spontaneous play and cooperative effort. In spontaneous play, children engage in whatever play activities interest them. Cooperative effort occurs when children engage in such activities as group projects, investigations, and constructions.

Conclusion

Spontaneous play is not the only alternative to early academic instruction. The data on children's learning suggests that preschool and kindergarten experiences require an intellectually oriented approach in which children interact in small groups as they work together on projects that help them make sense of their own experience. These projects should also strengthen their dispositions to observe, experiment, inquire, and examine more closely the worthwhile aspects of their environment.

For More Information

Donaldson, M. (1983). "Children's reasoning." In M. Donaldson, R. Grieve, and C. Pratt (editors), *Early Childhood Development and Education*. London: The Guilford Press.

Dweck, C. S. (1986). Motivational processes affecting learning. *American Psychologist, 41*:1040–48.

Katz, L. G. (1986). Current perspectives on child development. *Council for Research in Music Education Bulletin, 86*:1–9.

Katz, L. G. (1985). "Dispositions in early childhood education." *ERIC/EECE Bulletin 18*. Urbana, IL: ERIC Clearinghouse on Elementary and Early Childhood Education.

Morgan, M. (1984). Reward-induced decrements and increments in intrinsic motivation. *Review of Education Research, 54*:5-30.

Schweinhart, L. J., Weikart, D. P., Larner, M. B. (1986). Consequences of three preschool curriculum models through age 15. *Early Childhood Research Quarterly, 1*:15-46. Reprinted with permission from ERIC Clearinghouse on Elementary and Early Childhood Education, Urbana, Illinois.

Lilian G. Katz

Lilian G. Katz, PhD, Professor Emerita, University of Illinois, Urbana-Champaign, is Co-Director of the Clearinghouse on Early Education and Parenting and Editor of *Early Childhood Education and Parenting*.

The Effects of Culture on Thinking

by Barbara Bowman

Thinking is a high priority in the United States today. As brain, rather than brawn, power increases in importance, one of our most pressing economic priorities is to raise the educational achievement of our children. Yet, our goal of educating all children is made more difficult by our history of educationally excluding and marginalizing people who are not white, English speaking, and Christian. Until quite recently, schools (and the nation) shunned poor and minority children, contending they are inherently unable to master the academic curriculum. Genetic research over the past quarter century has challenged this assumption and concluded that the human capacity to learn exists across all racial and social groupings. With a growing population of people of color, speaking a variety of different languages, belonging to many religious groups and ethnic and national communities, the question is not can all children learn, but how to teach them. One of the barriers to teaching and learning is caused by differences in how people think.

We now know that there is a great deal of similarity in human thinking. Piaget's (1967) work is based on the genetic disposition of children to develop in certain ways. He contends that there are universal patterns in development caused by the interaction of the human genetic code and experience. This idea is consistent with the enormous biological overlap scientists have found in all human capabilities.

There is also considerable research that shows some individuals are able to think better than others — earlier, faster, and/or more profoundly. Presumably, their individual genetic make-up and their specific experiences better prepare them for thinking. More recently, Howard Gardner (1993) pointed out that there are different kinds of thinking and that some of us are better at some kinds than others. We may be more artistic and relational, rather than scientific and logical; or better at verbal tasks than at manual ones. What this tells us is that although people are similar in their potential for thinking, there are individual differences that reflect each person's unique blend of genetic potential and personal experience.

Culture is less often recognized as a factor in thinking. However, individuals are shaped not only by their individual genes and experiences, but also by the meaning these are given by the groups within which they live. Culture consists of patterns of beliefs, attitudes, and relationships that a group of people shares with one another, including values, morality, myths, language, as well as customs, practices, roles, communication styles. The role of culture in thinking has been highlighted in recent years by the work of Vygotsky (1978) and others who have focused on the role of social interaction in thinking. This has spawned a new understanding of group differences and the role of social experience and language in shaping our human capabilities. Barbara Rogoff (2003), Shirley Brice Heath (1983), and others have called our attention to how groups of people make sense of their world and teach it to their children. There are certainly individual differences within each group (the range for any characteristic is probably as broad within groups as it is between groups); nevertheless, groups do have shared social structures and practices that give meaning to their thinking.

Most American children share a culture; however, some of us live in more socially isolated groups than others. Children from these groups — segregated by ethnicity, social class, language, and religion — are most likely to have cultural patterns that are different than those found in the mainstream. Unfortunately, they and their parents are frequently misunderstood and they, in turn, often misunderstand the larger society. We miscommunicate because we think our culture's ways of thinking is the right way and if others do not see the world the way we do, there must be something wrong with them.

Most of us are aware that different groups have different practices; but we often assume that these express the same thinking, although we may think they are peculiar. Muslims show their respect for God by taking off their shoes and putting on their hats, while Christians do just the opposite. Both groups honor God, though they do it in different ways. Often when we think of cultural difference we expect just such minor variations — like whether you eat bagels, corn bread, or fry bread for Sunday breakfast. We tend to be blind to real differences in how people think, differences that set us wondering, "what is wrong with them?". For example, many of us see the weather mainly through a scientific lens. When a phenomenon — like thunder and lightning — are explained by science, we are satisfied, even if we are not scientists ourselves or prefer other types of thinking. Yet, there are groups who think that metaphysical events are more real than those that are explainable with science. They live in a world inhabited by ghosts and other magical objects that cause claps of thunder and flashes of light. We wonder why they don't use science to explain the world the way we do and they wonder why we don't believe in what seems real to them.

Does this mean there are no developmental regularities that cut across cultural differences? Not at all. At one level all humans have the same basic abilities. They can all use language and their senses, categorize, sequence, symbolize abstract experience, play with ideas. And these abilities come to fruition at similar times. For example, no matter what language children learn, it begins with babbling at 4 to 6 months and ends in community speech by six years. So, there are universal characteristics to thinking. However, the way children use these abilities is determined to a large extent by the cultural experiences they have. How children learn to talk, whom they talk to and who talks to them, and what they talk about is learned. The language children speak also affects their thinking. Most people who speak more than one language say that some ideas are more easily expressed in each language. For instance, base 10 is illustrated more clearly in Chinese where the word for twelve is ten and two than in English where there is a new word for this concept.

Early childhood professionals sometimes misunderstand culture because of our emphasis on developmental norms. We have studied some children, noted the similarities in their development, and assumed that the average represents what normal children do. Children whose ideas and behavior do not conform to normative expectations are often considered delayed, deviant, and or disadvantaged. While in some instances this is true, other times the differences have a cultural explanation. For example, American norms call for children as young as 3 months to sleep by themselves, while other cultures expect children to sleep with someone else most of their lives. Americans expect children to dress themselves by age 4 or 5. Many groups expect to dress children until they are 6 or 7. Americans often think children cannot sit still for long periods, and meals are usually completed quickly. In other countries, quite young children sit much longer as they finish three-course meals without showing the least discomfort. These differences mean that what is considered normal in one group may not be in another. The differences are neither bad nor good, but may be more or less adaptive in some situations. For example, an American child in a French child care center may not sit quietly through a long meal and be seen as hyperactive.

Adults with low incomes use fewer words in their interactions with their children than do middle class parents; consequently, their children learn fewer words (Hart & Risley, 1995). These children are developmentally competent in their own community, even though their vocabulary may be so small that learning to read is difficult. Children learn to think as their own culture; does it mean they can't learn others' ways of thinking? Not at all; it just means their prior knowledge may or may not easily support the new thing you want them to know. Many kinds of thinking transfer from one language to another, from one situation to another, from one culture to another. For example, if children know a home language in which they understand a concept, they can grasp the same idea in another language quickly, although they must still learn the new word. Similarly, if children are accustomed to responsive parents at home, they will expect alternative caregivers to also be responsive and be better able to get the care they need in a new situation.

Frequently, however, there is not an easy fit between what children already know and what we want them to know. This can create the illusion that there is something wrong with their development. This often is not the case. It may be simply a difference in how they have learned to think. For example, some African American children, accustomed to a more authoritarian interactional style with adults, are confused and misunderstand teachers who are more indirect (Delpit, 1988). Children whose families do not use much formal speech may not understand the language in a book. While listening to a story they may enjoy the rhythm and intonation and never think about what the words mean. For meaning, a child may look at facial expressions or body language and be quite skilled in interpreting these clues to adult thinking.

Children, from birth on, are exposed to their own culture's meaning system, expectations, and practices and their ways of thinking are deeply embedded in these. Understanding cultural differences is not easy. Many of them are subtle and the variations hard to see. Equally difficult is avoiding stereotyping; that is, attributing characteristics to children simply because they belong to a particular group. Children and families live in concentric cultural circles, drawing more from the heritage of one group this time and of the mainstream the next.

As early childhood professionals, we must challenge our cultural myopia and become more sensitive to these differences among groups in order to help children learn new ways of thinking. The onus is on us to find out how best to teach each child and to adapt curriculum to the differences among children, including their cultural differences.

References

Delpit, L. (1988). The silenced dialogue: power and pedagogy in educating other people's children. *Harvard Educational Review, 58*(3), 280–298.

Gardner, H. (1993). *Multiple intelligences: Theory in practice.* New York: Basic Books.

Hart, B., & Risley, T. R. (1995). *Meaningful differences in the everyday experience of young American children.* Baltimore: Paul H. Brookes Publishing Co.

Heath, S. (1983). *Ways with words: Life and work in communities and classrooms.* New York: Cambridge University Press.

Piaget, J. (1955). *The language and thought of the child.* New York: Norton, Meridian Books.

Rogoff, B. (2003). *The cultural nature of human development.* New York: Oxford University Press.

Vygotsky, L. S. (1978). *Mind in society*. Cambridge, MA: Harvard University Press.

Barbara Bowman

Early education expert and advocate Barbara Bowman earned her BA from Sarah Lawrence in 1950 and went on to receive her MA from the University of Chicago in 1952.

For many years, Bowman taught at both the preschool and elementary levels, but in 1966 she acted as one of the three founders of the Erickson Institute For Advanced Study in Child Development, where she pioneered the teaching of early childhood education and administration. She has become a sought-after expert and she tirelessly pursues higher quality and more extensive training for early education practitioners. Taking her expertise abroad, she has consulted with universities in China and Iran. In addition, she has directed training programs for Head Start teachers, teachers in inner-city schools, caregivers of at-risk infants, and for a Child Development Associate's program on Native American Reservations.

Bowman continues to act as the President of the Erickson Institute and of the National Association for the Education of Young Children. She has served on the boards of the Great Books Foundation, the National Board for Professional Teaching Standards, Roosevelt University and the Family Resource Coalition. She is the Chair of the Committee of Early Childhood Pedagogy for the National Research Council, for which she served as a member of their Committee on the Prevention of Reading Difficulties in Young Children. She and her husband, Dr. James Bowman, are the parents of one daughter, Valerie Jarrett, and the grandparents of Laura Jarrett.

Primed for Learning

The Young Child's Mind

by Karen Stephens

Are the kids running circles around you? Are you constantly on your mental toes trying to anticipate what little ones will get into or come up with next? Well, don't take it personally. It's just a matter of nature. Young minds are engineered to work twice as fast as adult's. YIKES! No wonder you're exhausted!

Sifting through Brain Breakthroughs . . . and the Baloney

I've waded through an explosion of brain research literature. Some of it was beyond my technical needs. A neuroscientist, I'm not! But I plodded on to find a gold mine of knowledge.

When hearing implications of brain studies, be a wise and thoughtful consumer. Inaccurate — or misapplied — information can harm children rather than help them. Don't accept everything you hear as absolute, final fact. For instance, actively learning to play music builds brain power; passively listening to music does not. Brain research is an emerging field, still in its infancy. New revelations, classifications, and implications surface regularly. Be moderately skeptical. Don't succumb to fads that supposedly stem from research. Follow your intuition and common sense.

Pay closest attention to information that triggers your "aha!" response. When brain research rings true, you'll feel it. After all, the human species has evolved to ensure survival of our young. *How wonderful that science now bears out that many instinctual parenting and caregiving responses are indeed the best ones!*

The Brain at Birth

At conception, children become a mix of each parent's genes. The time before birth (prenatal) is the most rapid period of human development, especially the brain's. Genetic groundwork to support a lifetime of experience is being laid.

For sound development, the prenatal infant (fetus) needs healthy genes from parents. Its brain growth is dependent upon good care, such as maternal attention to health, nutrition, and stress management.

Even at this early stage of life, children are affected by experience. The developing brain is especially vulnerable to insults that can hamper, distort, or depress its growth. Insults include poor maternal physical and mental health and malnutrition, as well as maternal smoking, alcohol consumption, and drug use.

The infant brain comes equipped with about 100 billion nerve cells, called neurons. An axon connects one neuron to another. Ends of axons have fibers called dendrites, which receive and transfer information from one cell to another. It is like achieving a telephone connection that allows information to be relayed from one neuron to another. When information comes together between neurons, it's called a synapse. All those synapses are firing two and a half times faster than ours. That's what primes children to be our most vigorous learners.

The number of brain cells (neurons) a child is born with doesn't change throughout life. What changes, and therefore allows learning and growth to take place, is the connections between brain neurons. Brain 'wiring' is made up of neuron networks. The brain's ability to acquire, apply, and benefit from information depends upon neural connections. Thus the challenge, the work of early childhood, is to make sense of the world — to make the connection.

Some fundamental 'survival' connections are established, or 'hard-wired,' before birth. That 'hard-wiring' is inherited from genes and controls involuntary body functions like breathing and heartbeat. This neuron activity takes place in the brain's interior, near the brain stem.

At birth, about 25% of neurons are networked, or connected together so information can flow between them. Gradually, brain development spreads throughout the brain, with higher order reasoning and thinking developing last. This development is completed during early adolescence. Portions of the brain governing these skills are located just beneath the protective skull. (Thus, Dr. Judy Helm reminds us of the importance of preventing brain injury through religious use of car safety restraints and bike helmets!)

The Brain after Birth

Following birth, rapid brain construction continues, neurons being the building blocks. Bridges between neurons, information pathways, are created to allow the brain to absorb and process increasing amounts of sensory information. At birth, there remains 75% of the brain that can be influenced by environmental factors in combination with genetic inheritance. *Capacity for such intricate, refined brain development means mom, dad, and the rest of us can have a great impact on nurturing kids' learning potential.* What a privilege! Oh what a responsibility!

During early childhood, children develop many more synapses than they need as adults. By the time the wiring process is complete, a single neuron can be connected to as many as 15,000 others! The synapses (or telephone connections) that aren't used regularly don't become ingrained in the brain, and are then pruned back. This process of pruning back accelerates after the first ten years of life. So the task of early childhood is to gather, gather, gather information. In the second decade of life, information storage is streamlined.

This neural network is the brain's infrastructure. Information flows between neurons by way of electrical impulses. Chemicals and hormones, called neurotransmitters, play a role in moving information along.

Some neurotransmitters facilitate learning, others hinder it. Calming hormones, such as seratonin, allow information to be transferred from one neuron to another. Stress hormones, such as cortisol, reduce, slow — or in severe cases — stop the brain's ability to transfer information. When functioning well, neural connections allow information to zip at about 200 mph to different brain centers, which then trigger body functions or responses, such as seeing, hearing, tasting, feeling, and thinking.

The more connections between neurons, the greater the brain's ability to take in, process, and make sense of information. The more successful connections, the greater the learning capacity. The neuron connections that create information highways develop early in life, *most significantly during the first ten years.* Brain density in terms of neural connections, rather than brain size, contributes most to intelligence. Properly stimulated brain circuits become increasingly complex, refined, and detailed. This translates into learning potential for kids!

Nurturing Brain Growth and Learning Potential

The child's learning process is choreographed by minuscule electrical synapses in the intricate dance of human intelligence. To trigger the ballet, children need a wide range of experiences for the brain to 'chew on,' meaning to decipher, analyze, and synthesize into meaningful concepts. Unfortunately, the ballet can also be impeded, if not halted. Environmental and personal stress impair brain development and functioning.

Following is what we have learned about the brain and how it works, and does not work. Early results give us clues on how to help children's brains grow and work well. And keep in mind that the practices mentioned are helpful for any age child, but especially those in early childhood, when the brain is primed by nature for learning.

- **Strong, secure attachments promote brain development.** Infants flourish when responsive caregivers are head-over-heels in love with them. Being gently held, cuddled and cradled, hearing soothing language (including songs and lullabies), and frequent loving touch all feed the brain with positive experiences.

  The most critical time for establishing secure bonds of attachment is the first year of life. When infants experience a strong attachment, hormones are secreted that induce relaxation and a sense of well-being. Strong attachment develops when caregivers are consistent and predictable.

- **The ability to trust cannot be formed without a secure attachment.** Secure attachment is a prerequisite to positive social adjustment. Familiarity of caregivers creates a comfort zone that literally stimulates release of chemicals and hormones that help a child access memories of experience and apply them to current situations. This is a critical process of learning.

- **The brain is impressionable.** The brain has 'plasticity'; it responds to positive nurturing and experience. Likewise, it reacts to negative experiences. Timing of experience is often critical, especially the first three years of life. Once again, consistent caregiving and secure attachment is vitally important. Without it, children don't develop well in terms of intellect, or their ability to regulate and control emotions.

- **The brain is resilient.** To an amazing degree, the brain can compensate when a portion of it is injured or under-stimulated. If *short-term stress* is endured, such as a one-time incident of domestic violence, the brain can bounce back in spite of the experience. *Prolonged exposure to stress* undermines the brain's natural ability and tendency to rebound and compensate. Such stress would include living in violent neighborhoods, or enduring extreme poverty or persistent malnutrition.

- **Brain development affects more than intellectual growth.** Brain development and function affects personality, temperament, and children's ability to regulate emotions. It affects social skills and the ability to function according to moral and ethical codes. Capacity for empathy and remorse stems from early childhood. Warm, supportive, and dependable relationships nurture it. *Consistency of good caregiving in the early years can never be overemphasized.*

- **Brain development is interrelated; growth in one area affects growth in another.** Connections, connections, connections. Their importance heeds us not to teach anything in isolation. Advancements in one area of development trigger advancements in others. For instance, growth in language spurs emotional and social growth. That's because self-control is more easily maintained when children learn to identify, express, and cope with emotions through language. As young children gradually master language, we have to consistently coach and support them in skills such as tolerance, patience, and peaceful conflict resolution.

- **Our brain is a social brain.** *Attentive, loving responsiveness to children is critical.* Children need interactions with peers as well as those older and younger. Physical as well as emotional responsiveness to children provides them with social interactions that literally trigger neural connections.

Primary caregivers who are depressed, withdrawn, and generally unresponsive to children don't stimulate brain connections. In fact, their behavior elicits in children emotional stress and self-doubt, which bring stress hormones into play. That in turn impairs brain function.

- **There are 'windows of opportunity' when a child's brain is primed to absorb specific types of knowledge and acquire specific skills more easily.** Different brain sectors store different information. Children learn easiest when experience corresponds to areas of the brain undergoing growth. Capitalizing on 'windows of opportunity' makes for successful learning. It helps children develop a strong self-image as capable and competent learners.

For instance, we know the first two years of life are critical for language development. During that time, it's especially important for children's communications — even babbling — to elicit interest and engagement from caregivers.

And while learning to play a musical instrument is possible at any age, because of the brain's particular sensitivity to music instruction in early childhood, it is much easier to learn music, even multiple instruments, if instruction begins by age ten.

- **Children rely heavily on learning through imitation.** By our actions we are teaching children the ways of the world. Through imitation children learn to speak. It's important to be a good role model of elaborate, clear language. Involve children in daily activities, such as running errands, so they can observe your adult skills and social 'know-how.'

- **Children learn best when experiences closely match their current level of knowledge and competency.** Children make sense of knowledge layer upon layer. Gradually, they develop concepts and theories of how the world works. This process of children building knowledge, through active investigation, is critical to brain development.

Too large of gaps between what children know, and what we expose them to, or try to teach them, leads to frustration and stress. Expecting children to develop skills in too many areas at once can also create stress. Pushing children to excel at a faster pace, or over-scheduling them in too many structured enrichment lessons at once, is counterproductive. *Nice and easy, step-by-step is the natural way children are primed to learn.*

When teaching, observe closely to assess current abilities and knowledge. Then build from there. Children's behavior will tell you if you are on the right track. For instance, infants send caregivers nonverbal cues to pace learning and interaction.

Eye contact, facial expression, and body posture reveal when a child is alert, tired, bored, or over-stimulated. Preschoolers' attention span, depth of concentration, and enthusiastic interest reveal whether experiences are properly timed. Ignoring cues or pressuring children to perform is counterproductive. It simply increases stress reactions, which impede learning.

- **Children need activity-based, hands-on, sensory experiences to build the brain's learning pathways.** Learning is most meaningful when self-initiated. Exploring through trial and error is very motivating. From birth, children find problem solving and exploring cause-and-effect relationships especially intriguing. Passive, less interactive experiences, such as many hours of daily television and computer play, do NOT build connnections effectively.

So Froebel, Montessori, Piaget, Vygotsky, and Dewey were right! Children learn best through play; they learn best by doing. Play materials should be safe and developmentally appropriate. Anything that allows children to explore through their senses feeds the brain, including, but not limited to: playing with paints and play dough; building with blocks and Legos® in conjunction with toy cars, people, and animals; playing with sound toys and simple music instruments; dressing up, using dolls, and playing house; using puppets and reading picture books; and messing about in natural elements like sand, dirt, and water.

■ **To become permanent, neural pathways (or learning pathways) must be strengthened through repetition.** Children benefit from repeated experiences so brain connections become ingrained. 'Use it or lose it' could never be more important.

Don't confuse repetition with drill. Drill focuses too narrowly on one skill, such as memorizing flash cards. *Repetition is experiencing the same types of activities as long as children find them moderately challenging, relaxing, and engaging.* Daily ritual activities, such as reading bedtime stories and playing peek-a-boo, are examples of repeated experience that reinforce learning.

■ **Children's innate curiosity of the world, joy of learning, and pride in accomplishment is the perfect motivation for brain development.** Threats, punishment, and excessive competition are not effective motivators for long lasting learning since they release stress hormones. In contrast, supportive coaching, collaboration and cooperation, teaching responsibility through respectful consequences, and other types of non-punitive teaching and guidance encourage calm.

Developmental successes inspire intrinsic satisfaction, which in turn creates a self-perpetuating spiral of learning and achievement. *Never underestimate the role of joy, pride, and self-respect as a motivator for learning.*

■ **The brain is 'programmed' to learn a system of language. Infants hear a much wider range of sounds than adults.** Gradually, they learn to attend only to those most important to their family's native language. This 'winnowing' out of sounds takes place during the first *ten months* of life. (This makes a strong case for the importance of hearing tests at birth, and for treating ear ailments without delay.)

Capacity for intricate language is unique to humans; it is especially important in building the brain. The portions of the brain that learn language(s) are most easily activated before age ten. Children enveloped in a rich, loving language environment are given an ideal incubator for brain development.

To facilitate language, speak with children from birth. (They attend to your voice even before birth!) Talk to them about what they are seeing or touching, or what you are doing. Respond to pre-language conversations so infants learn their babbling gets a response from a loved one. Read together daily throughout childhood.

As children grow, use open-ended questions to encourage expression of thoughts through words and sentences. Let them see you using writing tools and give them some to use, too. Build literacy by bringing their attention to meaningful ways language is used in daily life, spoken as well as written. Do this whether in the grocery store, post office, or a restaurant. Take advantage of 'teachable moments.'

■ **The brain is geared to recognize and make sense of patterns.** Noticing similarities and differences is how children go about making sense of the world. This is especially true in terms of sight and hearing. Children analyze patterns of sound in order to decipher their native language. From their earliest days, infants prefer patterns of the human face, even drawings.

Give children opportunities to play with patterns through matching games, building with blocks, coloring with crayons, and putting together puzzles. Help guide children's deductions and associations by encouraging them to observe patterns. How are objects alike and different? Which is bigger, smaller, taller, wider? What happens when seasons change?

- **Complementary experiences build connections.** The more ways children experience information, the more efficiently they construct knowledge and concepts. This establishes learning pathways so children can access stored memory, thereby increasing odds of repeated success.

To build connections, provide a rich variety of related experiences. *Link new skills and concepts to existing ones.* For instance, when exploring the fall season, go out and pick apples at the orchard. Compare sizes and colors. Sort good apples from rotten ones. Taste fresh apples. Which are sweet? Which are sour? At home, make an apple pie or applesauce together. Plant your own apple tree.

- **Each child's brain, and learning preference, is unique.** Over time most kids develop preferred ways for learning. Dr. Howard Gardner's theory of multiple intelligences addresses this issue. Some children are more visual learners, while others are more auditory. Some require a greater degree of learning through body movement, while others excel in musical intelligence. This probably happens when parts of the brain develop more fully than others. You can tune in to a child's unique strengths and inclinations by watching behavior. Provide experiences accordingly.

In Conclusion

The debate over whether children develop more due to nature versus nurture is obsolete. Brain research reveals it's both! *Genetic birthright and environmental blessings interlace in infinite ways to weave a lasting and visible imprint on children's developing minds.* That in turn affects their lifelong ability to function in society and create a dignified, fulfilling life.

You and I are the fortunate few who get ringside seats to watch the mysteries of the young brain unfold. We are the trusted few with the responsibility of supporting the process. Savor the experience, and respect your role in nurturing fertile minds primed for learning.

References

Begley, S. (1996, February 19). Your child's brain. *Newsweek.*

Blakeslee, S. (1997, April 17). Studies show talking with infants shapes basis of ability to think. *New York Times.*

Gardner, H. (1983). *Frames of mind: The theory of multiple intelligences.* New York: Basic Books.

Gardner, H. (1993). *Multiple intelligences: The theory in practice.* New York: Basic Books.

Greenspan, S. (1997). *Growth of the mind.* New York: Addison-Wesley.

Healy, J. (1990). *Endangered minds: Why children don't think and what we can do about it.* New York: Simon & Schuster.

Healy, J. (1994). *Your child's growing mind: A guide to learning and brain development from birth to adolescence.* New York: Doubleday.

Jabs, C. (1996, November). Your baby's brain. *Working Mother.*

Kotulak, R. (1997). *Inside the brain: Revolutionary discoveries of how the mind works.* Kansas City, MO: Andrews McMeel Publishing.

Nash, J. M. (1997, February 3). Fertile minds. *Time.*

Ramey, C. T., & Ramey, S. L. (1999). *Right from birth: Building your child's foundation for life.* New York: Goodard Press.

Shore, R. (1997). *Rethinking the brain: New insights into early development.* New York: Families and Work Institute.

Resources

"The Brain and the Developing Child Newsletter." Institute for Faculty Development Project on the Brain, Erikson Institute. Call (312) 755-2250.

"Your Child's Brain," Prime Time Live Video Segment, January 25, 1995, by Diane Sawyer. To purchase: (800) CALLABC — $39.95 plus $3.95 shipping.

Karen Stephens

Karen Stephens, MS in education specializing in early childhood, began her career as a teacher in a preschool classroom in 1975. From 1980 to May 2013 she served as campus child care director and taught child development and early childhood program administration courses for the Illinois State University's Department of Family and Consumer Sciences. Today she writes from her home and enjoys occasional travel to deliver staff development training and conference presentations.

Building Brains One Relationship at a Time

by Gina Lebedeva

Take a moment to celebrate by reflecting on all the ways you have observed or supported young children experiencing everyday interactions that were literally growing their brains, enriching their minds, and creating the blueprint for healthy lifelong learning:

- *An embrace, for as long as it takes, during a meltdown that tells a child, "I'm always here for you, even when your feelings are so overwhelming and scary to you, that you do scary things to yourself or others."*

- *A child being bathed in rich language, sophisticated vocabulary words, and open-ended questions that offer opportunities to wonder, connect, describe, create, or express.*

- *A child sharing a 'belly-laugh' with important people in her life, that comes in even the most ordinary moment.*

For more everyday examples, see Box 1 at end of article.

The Brain Science to Permeate the Early Learning Ecosystem

The examples above, and many others, can each be considered applied brain science, and are part of a 'neuro-relational' framework to early learning (Lillas & Turnbull, 2009) — an approach that transcends any single curriculum or educational setting serving young children and families. Importantly, when professionals across different disciplines — from pediatricians to home visitors, family resource specialists to therapists, educators to nannies — can all begin to see their work through the same lens, it becomes much deeper than a 'list of best practices' or 'strategies to try,' or assurance that a 'checklist of gold standards' or 'behavioral objectives' are met.

This article outlines the main tenets of a neuro-relational approach to help practitioners recognize what they already do well, using examples and guiding principles to prompt them to think differently about their service. The purpose is to create a platform for discussion and further exploration.

What is a Neuro-relational Approach and Why do Parts of it seem Familiar Already?

We begin with two basic assumptions that are likely familiar to many practitioners already:

- Experience, not simple maturation, changes the brain (neuro).

- All learning happens in the context of relationships (relational).

These two foundational themes are not new in themselves, but the recognition that they are inextricably intertwined is fortunately experiencing renewed attention and awareness. In short, it is the idea that the brain is an organ that is modified, in complex and interactive ways, by relational experiences with others.

Neuro-relational Approach: Not a New Concept, but a Refreshed Approach

The neuro-relational lens is rooted in decades of research in neurobiology, developmental psychology, psychopathology, cognitive neuroscience, family studies, and prevention/intervention science, and policies and practices can now be savvy enough to reflect these data (Shonkoff & Fisher, 2013). Though the early learning field has come a long way in connecting brain science to practice across different settings, current professional development efforts are being focused on how providers can become more aware, intentional, and articulate about the details.

A rapidly growing body of evidence describes the links between interpersonal relationships and brain development in the prenatal–age 8 period. These findings help providers know what details to look for and share in everyday moments and when engaging families. For examples of this evidence, see Box 2.

Beyond the Basics: Understanding Brain Systems, not just Brain Parts

Research in human brain mapping has revealed much about the functions of various structures and parts within the brain. A basic brain lesson might discuss the major brain regions and their functions such as the brain stem (survival functions like reflexes and breathing), cerebellum (movement and coordination), limbic system (emotion, mood, memory), and cortex (perception, thinking, language). Current research methods are now able to examine how various regions are interconnected during functional tasks. Instead of just taking static images of brains or even just seeing 'what areas are activated' in a single brain region, there are now ways of examining the physical pathways, or neural tracts, between regions that actually create our learning and behavior, and what factors make these pathways grow or deteriorate over time. In other words, research is beginning to examine the connectivity between related regions and how they work together in complex ways (*what is language processing like when we are mentally distracted or tired? how do children learn literacy when their brains have not calmed down from stress?*). This 'systems neuroscience' approach is in many ways aligned with the neuro-relational framework.

The Neuro-relational Framework: A Four-system Framework of Brain Function

Building on aspects of several different approaches, the neuro-relational framework emphasizes the following four brain systems: **Regulation, Sensory, Relevance,** and **Executive Systems**[1] (see Box 3). These systems are not discrete anatomically or functionally; there is overlap and interaction at many levels. When practitioners use this framework as a comprehensive lens, they can more accurately observe and map children's behaviors, reflect upon and refine their own individualized responses during interactions, and perhaps most importantly, engage with the family on building that child's relationships to support goals across learning domains. This approach can support practitioners' abilities to understand the process of how development reflects a person's internal and external environments, with

---

1 Descriptions of the four systems are adapted from Lillas & Turnbull, 2009.

relationships at the core of learning, rather than only addressing children's behaviors or outward skills.

Regulation System. This is considered the foundation of all other learning, and is highly developed at birth, as it is one of the oldest evolutionary structures important for survival. It includes basic aspects like nutrition, sleep/awake cycles, and the stress response and recovery systems. It explains the observations that when a child cannot regulate his energy or arousal levels due to stress, hunger, tiredness (meltdown!), there is no capacity to access language, reason, or take in any new information — no matter how well it is delivered. This system includes neurochemicals and hormones, a central hub being the hypothalamus. Chemical messenger systems (including dopamine, seratonin, and adrenaline) work with touch, balance, taste, sight, and smell (sensory systems), to give the body the right amount of energy or control needed to respond to the environment. Chronic or toxic levels of stress, even in infancy, can easily disrupt the chemical balance, and physically disrupt the brain's long-term ability to regulate the body. When the regulation system is not functional, the higher level brain systems responsible for higher-level processing and learning are also not able to function (see Box 4).

Regulation is learned in infancy, and is developed only face-to-face with others. It is not a system that develops 'in isolation' or 'automatically.' One dominant theory is the Mutual Regulation Model (Tronick & Beeghly, 2011), where it is the co-regulation of both the care provider and the infant (or child) that creates the brain patterns conducive to learning. A main way a body shows a regulated state is when its level of energy is adequate for the situation, and there is recovery (a return to calm) from stress. According to this model, the child's distress signals of dysregulation have evolved to cause the caregiver's brain to dysregulate as well. When the caregiver is able to show responsive, sensitive, and consistent behaviors toward the child, then both the child's and the caregiver's stress response systems will re-regulate together. In this way, the child's brain will 'learn' regulation only in the context of others' regulation response patterns. When the co-regulation flow does not occur, neither system can return to its regulated state (see Box 5).

Sensory System. This system takes information from the environment (sights, sounds, touches, smells) and processes it into some level of consciousness, dependent on the context. For instance, while you are able to feel your shoes on your feet, you are not necessarily conscious of it until your attention is drawn there. This is because you (your brain) have learned to desensitize so that it can focus on other sensations (the words you are now reading). There are several levels to decoding the incoming sensations, starting with 'primary' (more primitive and deep) areas of the brain, then moving to more advanced levels (higher up in the cortex). For instance, when you have experienced hearing someone talk, but not actually processed what he said, this is the sensory system interacting with the relevance (meaning) system. Both internal and external sensations need to be processed, including temperature, pain, sound, balance, itch, taste. With young children, the source of the sensation might not always be obvious — a provider might assume a child is reacting to the balloons in the activity, but really she may be hyper-focused on the tag in her shirt or the airplane outside, and perhaps unable to communicate that. Considering this level takes careful observation.

Relevance System. The relevance system, which connects the 'older/primitive' brain parts (like the limbic system) with the 'advanced/higher-level' parts (cortex), starts to give meaning and intention to the sensations and emotions that are experienced, creating memories that ultimately create the template for learning. Neuroscientsts refer to the notion that experience changes brains by strengthening the relevant connections, and eliminating the irrelevant ones; in other words, the brain is customized according to its experience ('neurons that fire together, wire together'). This is the basis for the highly efficient learning in the first three years, when neural organization rate is at it peak: a lack of stimulation will prevent and prune connections, and high stimulation will make connections stronger. In a classic example, when exposed to the sounds of Swahili, but not of French, the brain will assign meaning to only those sounds in Swahili, but not French, even before first words emerge. See Box 6 for more examples on how patterns in the relevance system from early childhood can influence lifelong relational patterns.

Executive System. This system is most advanced in evolutionary terms, residing in the brain's cortex, the outermost layers. These are the 'real-time, real-world' behaviors most easily observable that are informed by how the other three systems are functioning. It includes the conversational ability of a child in context ("*He has words, but doesn't seem to shift topics or hold a story very well*"), planning and sequencing ("*Wow, she knows that if she can wait a little while longer, she'll get two treats instead of one*"), and reasoning ("*It's great when all those practical tools of positive discipline are actually effective because this child's regulation, sensory, and relevance systems are now all ready to learn*").

Importantly, a well-functioning executive system needs to have **flexibility** (balancing between thinking and feeling, inhibiting and controlling responses appropriately, fluidly moving between rigidity and spontaneity, turning engagement on and off purposefully) and also **complexity** (able to adapt to various expectations, integrate new information with old, and show conscious awareness of one's self and of others' states of mind or actions). Practitioners can start to characterize their observations with regard to progress in those terms. Within the neuro-relational framework, it becomes easier to understand why a child whose regulation, sensory, or relevance systems are not properly functioning would have difficulties in the executive domain.

Putting it all Together: Working toward Interdisciplinary Practice

Again, the four systems are deeply interrelated, even though the lenses we use should consider each system. The source of any observed unexpected behaviors may be due to a breakdown in any number of other systems upon which the higher brain systems are built. The goal of the provider is to be attuned to these neural systems in order to make in-the-moment adaptations that respond to the child's current level and unmet needs, rather than to the level of the expectation — a concept at the heart of individualized instruction. In general, the more vulnerable or disrupted the systems are for the child or the provider, the more accommodations and intensity are needed in the setting for the systems to reestablish their patterns. Certainly these same principles apply to children performing at or above expected levels as well. See Box 7 for examples and prompts on using the neuro-relational lens in context.

Ultimately, it is up to the team of important people in the child's life — family, providers, and educators — to observe, wonder, and reflect together on the patterns of the four brain systems, both in children and in themselves. Taking this information together, providers can begin to make observations at deeper than face value, through a lens of how the brain systems are interacting. When providers are supported in seeing behaviors in the context of these systems, they are better able to understand that all behaviors have meaning, and are influenced by a child's earliest relationships. Thus, providers are not only equipped to serve the children more appropriately, but also to support the families and each other in building best practices.

Shifting to a Relationship-based Lens can Benefit Early Learners and Their Families

In summary, though there is no single 'right way' or core 'curriculum or approach' to address every finding from brain research, or resolve every issue, practitioners can always safely and securely return to the relationship, of both practitioner-child, and practitioner-family, through which all learning will take place. The exciting trend toward the increased training quality and professionalization throughout the early learning community is no longer having to hold back the more nuanced brain and social sciences that are critical to building the next generation of citizens and families. With this knowledge comes empowerment that makes some of the most difficult and critical aspects of our job infinitely more successful — and more rewarding. See Box 8 for Reflective Practice and Discussion Questions.

References

Lillas, C., & Turnbull, J. (2009). *Infant/child mental health, early intervention, and relationship-based therapies: A neurorelational framework for interdisciplinary practice.* New York: W. W. Norton.

Shonkoff, J. P., & Fisher, P. A. (2013). Rethinking evidence-based practice and two-generation programs to create the future of early childhood policy. *Developmental Psychopathology*, 25, 1635–1653.

Siegel, D. J. (2012). Mind, brain & relationships: The interpersonal neurobiology perspective. In *The developing mind: How relationships and the brain interact to shape who we are* (pp. 1–45). New York: Guilford Press.

Tronick, E., & Beeghly, M. (2011). Infants' meaning-making and the development of mental health problems. *American Psychology*, 66(2), 107–119.

Additional References and Resources

Beauchamp M., & Beauchamp, C. (2012). Understanding the neuroscience and education connection: Themes emerging from a review of the literature. In S. Della Salla & M. Anderson (eds.), *Neuroscience in education: The good, the bad, the ugly,* (pp. 337–355). Oxford: Oxford University Press. (Text available: www.oxfordscholarship.com)

Beauchemin M., et al. (2011). Mother and stranger: An electrophysiological study of voice processing in newborns. *Cereb. Cortex*, 21, 1705–1711.

Degotardi, S., Sweller, N., & Pearson, E. (2013). Why relationships matter: Parent and early childhood teacher perspectives about the provisions afforded by young children's relationships. *International Journal of Early Years Education*, 21, 4–21.

Degotardi, S., & Sweller, N. (2012). Mind-mindedness in infant day-care: Associations with practitioner sensitivity and stimulation during play interactions. *Early Childhood Research Quarterly*, 27, 253–265.

Eisenberger, N. (2012). Broken hearts and broken bones: A neural perspective on the similarities between social and physical pain. *Current Directions in Psychological Science* 21(2), 42–47.

Farmer-Dougan, V., & Alferink, L. A. (2013). Brain development, early childhood, and brain-based education: A critical analysis. In L. H. Wasserman & D. Zambo (eds.), *Early childhood and neuroscience: Links to development and learning* (pp. 55–76). New York: Springer Publications.

Fox, S. E., Levitt, P., & Nelson, C. A. (2010). How the timing and quality of early experiences influence the development of brain architecture. *Child Development*, 81(1), 28–40.

Graham, A. M., Fisher, P. A., & Pfeifer, J. H. (2013). What sleeping babies hear: A functional MRI study of interparental conflict and infants' emotion processing. *Psychological Science*, 24(5), 782–789.

Luby, J., et al. (2013). Effects of poverty on child brain development: Mediating effects of caregiving and stressful life events. *JAMA Ped.*, 167(12), 1135–1142.

McGrath, J. M. (2013). Important reminder: All neonatal caregivers are brain shapers. *Journal of Perinatal & Neonatal Nursing*, 27(3), 199–200.

Parise, E., & Csibra, G. (2012). Electrophysiological evidence for the understanding of maternal speech by 9-month-old infants. *Psychological Science*, 23, 728–733.

Power, J. D., Fair, D. A., Schlaggar, B. L., & Petersen, S. E. (2010). The development of human functional brain networks. *Neuron Review*, 67, 735–748.

Sabol, T. J., & Pianta, R. C. (2012). Recent trends in research on teacher-child relationships. *Attachment in Human Development*, 14(3), 213–31.

Swain J. E., Lorberbaum J. P., Kose S., & Strathearn L. (2007). Brain basis of early parent-infant interactions: Psychology, physiology, and in vivo functional neuroimaging studies. *J. Child Psychol. Psychiatry*, 48, 262–287

"Infant mental health and early care and education providers: A research synthesis." Center for the Social and Emotional Foundations of Learning, Vanderbilt University: http://csefel.vanderbilt.edu/documents/rs_infant_mental_health.pdf

World Association of Infant Mental Health: www.waimh.org/

Gina Lebedeva

Gina Lebedeva, PhD, CCC-SLP, a practicing early intervention speech-language pathologist, uses the lenses of infant mental health and family coaching and an interdisciplinary approach to support families and professionals in early learning. She teaches at the University of Washington in Early Childhood & Family Studies and was the founding director of Translation, Outreach, and Education at the Institute for Learning and Brain Sciences, where she connected developmental science to professionals and policymakers. Dr. Lebedeva holds a PhD in speech and hearing sciences from the University of Washington. She has three children. She can be reached at ginacc@uw.edu.

Box #1 — Everyday Brain-building Moments

Human survival depends on the ability of the brain to adapt and learn throughout the whole lifespan, but the timing and quality of a person's earliest experiences, and how she interacts with genetic predispositions, have a powerful influence on the brain's 'learning template' and lifelong behaviors.

As Jeree Pawl, the infant mental health pioneer, has championed, "How you are is as important as what you do." This could not be more accurate for applying modern brain science to early learning settings. Which of the following moments are most familiar to you? What are some others that you know are enriching a child's mind, brain, and lifelong learning? How are you empowering families to do the same?

- An embrace, for as long as it takes, during a meltdown that tells a child, "I'm always here for you, even when your feelings are so overwhelming and scary to you that you do scary things to yourself or others."

- An adult staying nearby that shows a child, "I'm happy when you explore the interesting things around you. There is no wrong idea, and I will make sure you stay safe. You can always come back to me."

- A child being bathed in rich language, sophisticated vocabulary words, and open-ended questions that offer opportunities to wonder, connect, describe, create, or express.

- An adult and child sharing a mutually new experience face-to-face: Running hands through birdseed, hearing rocks drop on the sidewalk, smelling fresh wet mud, or feeling light tickles with a feather.

- A child experiencing a sense of boundaries and routine, with flexibility and adaptation, teaching them confidence in both following and leading others.

- A child knowing what a true shared 'belly-laugh' feels like with important people in her life, and that they can come in even the most ordinary moments.

- A provider pausing to recognize his own intense feelings during a challenging moment, wondering about both his own and the child's triggers that caused the challenge, and making a plan to connect with the family around that moment to support next steps.

Box #2 — Relationships and Brain Development

A rapidly growing body of evidence describes the links between relationships and brain development, and in many forms provides information directly relatable to everyday interactions and support that can be shared with families and professionals. For instance:

- Pregnant mothers whose comments talking about what their unborn children might think, know, believe, or feel (mind-minded concepts) are more likely to have secure attachments up to two years later (Degotardi & Sweller, 2012).

- In newborns, the mother's voice elicits more activation in language-relevant brain areas compared to a stranger's voice (Beauchemin et al., 2011).

- Brain activity in infants nine months old show more mature patterns when they are listening to language from a primary caregiver compared to other people (Parise & Csbra, 2012).

- Caregivers with stronger attunement to their infants' cues show stronger brain responses in empathy and emotion centers (Swain et al., 2007).

- Sleeping infants show brain activity in emotional centers when their parents are in another room arguing loudly (Graham, Fisher & Pfeifer, 2013).

- Children 4-7 years old, whose parents used hostile or threatening tactics to control the child's behavior, showed less developed brain regions used for memory and learning (hippocampus and amygdala), compared to children whose parents used more supportive or positive tactics, where all families involved were living in poverty (Luby et al., 2013).

- In pre-adolescents and adults, the same brain network (anterior cingulate and insula) is activated for both physical and emotional pain (Eisenberger, 2012).

Box #3 — Key Components of the Neuro-relational Framework

Global Questions and Considerations for the Four Brain Systems of the Neuro-relational Framework

Regulation System: Reacting to and recovering from stress
- Are stress responses appropriate for the situation?
- Is there adequate recovery?
- Is energy use (seen in nutrition and sleep patterns) flexible (lower risk), rigid, or chaotic (higher risk)?

Risk Factors and Characteristics in both Children and Adults:
- Familial stress, limited resources, substance use or exposure
- Prenatal conditions (poor care, growth retardation, toxins in-utero)
- Premature/underweight birth or newborn medical condition
- Genetic anomalies/disorders
- Chronic allergies; sleep disorders
- Feeding challenges (poor suck/swallow, poor nutrition)

Sensory System: Perceiving and processing of information from all senses and body functions
- How efficiently is information from the child's internal and external environment processed?
- How reactive are responses?
- Are safe, rather than unsafe, sensations being sought?
- Sensory perception is highly individualized — what might be enjoyable to one person is not to another ("I wonder why this child hates swinging when so many other kids love it?").

Risk Factors and Characteristics in both Children and Adults:
- Unaddressed hearing or vision impairment
- Over- or under-reactive to sensory inputs
- Inaccurate or slow information processing
- Delays in speech or learning
- Over- or under-stimulation in the environment

Relevance System: Making sense of information, relating information to action
- Can a range of positive and negative emotions be expressed coherently?
- How do memories relate to new experiences?
- What kinds of meanings are assigned to experiences or information?

Risk Factors and Characteristics in both Children and Adults:
- Witnessing or experiencing violence, abuse, or neglect or other trauma
- Chronically depressed or anxious; rapid emotional swings, low frustration tolerance
- Low empathy for self or others; highly demanding or over-accommodating
- Inconsistencies between words and actions in communication
- Low ability to recognize the need to seek help

Executive System: Managing and controlling actions flexibly and contingently to each setting
- Can a conversation, thought, or action stay adequately 'on track' and be communicated effectively?
- Can tasks be planned and completed smoothly with minimal distraction?
- Can problem solving and decision-making be executed flexibly?

Risk Factors and Characteristics in both Children and Adults:
- Low ability to modify language for problem solving or social adaptations
- High distractibility and impulsivity, low ability to delay gratification
- Mental rigidity, unable to modify thinking patterns
- Low awareness of, or inaccurate judgment of strengths or weaknesses
- Difficulty using hindsight, foresight, cause-effect reasoning, or self-reflection
- Unable to separate and hold self from others in mind at the same time

Adapted with permission from Lillas & Turnbull, 2009

Box #4 — The Regulation System

- Like a high-performance sports car, the regulation system is so responsive that it can become fragile with misuse. A well-documented example is with chronic stress. Cortisol is a chemical produced to help cope with expected and 'healthy' stress, and to regulate arousal and excitability. Normal amounts of cortisol in the system are absorbed by the hippocampus, a deep brain structure that is also responsible for memory formation (a form of learning). When there is too much cortisol in the system from over-exposure to stress, the hippocampus cortisol receptors simply shut down, and stop working (perhaps like a boat that has too much cargo, causing it to break down and sink). This causes the cortisol production systems to also shut down (because it has been overloaded); thus, when stress from the environment continues, the brain is no longer producing the needed chemicals to deal with it, so the regulation system is fully out-of-balance. For instance, this non-coping system is what is observed in post-traumatic stress disorder, which can happen in all ages including infancy. Further, because the hippocampus is no longer doing its normal function, learning and memory become compromised, even when the stress is not actively occurring.

- An example of this in the classroom is a child who seems chronically to be in 'meltdown' or 'near-meltdown' mode, who cannot seem to regulate behaviors, might over- or under-react to stimuli (hitting or ignoring), or cannot adequately calm for nap or follow expected routines, let alone retain much new information. This is not a child who is being willfully defiant, but rather a child whose flooded brain is not able to create the necessary conditions to manage behavior and learn; this may be a frightened or overwhelmed child with no coping mechanism.

- The child's providers may try to externally manage the behaviors (e.g. time out), but because those strategies actually are addressing other brain systems (such as the executive or relevance systems, not the regulation system) the behaviors will not extinguish, and may even escalate. Many of these children even end up 'expelled' from centers even in the toddler years because providers themselves become dysregulated around the child, and are not equipped with tools to address this part of the brain system, and thus the interaction patterns become unsafe and unmanageable. The disrupted environment and rejection experienced by the child and family can worsen the underlying regulation dysfunction, not to mention the cascading effects (e.g. child's confidence, family pressure or humiliation, other children in the center, the teachers' sense of competency, and quality rating or improvement systems for the center — that may be tied to funds). Similarly, a child who seems to be chronically 'under-alert' and lethargic, very little emotional responsiveness or tone (floppy or sluggish) also may be showing signs of a dysfunctioning regulation system. Thus, strategies that are language or behavior based, though well-intended, will not be effective or sustainable unless the regulation system can be addressed.

Box #5 — How Regulation is Learned

- How does the Mutual Regulation Model work? In this model, when an infant shows some type of cue about his internal state, it affects the regulation system of the adult. For instance, a child's discomfort cry is quite noxious and annoying (an evolutionary adaptation), which directly affects the brain chemicals in the provider — putting that provider into a stressed zone of heightened alert, ready to respond. When the provider is responsive, sensitive, and consistent in attending to that infant such as through touch, voice, closeness, movement, food, comfort, the infant's system becomes more regulated (the need is starting to be met), thus reducing the overt behavior or crying. This also makes the provider's brain more regulated (her own stress chemicals are now balanced and no longer on alert), and she feels competent and successful at meeting the infant's needs. The couple can now engage in further positive interactions to sustain a calm and connected stance, and this builds mutual trust and communication. The brain regulation system has 'learned' what it is like to have a moment of dysregulation resolved through another person, and is now wired to continue that pattern in the future toward self-regulation — a necessary and healthy process.

- On the other hand, when a provider is not able to provide responsive, sensitive, or consistent reactions to the infants' signals, neither the infant nor the provider will regulate, and both their systems will stay in an imbalanced mode. This could happen for any number of reasons; perhaps the provider has experienced chronically unmet needs, and has a dysfunctional regulation system himself (e.g. over-reactive or under-reactive). Or, perhaps the provider is under-resourced or over-tasked, and his capacity is compromised. Or, perhaps the child is showing atypical signals that may need special responses due to an underlying disorder, and the provider has not been supported to recognize or respond appropriately. The result is that neither the child nor the provider can regulate from that instance, and they both feel frustrated, helpless, and become detached in order to protect themselves from experiencing that stress and failed repair again. This creates conflict and a ruptured relationship, and the brain circuits of that child 're-wire' accordingly to learn that regulation is not something that can easily happen, especially from others.

- Now, of course there are times when providers cannot meet every need of every child, in every instance. The regulation system is designed to adapt to those times. However, when the infant's experience is *by and large* one of non-mutual regulation, then that infant is likely to grow older with the same dysregulated tendencies because that is what the brain experienced, and will thus not have the brain basis available for other learning systems.

Box #6 — The Relevance System

- Patterns of learning in the relevance system early in life can influence lifelong tendencies in behaviors and in relationships. For example, cultural norms aside, the 'amazingly compliant' toddler who is able to sit much like an adult at an open table while calmly waiting for her parent to order lunch on the other side of the restaurant (a developmentally atypical presentation) may be operating on memories of what has happened when previous attempts at exploration were made. In that child's experience, it may be most relevant to be compliant and avoid any behaviors that result in repeated dysregulated states or otherwise unmet needs — a pattern that has higher risk for developing into avoidance tendencies into adulthood. (Have you ever met an adult who avoids emotional closeness or vulnerability, perhaps for fear of rejection, to avoid conflict, or assumptions of not getting emotional needs met?)

- In another example, a child with an early history of unpleasant sensations during feeding (e.g. reflux, intubation, or a hyper-sensitive sensory system) may have learned to associate feeding times with discomfort and fear, thus may adapt by restricting his preferences to only highly-preferred things rather than trying new textures, flavors, or even colors. A child who has experienced chronic regulatory or sensory disruptions early in life may have learned to anticipate or assume further negative experiences, and thus may actively re-regulate by preventing himself from exploring (*"Why does he hate new playgrounds?"*), by freezing or overly inhibiting or reacting (*"Is this extreme shyness, or this frequent giggling, normal?"*).

Box #7 — Thinking through the Lenses of the Four Brain Systems

- The four systems in the neuro-relational framework are all related to each other. Patterns of caregiver's responsiveness, sensitivity and consistency in everyday interactions largely influence how the four brain systems will develop. In addition, prematurity, trauma, genetic disorders (of known or unknown origin), family transitions, and interactions between temperament and parenting style play large roles. Once providers know what to look for in each system, they can begin to find brain-based solutions in the context of interactions. Using this lens can increase family engagement (taking the family's perspective in building a relationship with them to support their values, capacities, and goals), as well as interdisciplinary collaboration (referring to underlying developmental needs rather than only behaviors or skills).

- For instance, the sensory system strongly influences regulation, which in turn influences relevance — consider the therapeutic effects of deep pressure (weighted blankets, hugs, massage, chews) on children who need extra support to manage internal and external sensations in the process of co-regulation, well before they can be expected to communicate or engage socially. Sensory rooms are thus not only carefully planned for the sensations alone, but to aid in regulation, going back to the most basic system. Regulation patterns are learned through experiences and interactions. Executive functions are more challenging for children whose regulation, sensory, or relevance systems are not optimally developing. In general, the more vulnerable or disrupted the systems are for the child or the provider, the more accommodations and intensity are needed in the setting for the systems to re-establish their patterns:

    — *She knows she is not supposed to dump toys out, yet she does it all the time.*

    — *He seems to talk only in certain instances, but not others. Is that a conscious choice, or an indicator of a low capacity or unmet need in another brain system?*

    — *Though seeming regulated and engaged, this child has difficulty communicating with more than two words at a time. How can we make sure she is surrounded by input that matches and reciprocates her actual ability level, so that her relevance and executive systems can keep up with the demands, rather than overloading the system?*

    — *This child is performing lower than expected on a task. Are there regulation or sensory cues (visual or auditory) cues that might support the next step, or another memory we could relate this to?*

    — *We have identified some areas of unmet need in the child's experiences of responsive, sensitive, and consistent interactions outside of school. What are the appropriate steps to develop our relationships with the family to engage them in the process of meeting those needs effectively? How can I draw from and engage with disciplines other than my own to serve this family well?*

    — *No wonder why snack time is so fussy — perhaps we are offering too many foods too fast for her sensory system to re-learn how to take them.*

    — *Having considered the mom's perspective and her own story, I now understand why she expects these behaviors for her son.*

    — *Is this child struggling with naptime because we haven't provided a smooth or slow transition from playground to quiet time, that can help his body calm down?*

Box #8 — Reflective Practice and Discussion

- Which aspects of the neuro-relational framework are familiar to you? Which are new?

- What do you recognize in each of the four parts of the framework in your work with children and families, and in your personal life or childhood memories?

- Which areas are easiest to recognize? Which are more challenging for you?

- How might this lens influence or alter your current strategies or connections with children or families?

- What plan of action could you take to learn more about the many aspects of the neuro-relational framework?

The Wisdom of Children

by Ruth A. Wilson

> It's circle time, and a preschool teacher asks, "What makes you feel peaceful?" "Having a friend," suggests one child. The teacher notices that Amanda — who is new to the class — starts to cry. When asked what makes her sad, Amanda says, "I don't have any friends." Another child in the group, Trisha, gets up, walks over to Amanda, takes her hand, and invites her to sit next to her. Trisha then tells Amanda, "I'll be your friend."

This story of an actual happening in a Head Start classroom may surprise you in a number of ways. First, you may be surprised by the philosophical question, "What makes you feel peaceful?" presented to the children. You may also be surprised at Trisha's spontaneous empathetic response to the crying child.

While neither the teacher's question nor the child's response may be everyday occurrences in an early childhood classroom, they are consistent with what we know about young children and their ability to be intuitive thinkers. Too often, however, this understanding about young children tends to get lost or ignored in the mound of other perspectives, concerns, and priorities demanding our attention.

One way to sort through the varied and, at times, conflicting demands and priorities of the field, is to consider the wisdom of children. Wisdom, as defined here, is the ability to know what is true, right, or lasting. It's a type of knowing that is more intuitive and existential than academic or analytical. Wisdom resides more in the heart than in the head, more in the soul than in the mind. Trisha, in reaching out to a crying child, demonstrates this kind of knowing. No one told Trisha how to respond to the sadness of another child; no one even told her what it felt like to not have a friend. But Trisha knew. This type of knowing is one expression of wisdom.

Related Concepts

Wisdom isn't always the first thing we think of, or notice, about young children. Wisdom resides far deeper within a child than his or her ability to sing a song or walk on a balance beam. Children (and adults) rarely demonstrate wisdom on demand. A space needs to be open for expressions of wisdom to surface. The preschool teacher asking, "What makes you feel peaceful?" was creating an open and safe space for sharing — and like a butterfly from a pupa, wisdom emerged.

While the term 'wisdom of children' is rarely discussed in early childhood literature, a close examination of some of the research and theory relating to early childhood education reveals closely-connected concepts. Philosophical thinking, existential intelligence, and ecological perspective-taking are three such concepts.

Philosophical thinking. Philosophy for children isn't really all that new. In fact, as a worldwide educational movement, Philosophy for Children (P4C) has been around since 1972; and the Institute for the Advancement of Philosophy for Children (IAPC) has been developing curriculum and offering programs for children of all ages, including preschoolers, for almost 40 years.

A review of related literature indicates that there are multiple benefits of encouraging the philosophical thinking of children, including enhancing their cognitive, affective, and social skills (Christie, 2000; Gazzard, 2000; Lipman, 1993; Matthews, 1994; Pritchard, 1996; Wilson, 2001). Such skills, when integrated, often emerge as wisdom — as seen in the example of Trisha knowing what to do to comfort a child in need of a friend.

Existential intelligence. As an early childhood educator, you're probably aware of the theory of multiple intelligences and recognize its relationship to holistic child development. What you may not be aware of is that since this theory was first developed around the idea of seven types of intelligence (spatial, linguistic, bodily-kinesthetic, logical-mathematical, musical, interpersonal, and intrapersonal), it has been expanded to include a naturalistic intelligence and the possibility of an existential intelligence (Gardner, 1983; 1999). While naturalistic intelligence bears some relationship to wisdom in children, existential intelligence speaks to it more directly.

Existential intelligence is described by Gardner (1999) as a proclivity to ask fundamental questions — that is, questions relating to the meaning of existence. Existential intelligence is engaged when we reflect on the underlying truths of our existence: What does it mean to be alive? What is our purpose in life? How should we relate to other living things?

While children may use different words to ask these questions, the fact that they raise questions about the 'big issues' in life reflect a type of existential knowing; a knowing that says there is more to life than what we perceive through our senses or what can be measured, manipulated, or controlled.

Existential knowing goes right to the heart of an issue or the core of existence (Wilson, 2001); it involves a 'direct knowing' (Hart, 2005), often bypassing the need for analytical debate. Described in this way, it becomes obvious how existential knowing and wisdom overlap.

Suggestions of existential knowing in children are clearly evident in the literature:

- Rachel Carson (1956) speaks of children's "clear-eyed vision" and their "true instinct" for what is beautiful and awe-inspiring.

- Rachel Sebba (1991) wrote about children's "unique and unrepeatable ability" to understand the world around them.

- Joseph Clinton Pearce (1971) discussed the "primary perceptions" of a child which, he suggested, allow them to know the world in a deep and direct way.

- Louise Chawla (1994) suggests that children — who often relate to the world in an imaginative way — see the world like poets. This, she says, gives children the ability to know the "essential significance and moral influence of things" (p. 42).

Again, the overlap between wisdom and existential knowing becomes obvious.

Ecological perspective-taking. According to Chaille and Britain (1991), ecological perspective-taking involves being aware and considerate of the perspective of other living things. While Chaille and Britain first discussed this skill (or accomplishment) in the context of science, it certainly includes elements of wisdom — especially in relation to knowing what is right in our treatment of other living things.

A dramatic painting from the 1800s provides an example of ecological perspective-taking in children.

This painting, "An Experiment on a Bird in the Air Pump," shows a small white cockatiel fluttering in panic as air is slowly drawn from the glass bottle in which the bird has been placed. Onlookers of this experiment respond in various ways. The adults, for the most part, seem fascinated by the experiment. The children, however, are more concerned about what's happening to the bird. One of the girls watches with obvious distress as the bird begins to panic. Another girl is too upset to watch and covers her eyes with her hand.

The children in this scene seem to know that living things should be treated with respect and compassion. Such knowing is consistent with what we understand about the wisdom of children (Hart, 2005; Pearce, 1971).

Recognizing and Respecting the Wisdom of Children

The Head Start teacher who asked "What makes you feel peaceful?" did so with the belief that young children have the ability to reflect on ideas and feelings that reach beyond what they can experience through their senses. She also worked from the understanding that children's ideas are to be recognized and valued. She then provided an emotionally safe place for children to share their ideas and feelings. The children's responses confirmed this teacher's belief in the wisdom of children.

Following are four specific ideas on what you might do to encourage and show respect for the wisdom of children.

1. **Listen to children.** Because their vocabularies and their ability to express a focused idea are limited, young children sometimes have trouble explaining exactly what they think and how they feel. Adults would do well to recognize this and give children the extra time and support they need to help them find a way to fully express their ideas. Too many adults have a tendency to jump in and put words to what they think a child wants to say. It's certainly okay to help children express their thoughts, but to move on before checking to see that you got it right does a disservice to the intelligence — and wisdom — of a child. Really listening requires respect, patience, and a belief in the wisdom of a child.

   The benefits of listening and being listened to should not be underestimated. Being listened to "encourages deeper reflection and sharing on the part of everyone. When children realize that someone is really listening to what they have to say or how they are feeling, they may concentrate harder to make what they say authentic and meaningful" (Wilson & Schein, in press).

2. **Engage in authentic dialogue with children.** 'Real talk' is the basis for authentic dialogue. The discussion in 'real talk' is directed by the interests of all the participants — not just the teacher or a designated discussion leader. 'Real talk' requires an environment in which everyone knows that their voices count and that their thoughts and ideas will be respected (Thayer-Bacon, 1995).

3. **Encourage 'wondering' questions and comments.** Wondering questions usually start with "I wonder about…." Some teachers use 'wondering' questions as story stretchers. After reading a book — especially a book with a philosophical theme — the teacher might start a discussion by asking, "What does this story make you wonder about?" The teacher might also start a discussion by sharing something he wonders about. After reading *The Other Way to Listen* by Baylor and Parnall (1978), for example, the teacher might say something like "I wonder if stars whisper to each other."

   'Wondering' questions can also be used to stimulate reflection and sharing related to many different topics and experiences outside of story time. For example, on Valentine's Day in the midst of sharing 'love notes,' one teacher invited reflection and sharing by saying, "I wonder what love really is." The children's responses were amazing. According to one child, love is when Grandpa rubs Grandma's feet — even when his fingers hurt. Another child suggested that love is when you share something that you really want to keep. It's important to recognize that 'wondering' questions should come from the children, as well as from the teacher. Keep in mind, as well, that 'wondering' questions don't always require an answer. Wisdom — in both children and adults — is often expressed as much in the questions as in the answers.

4. **Encourage and respect imaginative expressions of ideas.** If children see the world as poets, it seems only right that we should encourage poetic forms of expressions. If children know the world in a non-literal, intuitive way, it seems that adults would do well to recognize and honor this way of knowing. We can do this by encouraging children to sing, dance, draw, and paint their feelings and ideas about the world around them. We can then help them document their artistic feelings and expressions through photos, videos, and narrative text. Allowing children to tell you what their painting, dance, or sculpture means or represents and recording this for them is one way to demonstrate that you recognize and value their wisdom and their special way of knowing the world.

5. **Foster a sense of wonder through frequent opportunities for positive experiences with nature.** Over the past several years many have spoken eloquently about the benefits for children of time in nature. (For a summary of related research, see White, 2011.) These benefits include improved concentration and impulse control, enhanced sense of well-being, improved quality of play, and improved powers of observation and creativity (Chawla, 2007; White, 2011; Wilson, 2008).

   In addition to fostering all areas of development (physical, social, emotional, cognitive), positive experiences with nature also foster a child's sense of wonder. In fact, as Hart (2005) states, "It appears that time in nature is the most common catalyst for moments of wonder" (p. 165). Hart identifies wonder as one of the spiritual experiences and capacities of children and describes it as a type of knowing that is "non-rational or trans-rational" and says that it involves "direct knowing" (p. 166).

Children — in their moments of wonder — know the world the way it truly is: more of a "gorgeous celebratory event" (Berry, 2002, p. 5) than an object to be used, manipulated, or studied. Children know intuitively — as do many poets and mystics — that every being has its own voice and its own dignity (Berry, 2002).

Summary

Recognizing and respecting the wisdom of children can be a powerful force in fostering their holistic development. An additional benefit of attending to the wisdom of children is that it has the potential for helping us re-discover wisdom within ourselves. This wisdom will not only enhance our individual lives, but may also lead to a healthier and more beautiful way of relating to the social and physical world around us.

References

Baylor, B., & Parnall, P. (1978). *The other way to listen*. New York: Charles Scribner's Sons.

Berry, T. (2002). *Dream of the earth*. Berkeley: University of California Press.

Carson, R. (1956). *The sense of wonder*. New York: Harper & Row.

Chaille, C., & Britain, L. (1991). *The young child as scientist*. New York: Harper-Collins.

Chawla, L. (2007). *Benefits of nature for children's health*. Available: www.peecworks.org/PEEC/PEEC_Research/01C101B8-007EA7AB.0Benefits_of_nature_Fact_Sheet_1_April_2007%5B1%5D.pdf (Accessed February 19, 2011).

Chawla, L. (1994). *In the first country of places*. Albany, NY: State University of New York.

Christie, J. (2000). Introduction of philosophy for children into the Montessori curriculum. *Thinking, 15*(1), 22–29.

Gardner, H. (1983). *Frames of mind: The theory of multiple intelligences*. New York: Harper Collins.

Gardner, H. (1999). *Intelligence reframed: Multiple intelligences for the 21st century*. New York: Basic Books.

Gazzard, A. (2000). What does philosophy for children have to do with emotional intelligence? *Thinking, 15*(1), 39–45.

Hart, T. (2005), Spiritual experiences and capacities of children and youth. In E. C. Rhehlkepartain, P. E. King, L. Wagener, & P. L. Benson (eds.), *The handbook of spiritual development in childhood and adolescence*. Thousand Oaks, CA: Sage Publications.

Lipman, M. (1993). *Thinking children and education*. Dubuque, IA: Kendall/Hunt.

Matthews, G. (1994). *The philosophy of childhood*. Cambridge, MA: Harvard University Press.

Pearce, J. C. (1971). *Magical child*. New York: Dutton.

Pritchard, M. S. (1996). *Reasonable children*. Lawrence, KS: University Press of Kansas.

Sebba, R. (1991). The landscapes of childhood. *Environment and Behavior, 23*(4), 395–422.

Schein, D. L. (2010). "A social constructivist grounded theory on spiritual development beginning at birth." Unpublished doctoral thesis, Walden University.

Thayer-Bacon, B. (1995). Constructive thinking: Personal voice. *Journal of Thought, 30*(1), 55–70.

White, R. (2011). Benefits for children of play in nature. Available: www.whitehutchinson.com/children/articles/benefits.shtml (Accessed: February 19, 2011).

Wilson, R. A. (2001, May/June). Encouraging philosophical thinking in young children. *Early Childhood News*, 54–61.

Wilson, R. (2008). *Nature and young children*. London: Routledge.

Wilson, R. A., & Schein, D. (in press). Supporting the spiritual development of young children. *Exchange*.

Ruth A. Wilson

Dr. Ruth Wilson has been a teacher, teacher educator, and consultant in early childhood education for over 30 years. She currently devotes most of her time to developing curriculum in the area of environmental education for young children. Most recently, Dr. Wilson worked as a curriculum writer for California's Education and Environment Initiative and as a consultant with Sesame Street in planning environmental programs for young children. Dr. Wilson has published several books and numerous articles. Her most recent book is *Nature and Young Children: Encouraging Creative Play and Learning in Natural Environments*. Dr. Wilson can be contacted at wilson.rutha@gmail.com.

CHAPTER 2
Crafting the Curriculum

Designing a Curriculum for Early Childhood Teachers and Caregivers *by Lawrence J. Schweinhart* 46

Everyday Differentiation: How Administrators Support Differentiation of Curriculum and Instruction in Early Childhood Classrooms *by Ann Gadzikowski* 51

The Importance of Order *by Jim Greenman* 58

Taking a Stand on Standards of Experience *by Lilian G. Katz* 61

Responding to Racial and Ethnic Diversity in Early Childhood Programs *by Francis Wardle* 64

Preparing Bicultural, Bilingual Children to Succeed in School *by Hazel Osborn* 69

A Journey towards Inclusion *by Kate Jordan-Downs* 73

The Intangibles in the Early Childhood Classroom *by Carol B. Hillman* 78

Universal Early Childhood Curriculum Principles
by Lawrence J. Schweinhart and Diane Trister Dodge... 82

Designing a Curriculum for Early Childhood Teachers and Caregivers

by Lawrence J. Schweinhart

> This article is written from the perspective of Larry Schweinhart's work with HighScope. It is the intention of the provocations presented here to stimulate discussion and thinking around issues of teachers and caregivers, whatever a program's curriculum might be.

Early childhood programs are not institutionalized like educational programs for children and youth. Instead, they operate in schools, several types of community agencies, other people's homes, and parents' own homes. Several long-term studies show that high-quality preschool programs can have long-term effects and strong return on investment. However, several other short-term studies show that most existing preschool programs have, at best, modest effects on children's development.

A central task of university-based early childhood teacher educators is to provide prospective early childhood teachers with coursework towards bachelors' degrees and certification. But these apply mainly to school teachers and are not required of most teachers and caregivers in community agencies or private homes or parents in their own homes. Early childhood teacher educators in community colleges and pre- and in-service training programs of all sorts must train adults for these roles as well, beginning in high school. Thus, an early childhood curriculum must not only provide basic principles and practices of teaching and learning that are accessible to caregivers and parents as well as teachers; it must also provide teachers with a fully articulated structure that specifies content objectives consistently with a lifelong curriculum supported by an assessment system. The *HighScope Curriculum*, for example, serves these two purposes.

A national U.S. survey found that in 2001, the country had 20.2 million children under 6 years old who had not yet entered kindergarten (Mulligan et al., 2005). Three-fifths of these children had some type of nonparental care and education arrangement at least weekly: one-third received care and education in a center under various auspices, a proportion that grew steadily from 8% of infants to 65% of four-year-olds; 16% received care and education from a nonrelative in a home; and 22% received care and education from a relative in a home.

The Need to Emulate Model Programs

Longitudinal research on the effects of early childhood programs shows that they vary greatly in what they can achieve. Three studies show that high-quality preschool programs can have long-term effects and strong return on investment — the *HighScope Perry Preschool Study* (Schweinhart et al., 2005), the *Carolina Abecedarian Study* (Campbell et al., 2002), and the *Chicago Child-Parent Centers Study* (Reynolds et al., 2001). At least two of these three studies found positive effects on children's intellectual performance in childhood, school achievement in adolescence, reduced placements in special education, reduced retentions in grades, improved high school graduation rates, reduced arrest rates, and reduced teen pregnancies. All three studies found economic returns that were at least several times as great as the initial program investment. Leading economists regard this evidence as stronger than the evidence for most other public investments (Heckman, 2006).

In contrast, three recent studies of government-sponsored preschool programs in the United States show that typical Head Start and state preschool programs — some of the best-funded early childhood programs in the U.S. today — have no more than modest effects on children's development. These three studies are the Head Start Family and Child Experiences Survey or FACES (Zill et al., 2003); the *Head Start Impact Study* (Administration for Children and Families, 2005), and a study of the effects of five state-funded preschool programs (Barnett et al., 2005). Looking at representative samples of children, these studies found small to moderate effects on children's literacy and mathematics skills, less than half as large as the effects of the model programs studied longitudinally.

Effects have been found for these various programs in schools and community agencies in contrast to parents raising children at home or child care in other settings. Further, the studies finding effects have almost all focused on children living in poverty. Few studies have been conducted, hence few effects found, for programs serving children in middle-income families, except for one conducted in Tulsa, Oklahoma, by Gormley, Gayer, Phillips, and Dawson (2005), which found strong program effects on reading and mathematics achievement test scores.

Generalizing Findings

Narrowly defined, the task of university-based early childhood teacher educators is to provide prospective early childhood teachers with coursework towards whatever degree or certification they are seeking. Even then, the match between these degrees and available jobs shapes the content of the coursework. Teachers with bachelors' or masters' degrees will probably focus on teacher certification and jobs in schools, not only in pre-kindergarten but also in the elementary grades. Some of them will find teaching jobs in community agencies. But they will serve only a small fraction of young children in child care.

The gap between professional recommendations and government regulations regarding child care in the U.S. is very wide. The National Association of Child Care Resource and Referral Agencies (NACCRRA, 2007) recommends that child care center directors have at least a bachelor's degree, but only one state has this requirement; and that child care center teachers have at least a Child Development Associate credential or associate's degree in early childhood education, but 21 states require no education and 28 require only a high school diploma or the equivalent. Various states require teachers to have from 0 to 30 hours of training a year, an average of 12.6 hours, while NACCRRA recommends that states require that child care center teachers have 24 hours of training a year. As long as the government expects so little of child care teachers, it is difficult for child care directors to insist that more training and professional development is necessary. It is estimated that only 33% of center teachers and 17% of family child care providers have a bachelor's degree or more (Center for the Child Care Workforce and Human Services Policy Center, 2002).

An expansive, inclusive definition of early childhood teacher education is needed, one that goes well beyond coursework in universities to include community colleges and pre- and in-service training programs of all sorts. Because the U.S. states do not require much training or education for child caregivers, some might be tempted to write off the training that they are required to receive as hopelessly inadequate to the task. Put in terms of the longitudinal studies cited above, high-quality early childhood programs with well-trained teachers have the capacity to make an extraordinary contribution to the development of young children. One reasonable response is to work hard to secure high-quality early childhood programs for as many young children as possible. At the same time, it is important to educate people who become home and center caregivers and parents to do the best job possible. Such education should begin in high school if not earlier; because high school, required of all citizens, is the way to reach as many future caregivers and parents as possible.

Implications for Early Childhood Curriculum

Epstein (1993) identified ingredients of effective early childhood teacher training in a sequence of studies of HighScope training of trainers programs. For in-service training to be effective, it needs to have consistent trainers; distributive, cumulative learning rather than one-shot workshops; hands-on learning rather than just lectures; opportunities for sharing and reflection among practitioners; and, most importantly, a coherent curriculum that guides practice.

Early childhood curriculum is what early childhood teachers and caregivers do and ought to do and is the content of early childhood teacher training. The research findings presented here combine to present a strong rationale that an early childhood curriculum should embody the teaching practices of these model programs. But the analysis of early childhood teacher training here also has direct implications for the nature of early childhood curriculum, specifically that it has two distinct audiences: teachers, on the one hand, and caregivers and parents, on the other. Certainly, these two audiences overlap and some parents and caregivers contribute much more to children's development than do some teachers. The point is that the two audiences have different needs and perceptions of what early childhood curriculum is for.

To meet the needs of teachers, an early childhood curriculum needs a fully articulated structure that fits with, and indeed serves as the foundation of, the lifelong educational curriculum. This means it has content objectives in language, literacy, mathematics, science, the arts, socio-emotional development, and physical education. It is supported by psychometrically adequate tools for the assessment of children's learning and curriculum implementation. It specifies basic principles of teaching and learning and teaching practices consistent with these principles.

To meet the needs of caregivers and parents, an early childhood curriculum must be accessible to them regardless of their educational backgrounds. It identifies basic principles of teaching and learning and teaching practices consistent with these principles and does so in a way that can be clearly communicated, at least initially, in a matter of hours, through instruction and coached practice. These principles and practices should apply in homes as well as classrooms, to parents as well as caregivers. They should be accessible to students in high schools and community colleges, to caregivers receiving in-service training, and to parents taking parenting courses.

This is not a proposal for two early childhood curriculum models, but rather for one early childhood curriculum model that meets the needs of two different audiences. An early childhood curriculum needs to fit into the educational system and the parenting/caregiving system. The educational system emphasizes what children must learn and do as they get older. The parenting/caregiving system emphasizes the present needs of children and families

The *HighScope Curriculum*, for example, was originally designed by teachers and administrators to fit the needs of a public school setting. During the home visits of the HighScope Perry Preschool program, it was adapted for parents. From its beginnings, it was adapted to fit well into Head Start programs. It was extended from infancy to elementary school through various projects funded by foundations and the federal government. It has all the components of a fully articulated early childhood curriculum.

It has also been framed for children's caregivers and parents. HighScope publications and workshops address family child care and caregiving practices for infants and toddlers as well as preschoolers. The curriculum's central focus, on adult-child interaction in which adults respect children and their thinking abilities, is accessible to parents and caregivers as well as teachers. Its emphases on room arrangement and daily routine are accessible to everyone.

Many people who take care of and raise children will never get a degree in child development or early education. Our continuing challenge is to make the basic principles of good child development and early education available to them within the educational opportunities available to them.

References

Administration for Children and Families, U.S. Department of Health and Human Services. (2005). "Head Start Impact Study: First year findings." Washington, DC: Author. Retrieved December 3, 2007: www.acf.hhs.gov/programs/opre/hs/impact_study/reports/first_yr_finds/first_yr_finds.pdf

Barnett, W. S., Lamy, C., & Jung, K. (2005). "The effects of state prekindergarten programs on young children's school readiness in five states." New Brunswick, NJ: National Institute for Early Education Research, Rutgers University. Retrieved December 3, 2007: nieer.org/docs/index.php?DocID=129

Campbell, F. A., Ramey, C. T., Pungello, E. P., Sparling, J., & Miller-Johnson, S. (2002). Early childhood education: Young adult outcomes from the Abecedarian project. *Applied Developmental Science, 6*, 42–57.

Center for the Child Care Workforce and Human Services Policy Center. (2002). "Estimating the size and components of the U.S. child care workforce and caregiving population." Washington, DC: Author. Retrieved May 19, 2008: www.ccw.org/pubs/workforceestimatereport.pdf

Epstein, A. S. (1993). *Training for quality: Improving early childhood programs through systematic inservice training.* Monographs of the HighScope Educational Research Foundation, 9). Ypsilanti, MI: HighScope Press.

Gormley, Jr., W. T., Gayer, T., Phillips, D., & Dawson, B. (2005). The effects of universal pre-k on cognitive development. *Developmental Psychology, 41*, 872–884. Retrieved December 3, 2007: www.crocus.georgetown.edu/reports/oklahoma9z.pdf

Heckman, J. (2006, January 10). Catch 'em young. *Wall Street Journal*, page A14. Retrieved December 3, 2007: www.tompaine.com/articles/2006/01/11/catch_em_young.php

Mulligan, G., Brimhall, D., West, J., & Chapman, C. (2005). "Child care and early education arrangements of infants, toddlers, and preschoolers: 2001." (NCES 2006–039). Washington, DC: National Center for Education Statistics, U.S. Department of Education. Retrieved December 3, 2007: http://nces.ed.gov/pubs2006/2006039.pdf

National Association of Child Care Resource and Referral Agencies. (2007). "We can do better: NACCRRA's ranking of state child care center standards and oversight." Washington, DC: Author. Retrieved March 22, 2008: www.naccrra.org/policy/recent_reports/scorecard.php.

Reynolds, A. J., Temple, J. A., Robertson, D. L., & Mann, E. A. (2001). Long-term effects of an early childhood intervention on educational achievement and juvenile arrest: A 15-year follow-up of low-income children in public schools. *Journal of the American Medical Association, 285*, 2339–2346.

Schweinhart, L. J., Montie, J., Xiang, Z., Barnett, W. S., Belfield, C. R., & Nores, M. (2005). *Lifetime effects: The HighScope Perry Preschool Study through age 40.* Ypsilanti, MI: HighScope Press.

Zill, N., Resnick, G., Kim, K., O'Donnell, K., Sorongon, A., McKey, R. H., Pai-Samant, S., Clark, C., O'Brien, R., & D'Elio, M. A. (May 2003). "Head Start FACES (2000): A whole child perspective on program performance — Fourth progress report." Prepared for the Administration for Children and Families, U.S. Department of Health and Human Services (DHHS) under contract HHS-105-96-1912, Head Start Quality Research Consortium's Performance Measures Center. Retrieved December 3, 2007: www.acf.hhs.gov/programs/opre/hs/faces/reports/faces00_4thprogress/faces00_4thprogress.pdf

Lawrence J. Schweinhart

Larry Schweinhart is an early childhood program researcher and speaker throughout the U.S. and around the world. He has conducted research at HighScope Educational Research Foundation in Ypsilanti, Michigan, since 1975 and has served as its president since 2003. He has directed: *The landmark HighScope Perry Preschool Study through age 40*, establishing the great human and financial potential of high-quality early childhood programs; *The HighScope Preschool Curriculum Comparison Study*, which shows that child-initiated learning activities are critical to the success of early childhood programs; and studies of the effectiveness of Head Start training and of Michigan's Great Start Readiness Program. He received his PhD in Education from Indiana University in 1975 and has taught elementary school and college courses. He and his wife Sue have two children and five grandchildren.

Everyday Differentiation

How Administrators Support Differentiation of Curriculum and Instruction in Early Childhood Classrooms

by Ann Gadzikowski

Most early childhood administrators differentiate every day in their supervisory practices. For example, a new teacher in a toddler room may need practical suggestions for managing the transition from lunch to nap, while a veteran preschool teacher may need a responsive sounding board as she reflects on her latest emergent curriculum project. When administrators individualize their approach to staff supervision, they are modeling differentiation strategies that are among the hallmarks of excellent teaching.

What is Differentiation?

Differentiation means adjusting or changing instructional practices, plans, or materials to meet the individual needs of each learner. The term 'differentiation' is often used in special education or in gifted education to describe the ways teachers adapt activities or assignments to meet the unique needs of struggling or advanced students. But even among a general population of typically-developing young learners, differentiation of instructional practices, as well as of curriculum and materials, results in a richer and deeper learning experience for all.

Differentiation vs. Individualization

In early childhood education, we often use the word 'individualization' instead of differentiation, at least in terms of the physical care and social-emotional support of each child. We strive to get to know each child and her family, to build trusting relationships. Most teachers and caregivers individualize every day, often through one-on-one conversations and caregiving tasks, from helping children put on their shoes to serving snacks.

The term 'differentiation,' however, is more specific than 'individualization' because it is most often used in relation to cognitive development, to curriculum, to assessment, and to the learning environment. While many early childhood teachers are accustomed to individualizing the care of young children and may also be familiar with individualized assessment practices, many are not trained or experienced in incorporating differentiation strategies into curriculum planning, teaching practices, and the preparation of the learning environment. Let's take a look at the following scenario.

Meet Beth

Beth Jameson is the director of Westside Child Care Center, a small non-profit program offering full-day child care services to families with preschool-aged children. Beth has led the program for five years and, before that, she worked as a teacher at Westside. When Beth talks with prospective parents about the strengths of her program, she describes the benefits of their mixed-age classrooms: children from ages three to five, together in the same group. At Westside, children stay with the same pair of teachers from the time they enter the program at three years old until they leave for kindergarten at five. This continuity of care means the teachers are able to build strong, trusting relationships with children and their families over time.

Beth also enjoys talking with parents about the strength of their curriculum at Westside, praising the teachers' ability to create engaging curriculum plans that are organized into weekly units based on broad early childhood themes, such as weather, farm animals, insects, community helpers, and 'things that go.' The planning process that Beth has developed for the center requires that teachers create weekly curriculum plans in advance. Beth reviews these plans with each teaching team at their weekly planning meetings, and then the teachers post them on the bulletin boards outside their classrooms. The plans describe the focus of the unit, the plans for activities, materials that will be offered in each interest area in the classroom, and a list of state early learning standards that will be addressed through the week's curriculum.

Although Beth is usually satisfied with the weekly curriculum plans when she reviews them in advance, recently Beth has noticed during her regular, informal classroom observations, that some weekly plans tend to engage mostly the younger children, the three-year-olds and younger fours, while some weekly plans seem to engage mostly the older children, the older fours and the five-year-olds. For example, the teachers in the Blue Room recently developed a curriculum plan for a unit on farm animals, which seemed very engaging to the younger children but the older children were often restless, wandering and getting into mischief. The activities planned for the next curriculum unit on the topic of machines and robots, Beth recognizes, generally appeal to the older children; many of the younger children are reluctant to participate. Beth wonders how she might help the teachers differentiate the curriculum to ensure they are challenging and engaging both the younger and the older children in every unit.

Applying Differentiation to a Traditional Lesson-planning Process

A common curriculum planning process among early childhood practitioners is the creation of one weekly curriculum plan for the whole class. These plans are usually not differentiated. Teachers may need support from administrators and supervisors to:

- find ways to differentiate to meet the needs of the children who are struggling and those who are advanced and have already learned most of the content of the lesson.

- write differentiated lesson plans or revise their plans to include differentiation.

- modify the forms or tools they use to document their plans.

- add pages or sections where they can note how they might adapt activities to make them more accessible or more challenging for the children.

Although differentiation has not been widely studied in early childhood classrooms, a growing body of research supports differentiation as an effective teaching practice in general, mixed-ability classrooms at the elementary and secondary level (Hueber, 2010). Among the most useful and practical strategies for differentiation that are relevant in an early childhood classroom are: increasing complexity, creating flexible groupings, adjusting the pace, and offering choices.

Increasing Complexity

The first strategy, increasing complexity, is particularly important for ensuring that children who have already mastered prescribed learning outcomes are still challenged by the curriculum. One of the roles of the administrator in differentiation is reviewing lesson plans to ensure that there is a process in place for pre-assessment, to measure what prior knowledge children have about a topic.

> If a team of Pre-K teachers are developing a project or unit on the topic of farm animals, a developmentally appropriate pre-assessment activity would be to interview children with open-ended questions, such as "What are some examples of animals that live on farms? What do they look like? What do they do all day?" and to observe children's actions and conversations during open-ended play with toy farm animals or during dramatic play related to farms.

Through these pre-assessment activities, teachers can gather information about children's prior knowledge and adjust their plans in order to avoid spending time teaching children what they already know and to prepare activities that will truly challenge the children.

A helpful tool for measuring the complexity of the concepts and experiences in a lesson plan is Bloom's taxonomy. Educational psychologist Benjamin Bloom created a taxonomy as a tool to help teachers identify and categorize learning objectives that promote higher-order thinking. 'Higher order' means thinking with increasing complexity and creativity. Bloom's taxonomy, as revised and updated by Lorin Anderson and David Krathwohl (2001), has six levels, with the first level representing the least complex thought and each level thereafter involving greater abstraction and sophistication of thought:

- Remembering
- Understanding
- Applying
- Analyzing
- Evaluating
- Creating

Administrators and supervisors can use Bloom's taxonomy to evaluate curriculum. A review of curriculum documents or lessons plans can incorporate the use of a checklist or a list of questions that ensure there are opportunities for learning at each level of Bloom's taxonomy.

> A Pre-K unit on farm animals would include opportunities to recall the name of each animal (Level 1); to describe the sounds, movements, and appearance of each animal (Level 2); to apply the concept that animals need to eat, to how a farmer cares for the animals (Level 3); to analyze the similarities and differences between animals (Level 4); to evaluate the appropriateness of a farm structure, such as a barn, as a home for farm animals (Level 5); and to create a model of a farm out of blocks or clay (Level 6).

Creating Flexible Groupings

Creating flexible groups means that teachers create groups based on children's interests and their abilities. The groups are called 'flexible' because they are temporary. Children grow and learn at a rapid pace during the early childhood years and their abilities and interests shift and change rapidly. Children shouldn't be 'tracked' by having to stay in the same group assignment over a long period of time, but teachers can be intentional about structuring activities and lessons by working with small groups of children with similar interests and abilities.

> ### Beth Suggests Flexible Groups
>
> At Westside Child Care Center, where every mixed-age class includes children as young as three and as old as five, the children's participation in some of the activities and centers could be structured by age. For the curriculum topic related to farm animals, the youngest children might participate in dramatic play, pretending to be farm animals, while the older children might participate in a more challenging activity, such as creating a map of a farmyard.

Adjusting the Pace

Another differentiation strategy is to adapt the pace of a specific activity or adapt the pace of a whole curriculum unit. Increasing the pace of an activity, such as a matching game, challenges students by demanding greater expertise and faster thinking. A faster pace during a curriculum unit means more information and concepts are covered over a shorter period of time, preventing boredom and maximizing learning. Sometimes slowing the pace can add challenge too, because adding more depth and detail to an activity or curriculum sequence may also add complexity and creativity. For example, a unit on farm animals could be extended to include a study of the design and function of the barns and stables where the animals live.

During a curriculum unit on farm animals, teachers can create a temporary learning center for each type of animal — from pigs to chickens to horses — with activities, nonfiction books, and toy animal figures. Children can choose which center to visit in order to learn in-depth about one type of animal.

Offering Choices

When teachers offer children choices, we can be confident that the learning experiences are aligned with their interests. Offering choices allows children to take an active role in their own learning because the decision-making process engages them and increases their sense of responsibility for what happens in the classroom.

One way to offer choices to children is to create learning experiences at 'centers' and invite children to choose which center they want to visit. Giving children the choices about which activity to try increases the likelihood that children will be engaged in the activity and stick with the ones that are at their appropriate level of challenge.

Beth Suggests Offering Choices

In the example of the Westside Child Care Center, where some of the younger children were still learning the names of farm animals while some of the older children were ready to explore the characteristics of farm animals in greater depth, the teachers could offer activity choices at learning centers that might include a matching game that teaches and reinforces vocabulary, as well as a letter-writing station where children can dictate letters to a farmer, asking questions about the animals on the farm. The younger children with less experience and expertise will likely choose the matching game and the older children will likely choose the letter station.

The Administrator's Role in Differentiation

The administrator's role in supporting differentiation is to determine how differentiated instruction fits into the current curriculum practices. Even if differentiation has not been a topic of discussion or attention, teachers are probably already practicing it to some extent. Administrators who supervise teachers and lead curriculum development can help teachers become more intentional about differentiation by shining a light on the successful examples of differentiation and by developing structures and practices that allow teachers to differentiate. It may be helpful to communicate to teachers that differentiation is not a new task to add to their long list of things to do, but an enhancement, a thread that runs through what they are already doing.

Early childhood programs that use a formal child assessment system, such as *Teaching Strategies Gold®*, already individualize in the gathering of assessment information. In these cases, it can be helpful for teachers to think more intentionally about differentiation at the front end: to focus on pre-assessment at the beginning of each unit or project.

In early childhood education, because the children we work with are so young, we have a tendency to ignore the possibility that children may already have prior knowledge about a topic.

Administrators demonstrate that they value differentiation by creating and providing structures that support differentiation. The lesson-planning process must allow time for reflection and documentation of alternative activities for children who need more supports or greater challenge. The forms and documents used for planning should include space for writing differentiated plans and teachers need information, resources, and training on how to differentiate.

Differentiated Teacher Training

Teacher training on differentiation can be delivered as a stand-alone topic at staff meetings or conferences. As illustrated in the example above, differentiation techniques can also be demonstrated for teachers during training sessions on other topics. The administrator can use a parallel process, modeling instructional practices in the delivery of the training session that the teachers can practice in the delivery of their own instruction of the children. Any differentiation strategies used in a classroom with children can be modeled in teacher training with a group of adults.

Modeling is a powerful professional development tool, but it is most effective when partnered with other activities that will support and inform teachers' efforts to improve the quality of their curriculum and instruction.

> Many early childhood programs implement a curriculum unit related to cold weather at the start of the winter season. Children are taught introductory information about snow, ice, and snowflakes in a very similar manner at age two, three, four, and five. A pre-assessment activity, such as inviting children to create snow scenes using white clay, while asking children open-ended questions about snow and winter, is an informal yet effective method for measuring what children already know about winter weather. This process allows teachers to differentiate their approach to the curriculum plan, creating opportunities for children new to the topic to learn the introductory concepts and the children who are already somewhat knowledgeable about the topic to delve deeper.

In the example on the following page, Beth will need to provide teachers with resources, such as print materials, webinars, and videos that provide further details and specifics about differentiation strategies. She will need to provide encouragement and coaching for teachers as they experiment with different ways to group children and adjust the pace of their curriculum plans. Beth, like most early childhood administrators who supervise teachers, is in a position to challenge the teachers to continually improve the quality of their curriculum and their teaching practices while, at the same time, she is also responsible for making sure the teachers

---

Beth Models Differentiation in Teacher Training

Back at Westside Child Care Center, Beth wants to find more ways to encourage and support differentiated instruction in the mixed-age classrooms. She considers using the next all-staff meeting to present her ideas to the teachers, but she has already made a plan to use that meeting to review important playground safety procedures. Then she realizes that she can use the playground training session to demonstrate differentiation strategies. At the beginning of the meeting, Beth tells the teachers that she will be demonstrating two differentiation strategies during the training session, pre-assessment and flexible grouping, and asks the group to pay attention to how these strategies work with adults and to consider whether these strategies could also be relevant for children.

Then Beth implements the training by beginning with a pre-assessment activity. She presents a scenario to the teachers, describing a playground situation that demonstrates a number of different common safety hazards. Then she asks teachers to complete a self-assessment survey in which they rate their own knowledge and confidence in their ability to respond to the scenario. Beth does not collect or read the surveys, but she asks each participant to choose, based on the results of their reflections and survey responses, a training activity that is specific to her experience and interests:

- One activity, which involves a basic read-through review of procedures from the staff handbook and the creation of a scenario that demonstrates and summarizes best practices, is intended for new or inexperienced teachers who feel they need a review of the written materials.

- Another activity is a playground inspection, where a group of teachers uses a checklist (prepared by Beth) to walk around the playground while reviewing and evaluating the playground. This activity is intended for teachers who are familiar with the procedures, but may benefit from thinking deeply about how the procedures are implemented on a daily basis.

- And the third choice of activity is to create a skit that illustrates the importance of following playground procedures. This activity is intended for staff members who are very informed and experienced and can take a leadership role in demonstrating safety procedures to the rest of the team.

Beth allows the teachers to choose their own group, based on their self-assessment. After they select their activities and get to work on the tasks, Beth is pleased to find that the make-up of their self-selected groups pretty much matches the selections she would have made if she had directed them to groups based on their job performance and teaching experience. As the leader, she chooses to work with the first group, to help the less experienced or less confident teachers review and summarize the written safety policies.

At the conclusion of the training, Beth allows time for the whole group to come together and discuss how the differentiated instruction worked for them and how these practices might be applied to their own teaching with children.

have the time and resources they need to reflect, plan, and implement a differentiated curriculum.

Parallel Process

Differentiation by administrators in teacher supervision and differentiation by teachers in classroom instruction are two separate but parallel processes. Both teachers and children benefit from these practices. Yet differentiation is not a simple, discrete task to add to your center's list of things to do, an item to be checked off and forgotten. Differentiation is an enhancement that deepens growth and understanding for every learner. In early childhood education, one size does not fit all. When administrators tailor each supervisory experience to the interests and ability of each staff member, the teachers will be inspired to do the same with the children in their classroom.

Reference

Anderson, L., & Krathwohl, D. (2001). *A taxonomy for learning, teaching, and assessing: A revision of Bloom's Taxonomy of Educational Objectives.* New York: Pearson.

Resources

Gadzikowski, A. (2013). *Challenging exceptionally bright children in early childhood classrooms.* St. Paul, MN: Redleaf Press.

Heacox, D. (2012). *Differentiating instruction in the regular classroom.* Minneapolis, MN: Free Spirit Publishing.

Huebner, T. A. (2010, February). What research says about differentiated learning. *Educational Leadership, 67*(5), 79–81.

Ann Gadzikowski

Ann Gadzikowski is an author and educator with more than 25 years' experience teaching and directing early childhood programs. Her recent book, *Creating a Beautiful Mess: Ten Essential Play Experiences for a Joyous Childhood*, won gold in the 2015 National Parenting Publications Awards. She currently serves as the Early Childhood Coordinator for Northwestern University's Center for Talent Development. Visit her website: www.anngadzikowski.com

The Importance of Order

by Jim Greenman

> The new three-year-old looked into my eyes with a mixture of panic and fear and a hint of excitement, as if to say, "What the hell is happening here?" I recognized the expression. It was almost identical to the look on the face of the new student teacher or the look on my face the first time I set foot in México City.

We all need order in our spaces to make them tolerable. Our homes are our homes because we create within them an order that expresses our personalities, values, culture, geography, logic, goals, and concerns related to living. Our homes are where we feel secure and competent when it reflects us and when it is familiar and predictable. The same need applies to children's programs. Children's places need ordered time and space that furthers the program goals while making the program a pleasant place to live and work for all those (large and small) who inhabit the program. We need planned complexity — an environment rich enough to challenge, but not so complex as to frustrate. The order provides a comforting framework that does not harshly interrupt the activities of children; instead, the order allows for more experiences and for children to anticipate their day.

We regulate our days by routine and time, welding actions and expectations to the clock. When we ignore the clock for a while, it can be liberating. But after a while, we may become anxious or disoriented, even if we know why we are off the clock. Young children, who rarely understand why the fabric of order woven by schedules is torn, are likely to feel the loss more — unless we take responsibility for always keeping them in the know.

Of course, we are all not the same. There are those who feed and flourish on disorder and other meticulous souls who are thrown off balance by anything out of place. Teachers in a single classroom often seem to span this range, and certainly it is true of the children. And then, of course, there are toddlers, little anarchists with a herd instinct who seem to have a sense of order based on some vision undecipherable to the adult mind.

Structuring Space

The job of a young child is to make the world sensible, to construct or discover the properties, patterns, relationships that exist in the material world of people and things and to figure out where he or she might fit in. The path of learning and development is more like that of a butterfly than that of a bullet. Our job is to provide a setting where a group of energetic, idiosyncratic seekers go about this task and where all — adults and children — thrive amidst the daily rigors of group living. To accomplish this, the setting must have an order that is comprehensible to and functional for all occupants. The look of the order is busy and alive. Some guidelines:

The order should be based on program goals and values (which may well include individualization). Order for order's sake is often mere tidiness and control. If independence, competence, and individual growth are primary goals, then the materials should be stored and displayed for independent use for all developmental levels of children. If the goals include the development of language and math skills, the display and function of learning centers should form the order of the building. The order should be understood by children as well as adults. The more turnover in adults and children, the more obvious and predictable the order needs to be. Understanding the developmental abilities of the children is important. An understandable order for toddlers requires anchoring objects and activities to the same times and places and using the simplest classification categories for child-access storage, like using duplicates and photographs to identify the object's place.

The order should be restorable by children and adults. The order should be obvious; labels should include photographs, pictures, symbols, and language depending on the cognitive skills of the children. The storage sites and routines should accommodate child capabilities. If the order is not easily restorable, then the adults will inevitably reduce the potential for disorder, usually barring child access or removing materials, particularly those with many small parts. The program order should be functional, working to make life easier, better, and more productive. This is obvious but necessary to keep in mind. Sometimes the order has the opposite effect. A too precise order can bring program life to a halt. There is a need for toy bins and chests for quick dump-it-in storage to keep the action flowing, just as there is a need for carefully ordered shelves.

The order should reflect changing conditions. This is not always easy, as people become accustomed to a familiar order. When an order is designed to achieve goals, change is necessary because the children change as they become familiar with the room and grow. In a good classroom, observing children leads to ordering and reordering with the children's involvement.

The order should contribute to a sense of aesthetic harmony. There is more to life than function. When going about the business of positioning objects and display, it is always important to keep in mind the overall aesthetic, the rich normality created by the harmony in size, colors, and shapes.

Structuring Time

The structuring of time has an enormous impact on how we feel. Feeling powerless over the rhythms of living within a rigid order, or trying to keep up with an assembly line that speeds up, or waiting for something, anything, interesting to happen, are all unpleasant feelings. And a too casual approach to the clock can limit program achievements and deprive children and adults of the security that comes with predictable routines (to say nothing of a prompt, regular meal and a dry diaper).

Basic time blocks and the day's rhythms are defined by the tasks of living: eating, diapering and toileting, sleeping, and housekeeping; by staffing schedules and breaks; and by the physical space, particularly the amount of scheduled shared space. Routine weds the tasks and times. In some programs if staff are not careful, achieving some important goals, for example staff breaks, a prescribed set of learning experiences, or use of more space can result in rigid, assembly-line scheduling of time. If every activity must be completed in a short, fixed time period, obviously both children and teachers are severely constricted in what they can do. "I never get to finish anything" can be a common complaint of preschoolers and is a clear indication about the social value of depth and concentration, as well as to who is in charge.

Timetables for children, like space, need some flexibility if learning and caring are to take place. Building a cardboard castle, cooking breakfast, visiting a farm, or reading a book may be hard to fit into the schedule. Waking up after napping, diapering two babies, successfully completing the training mission to the potty chair, and other caring elements don't always lend themselves to the clock.

What makes life worth living is the chance, the hope, that wonderful things might just happen — a hope based on experience with random surprises. Many children delight when the order wavers, by chance or design, although some find any surprise disconcerting. Breakfast outside or waffles for lunch, a change in nap, mixed-up space — these are memorable experiences that open eyes to possibilities.

Routines and Rituals

Our lives are ordered with daily routines and rituals: the first cup of coffee, good-bye kisses, how we enter sleep, the routes taken to work or school. What's the difference between routine and ritual? The morning cup of coffee is a routine; having it in your favorite cup or at your favorite spot turns it into a ritual — rituals tend to be personal routines that generate feelings of pleasure. Adult group life has its own rites: holiday ceremonies, pre-game warm-ups, pledges of allegiance. Ritual joins routine and the physical order as the secure skeleton that holds individuals and groups together in times of stress, amidst the uncertainties of staff and children who come and go and change from mood to mood, day to day.

Rituals serve the same purpose in children's programs. Group daily activities, like sharing the same song or the same story day after day, reassure against the unknown. Children under three will listen to *Good Night Moon* by Margaret Wise Brown with delight every rest time. There are acknowledged rites of passage as children give up diapers and bottles, enter older groups, and leave for school. Individual rituals between children and caregivers can become pinions of security — a special touch, a shared joke, any regular shared exchange. Groups might experiment, even with rites of destruction perhaps.

Consider this excerpt from the journal of writer Katherine Mansfield: "Tidied all my papers. Tore up and ruthlessly destroyed much. This is always a great satisfaction." There is always occasion to restore the order through ruthless destruction — the collapsing of a block tower, the exuberant balling up of paper and tossing it into the trash.

Avoiding a rigid order that chokes or constricts or a too loose order that frightens or intoxicates generally requires a thoughtful and complete analysis of how all the program structural elements interact — time, space, goals, organization, and people — and creative problem solving to minimize negative side effects. Goals are statements about what matters. Used as a constant reference, goals prevent an order based on an individual's fussiness, territoriality, need for control, laziness, or lack of concern; or an order based on historical conditions, the last director's logic, the current director's logic, or institutional mindsets. And frequent analysis reduces the chance that order itself and smooth management — ostensible efficiency — become the goals, rather than what should be the real goals: learning and better care.

Jim Greenman

Jim Greenman dedicated more than 30 years to the early childhood field as an educator, early childhood administrator, and author. Throughout his career, he worked with employer-sponsored, inner city, hospital, and university programs; early childhood and family education programs; Head Start; family child care; and public and private schools. Jim played a significant role in the facility and program design process for more than 100 early childhood projects, taught at the Institute on Child Care Design at the Harvard Graduate School of Design, and was senior vice president for education and program development at Bright Horizons Family Solutions. He held a master's degree from the University of California at Berkeley, where he also completed additional advanced graduate courses. Jim passed away in 2009 after a courageous battle with cancer. He inspired many people in the early childhood field through his dedication and work in the early childhood field; Jim's legacy leaves an ever-lasting gift to children and educators.

Taking a Stand on Standards of Experience

by Lilian G. Katz

The adoption of state and national education standards has been steadily increasing in recent years. Sometimes they are referred to as 'standards of achievement,' sometimes as 'standards of performance,' and often as 'education outcomes.' Most recently, national "Common Core Standards" have been introduced to encourage all educators to improve their efforts to meet standards and to produce outcomes of educational programs around the country.

This increasing reference to performance standards and outcomes has become part of the new clichés in the field. Clichés are usually defined as broad, stereotyped, and over-used expressions that are sufficiently vague that large numbers of people can readily agree with them. They also have a kind of 'common sense' quality to them. But, the increasing efforts to adopt standards for the wide variety of early childhood provisions we have raises some troubling questions about their appropriateness, and perhaps also their potentially damaging effects.

By way of example, the state of Illinois issued a manual entitled "Illinois Early Learning Standards for Children 3-5"[1] in 2004 that refers to 'benchmarks' for all children within that age group. Seven guiding principles are listed, such as: "Early learning and development are multidimensional," "Young children are capable and competent," "Children are individuals who develop at different rates," and so forth.

In addition to the list of quite reasonable assumptions, eight 'learning areas' are suggested. They include language arts, mathematics, science, social studies, and so on. However, when specific subject- or content-related standards are presented, they become performance standards that are often referred to as outcomes. These outcomes are rationalized as ways to get children 'ready' for school, ready to 'succeed' in school, and to perform well on tests of academic skills.[2] During discussions about standards and outcomes, allusions are frequently made to the 'delivery' of the curriculum (as in delivering the mail or the milk), and discussions of 'inputs' designed to produce specific 'outcomes' are increasingly frequent. Some even refer to child care and early childhood programs as an industry, rather than as a service.

It seems to me that using terms like *outcomes* and *performance standards* is based on an industrial or manufacturing analogy. In an industry, raw material is placed on an assembly line, and is then run through a sequence of processes, at the end of which out come identical shoes or cups or pencils or whatever else is being manufactured.

I suggest that a more appropriate way to assess provisions for our young children is to answer questions like "What does it feel like to be a child in this environment day after day after day?" This question provokes another one: "What experiences should all children have much of the time?" (not every minute). In other words, what *standards of experience* should we provide for our young children?

Below is a preliminary list of possible experiences that I suggest all children should have much of the time; the matter of exactly how much time is needed depends on many factors worthy of further discussion. Let's start with the following list:

- Feelings of belonging and feeling welcomed

- Feelings of being taken seriously and respected

- Feeling what it is like to understand some things better (or more deeply)

- Experience of applying their developing skills in purposeful and meaningful ways

- Being intellectually engaged and challenged

- Experience of overcoming setbacks and obstacles

- Experience of offering suggestions to peers and helping them understand something better

- Experience of taking initiative, appropriate responsibilities, making some choices, and so forth.

The first of the proposed experiences — **feelings of belonging and feeling welcomed** — is included to suggest that, on most days, a young child should feel welcomed and included as a member of a group. There may be one or two days over an extended period when the child experiences the feeling of wanting to be home, to be with family or siblings. His teachers can identify these moments and take the opportunity to reassure the child that he is welcome, and that going-home time will come soon.

The second item on this list — **feelings of being taken seriously and respected** — has long been a concern among those who care for young children; most likely in every profession several years of practice leads to automatic responses. Working daily over a long period of time with young children may account for frequent and almost automatic use of phrases that are warm and kind and positive, but that do not really take children seriously. I often observe busy and certainly well-meaning teachers saying to children every other minute: "Awesome," "Super," "Well done," and many other positive, but empty phrases. Research on this 'over-justification effect' indicates that frequent praise lacking in content does not increase the desired behavior as well as does occasional, but informative, feedback.[3]

The third kind of experience listed above — **feeling what it is like to understand some things better (or more deeply)** — is included to emphasize that even very young children can benefit from deepening their understanding of matters — objects or events — in their own firsthand experience. Occasional experiences of that kind are likely to support the development of the disposition to seek in-depth understanding throughout life.

The fourth recommended experience — **experience of applying their developing skills in purposeful and meaningful ways** — relates to what it feels like for young children when they are engaged in a variety of projects during which they ask their teachers how to use their emerging skills like measuring things, writing titles and headings for their displays, and other contexts in which they are motivated to make sure that others can read the information they want to convey. (See for example the project titled Cheesy Pizza http://ecrp.illinois.edu/v11n2/gallick.html) that shows children tracing and cutting, signing names to a thank-you letter, labeling knobs on a cardboard 'oven').

The fifth item — **being intellectually engaged and challenged** — is included to emphasize the value of frequently engaging young children's minds and resisting the temptation to revert to long-standing traditions of too many experiences that are amusing or entertaining and exciting rather than interesting. The concept of interest refers to the capacity to lose oneself in a topic or activity, and to do so sufficiently to overcome setbacks and obstacles. We want to see this lifelong disposition early in young children; for that to happen, they need our support.

Similarly, the sixth item — **experience of overcoming setbacks and obstacles** — is included to suggest that occasional, real experiences of solving a problem, re-making something that was not successful the first time, and other experiences of overcoming difficulties can strengthen a child's confidence and become a lifelong disposition.

The seventh and eighth suggestions on the list — **experience of offering suggestions to peers and helping them understand something better** and **experience of taking initiative, appropriate responsibilities, making some choices, and so forth** — refer to the importance not only of building and supporting the dispositions to interact positively and helpfully with peers, but in the processes of doing so, to learn many complex interactive skills.

The value of the suggested experiences on the end of this list are likely to form the basis for lifelong dispositions to participate in one's community and society responsibly and helpfully.

The list offered above can be amended, added to, and perhaps also reduced. I suggest that it could be useful for leaders, staff, *and* parents to come together to create their own list of answers to the question: "What experiences should our children have *much of the time* in their early years, and no doubt in their later years as well?"

Endnotes

1. Illinois State Board of Education: Division of Early Childhood Education (2004). Springfield, Illinois.

2. The Illinois benchmarks are currently undergoing review and revision.

3. Warneken, F., & Tomasella, M. (2008). Extrinsic rewards undermine altruistic tendencies in 20-month olds. *Developmental Psychology, 44*(6), 1785–1788.

Lilian G. Katz

Lilian G. Katz, PhD, is Professor Emerita of Early Childhood Education at the University of Illinois (Urbana-Champaign) and is Co-Director of the Clearinghouse on Early Education and Parenting (CEEP) at the University of Illinois. Dr. Katz served as Director of the ERIC Clearinghouse on Elementary and Early Childhood Education for 33 years and as Past President of the National Association for the Education of Young Children, and is Editor of the first on-line peer reviewed trilingual early childhood journal, *Early Childhood Research & Practice*.

Responding to Racial and Ethnic Diversity in Early Childhood Programs

by Francis Wardle

In today's society professionals working with children want to provide what is best for all children. This requires them to be culturally responsive in their approach to children and their families. Part of being culturally responsive is to be knowledgeable and sensitive to issues of race and ethnicity. However, this is difficult to do, because race and ethnicity are concepts that young children simply do not understand. However, psychologists, multicultural educators, and practitioners know that race and ethnicity are central components of each person's individual identity; further, that racism in society can have a negative impact on a child's school success. Given all of these realities, what are professionals who work with diverse populations of young children supposed to do?

Provide a Culturally Responsive Approach to Children and Their Families

Each of us has created in our minds a unique, complex identity based on the interaction between many characteristics (West, 2001). These characteristics include, family, education, languages, abilities and disabilities, religion, gender, community, and race and ethnicity (Wardle, 1996). It is critical that professionals help children develop a secure and accurate identity, and a sense of pride and respect in that identity. Young children are beginning to notice physical characteristics of themselves and their peers, and also beginning to pick up some of society's views and attitudes around issues of race and ethnicity. Here are some ideas to assist teachers in this critical task.

Be Knowledgeable and Sensitive to Issues of Race and Ethnicity

The U.S. government has divided race and ethnicity into five broad categories: American Indian or Alaskan Native; Asian or Pacific Islander; Hispanic (can be any race); Black, not Hispanic; and White, not Hispanic. However, sensitivity to race and ethnicity requires us to go far beyond these categories in several important ways.

First, much of the world does not see race as we do. For example, Brazilians do not view themselves as Latinos, but rather as Afro Brazilian, Amerindian, Asian, European, and Mixed-race (Carvalho-Silva et al., 2000). Mayans from Guatemala are also classified under the Latino category, but view themselves as

Indigenous Peoples. With the increased number of immigrant families attending our programs, we must be sensitive to this reality.

Secondly, the U.S. approach lumps Japanese, Hmong, Koreans, Indians, Chinese, Vietnamese, and many other national groups into a general Asian category. Yet these countries have long been historical enemies, and each has its own unique history, culture, language, and identity.

And, thirdly, we must appreciate diversity within diversity (Wardle & Cruz-Janzen, 2004). It is a well-known fact that there is much more diversity within any large group than between two groups, whether the group is based on gender, race, ethnicity, income, age, ability, profession, or national origin. For example, my wife is African American, her mother was Catholic, she attended K-12 Catholic schools, and her family has a proud heritage of college graduates. She is also enrolled in the Chickasaw tribe.

There are many ways we can honor this wonderful complexity! On application forms the race/ethnicity question can be open-ended, so parents can record their family identity. We can ask families to provide us with books, artifacts, songs, and other aspects of their unique backgrounds; and we can learn about the wonderful diversity of each of our children and their families. Each of us also needs to expand our own understanding of global diversity beyond the limitations of our American view.

Help Children Develop a Secure and Accurate Identity and a Sense of Pride in that Identity

When my son, Kealan, traveled to Brazil, he left as a Black person (his mother is African American) but arrived as a mixed-race person (the Brazilian government's category for people of European, Indian, and Black heritage). Race and ethnicity are socio-political category systems. This means they are created and maintained for social and political reasons.

Further, young children do not understand race as adults do. Sure, they notice physical differences (i.e., skin color, height, body build, eye shape) and they also pick up language and behavior used by peers and adults. But they don't understand what this means in racial terms. In fact, race is very confusing to a young child! The other day a little girl from Bangladesh asked in puzzlement, "I am darker than Johnny, does that make me Black like him?" And when told by a peer from México that she was Black and he was not, my own biracial daughter asked, "How come I'm Black and he's not, when he is darker than me?" Therefore, we must find ways to help children see how they are similar to and different from other children. And we must help them feel good about their unique physical characteristics.

Since children this age are concrete learners, we should focus on concrete aspects of skin and hair color, eye color and shape, physical abilities and disabilities, and natural expressions of likes and dislikes. Also, since children this age love to experiment with language, we can use this to explore issues of empowerment, support, kindness, and hurtful expressions.

All age-appropriate activities can support this effort. Activities that are particularly helpful in developing and solidifying children's identity include, painting, music, dance, dress-ups, dramatic play, face painting and hair care, looking at picture books, reading (and being read to), crafts, writing songs, writing personal journals, painting murals, and creating literary and photographic records of the family and of the community. Various technology projects, from biographies and families' histories, to photographic documentaries and creating a website, can be created by older children.

Finally, we must make sure all of our children are successful in as many activities as possible. Self-image at this age is largely based on what children can do (Erikson, 1963; Wardle, 1993). We must never limit what a child can do because of a disability, gender, race/ethnicity, or because they have not completed an assigned task. A central role for identity development is to enable children to be successful in as many ways as possible.

Start with the Child to Learn about Their Family and Community

We must always start with the individual child, and not a racial, ethnic, cultural, or other group. Further, we cannot automatically assign a child with the characteristics or attributes assumed to be stereotypical of a group, be it racial, disability, gender, income, and so on. What we should do is learn about individual children, their families, communities, and the other important ecological contexts of the child and his family (Bronfenbrenner, 1979).

Early childhood professionals are good at focusing on individual children. We carefully observe children to determine their strengths and areas where they need extra assistance (Wardle, 2003). Emergent curriculum approaches require that we carefully observe children in natural settings — play, peer interactions, private speech — to discover their interests, language, past experiences, and dispositions; the Reggio Emilia philosophy focuses on each child documenting her strengths, development, and progress (Edwards, Gandini, & Forman, 1998). These skills should be used to determine the child's family, community, and overall national, racial, linguistic, and ethnic contexts.

Let the Child and His Family Inform Us about Their Values, Behaviors, and Beliefs

We need to extend our observations and insights of the child and family mentioned above to inform us about values, behaviors, and beliefs important to them.

- How does the child acknowledge and celebrate his skin color and nation of origin?
- How do parents want their child's first language to be acknowledged?
- How does the family support the child's race and ethnicity outside the school or child care program?
- How does the family want children to respond to older people, to people outside their community, and to people in authority?

The child and her family can inform us about their community: religion, food, traditions, male and female roles, importance of grandparents, role of the child in the home. Again, a variety of methods can be used in collecting this information:

- Questionnaires
- Questions on application forms
- Open discussions at parents-teacher conferences
- Input from parents during parent-education activities
- Casual, informal discussions between teachers and parents
- Visits to the communities where your children live, both through field trips and by frequenting local stores and cultural centers.

When I was a Head Start director, we had a large influx of Hmong families. No one in the program knew much about these children and their families. I discovered a Hmong church in their community where the elders provided us with a great deal of helpful information and support.

Always View the Whole Child with All the Factors that Make Up His Identity

All the factors that make up a child's identity — race, ethnicity, language, personality, income, gender, family structure, and so on — should be integrated throughout the curriculum. Do not use a tourist approach; do not use a curriculum by celebration approach, either. These approaches are not inclusive and are not developmental.

And we should not engage in what is called essentialism — just focusing on a few components of a child's full identity (Fish, 2002). We should always look at all the aspects that make-up the child's identity, and also look at the sum of these parts — the Gestalt. Martha West reminds us that children construct their own meaning of their unique realities (2001). This includes their social and contextual reality. Teachers can support this developmental effort that continues throughout a child's entire school life. Provide multiple opportunities for children to explore all the factors that make up their unique identity, and the integration of these factors into their overall, unique Gestalt. A variety of activities that engage children in exploring themselves, their family background, and their community work well here. But of most importance is not to isolate race and ethnicity, and not to use curricula approaches that focus on these factors above all others. My ecological and anti-bias model (Wardle, 1996) can be used effectively in this process.

Do Not Impose Your Ideas of Race/Ethnicity on the Child

Never, ever, impose your ideas of race or ethnicity on a child. This includes forcing a child to select a specific federal racial category. Further, a child should never be prejudged based on their racial or ethnic identity, including behaviors, academic expectations, or specific skills and dispositions. Allow the child — and her family — to define herself, and to define her own values, dispositions, likes and dislikes, and behaviors. Clearly this mandate also includes children with complex elements that create unique identities (multiethnic and multiracial), adopted children, and the increasing number of children who do not fit neatly into the U.S. census categories. It is not our job to define a child or to determine that child's behaviors, predispositions, and world view. This does not mean children do not have racial, ethnic, and cultural attributes that impact their behavior and learning. But it means that we must follow the child's (and the family's) lead.

One of the best ways to encourage children to be everything they can be is through modeling. Modeling includes books, pictures and posters on the walls, visitors to the classroom, and visits to the community — workplaces, museums, stores. I work with a school in Brazil that serves children who are poor from the local *favelas* (slums). Central to their curriculum is a Professional Day. The purpose of this activity is to model to these children that people like them can be successful.

Teach Another Language to English-speaking Students

It is interesting to note the number of early childhood experts who advocate for bilingual activities in our early childhood programs and schools (Nieto, 2004; York, 2003). While all these recommendations are for programs to teach the child's home language and English, to be truly diverse we must also teach a second language to English-speaking students; further, that second language should be one of the world's major languages. These include Russian, Japanese, Chinese, Portuguese, and French. There are a variety of approaches that programs can take to implement foreign language efforts in their programs (Neugebauer, 2005).

Evaluate Curricula and Policies and Differentiate Activities for All Students

All policies, procedures, curricular content, and curricular materials and activities should be carefully evaluated to determine if they are good for all children, and not just for specific groups of children. Criteria to consider in this evaluation include the use of all of Gardner's eight learning styles (1983), use of field dependent and field independent approaches to learning, cooperative and individual activities and projects, hands-on learning, technology learning, and enactive, iconic, and abstract-symbolic learning.

Differentiation for gifted students, special needs students, and twice exceptional students must also be integral to the curriculum and activities. These changes, adaptations, and new approaches should not be designed for groups of children, but rather for individual children. This requires a flexible approach to time and schedules, with the possibility of advanced students pursuing projects and tangential activities, while other students might need to move on to new activities. Further, it requires us to allow students to be successful at what they are good at, not what the standards or curriculum say they should be good at.

Conclusion

It is important for professionals working with young children to be sensitive to issues of race and ethnicity. We can do this by always beginning with the individual child and his family, viewing race as one of the child's many ecological contexts (Bronfenbrenner, 1979), and understanding that children actively construct their own reality, including their racial and ethnic identity (West, 2001). We must never automatically respond to a child as a member of a racial or ethnic group; rather, we must respond to the child as a unique individual with a dynamic identity that includes, but is not limited to, race and ethnicity. Our goal is to provide the best possible environments, curricula, activities, and interactions for all the children we serve.

References

Bronfenbrenner, U. (1979). Context of child rearing: Problems and prospect. *American Psychologist, 34*, 844–850.

Carvalho-Silva, D. R., Santos, F. R., Rocha, J., & Pena, D. J. (2000). The phylogeography of Brazilian Y-chromosome lineages. *American Journal of Human Genetics, 68*.

Edwards, C., Gandini, L., & Forman, G. (1998). *The hundred languages of children: The Reggio Emilia approach — advance reflections* (2nd edition). Greenwich, CT: Ablex Publishing Co.

Erikson, E. (1963). *Childhood and society* (2nd edition). New York: Norton.

Fish, J. M. (ed.). (2002). *Race and intelligence: Separating science from myth*. Mahwah, NJ: Lawrence Erlbaum Associates.

Gardner, H. (1983). *Frames of mind: The theory of multiple intelligences*. New York: Basic Books.

Neugebauer, B. (ed.). (2005). *Literacy: A Beginnings Workshop book*. Redmond, WA: Exchange Press.

Nieto, S. (2004). *Affirming diversity. The sociopolitical context of multicultural education* (4th edition). Boston: Allyn and Bacon.

Wardle, F. (2003). *Introduction to early childhood education: A multidimensional approach to child-centered care and learning*. Boston: Allyn and Bacon.

Wardle, F. (1996). Proposal: An anti-bias and ecological model for multicultural education. *Childhood Education, 72*(3) 152–156.

Wardle, F. (1993, March). How young children build images of themselves. *Exchange, 104*, 44–47.

Wardle, F., & Cruz-Janzen, M. I. (2004). *Meeting the needs of multiethnic and multiracial children in schools*. Boston: Allyn and Bacon.

West, M. M. (2001). Teaching the third culture child. *Young Children, 56*(6), 27-32.

York, S. (2003). *Roots and wings: Affirming culture in early childhood programs* (Revised edition). St. Paul, MN: Redleaf Press.

Francis Wardle

Francis Wardle, PhD, teaches for the University of Phoenix (online) and Red Rocks Community College. He has been a Head Start director and national program evaluator, and is currently the president of the Colorado Chapter of Partners of the Americas, and a past board member of Partners of the Americas International. He has four multiracial children, and is the director of the Center for the Study of Biracial Children; his newest book is *Children and Families: Understanding Behavior and Dynamics*. He is working on his ninth book, *Challenge of Boys in Early Childhood Programs*, which will be published by Redleaf Press.

Preparing Bicultural, Bilingual Children to Succeed in School

by Hazel Osborn

> Parents lined up at the "Ask the Parenting Expert" booth at N.I.H.'s Parenting Fair. A young Chinese researcher sat across from me, struggling with newly-acquired English, asking how to be sure her son would get into Thomas Jefferson High School for Science and Technology (a highly competitive governor's school outside Washington, DC). My thoughts lined up: tutoring, entry exam prep class, science fair, computer camp. "Tell me about your son. What grade is he in now?" I asked. "He two years old," she answered.

Parents who move their families to the United States want their children to have full advantage of the educational opportunities available, and they often worry about language or cultural barriers. They need the support of early childhood educators to prepare their children for a good educational experience. And child care providers need to understand the special challenges these families confront.

Language Challenges

The first concern for parents is often teaching their children to speak English, especially when they are not fluent themselves. Research indicates children will learn English from peers and teachers at preschool and in elementary school, or even later for older children. As California's National University Education Professor Margot Kinberg (2001) writes, "The target language is the medium of instruction, rather than its topic." However, some parents resort to extreme measures to teach English, such as forbidding the child to speak the family's language at home, or limiting interactions with their children to English.

> The Salvadorian father of a four-year-old girl refused to answer her or interact with her in anything but the English neither of them spoke comfortably. Within a few weeks, her mother reported the child had become angry and withdrawn, acting out in school. I encouraged the child's teacher to urge the father to speak Spanish with his child, suggesting her behavior was the result of a new and upsetting distance from her dad. They tried this new approach, and she returned to her normal happy disposition.

Child care providers and teachers can re-assure non-English-speaking families that their children will learn English as naturally as they learned their family's language, through interactions and relationships with English speakers. But we can do more, by including first-language speakers and materials in programs serving bilingual children. Stephen Krashen (1997) writes, "The biggest problem… is the absence of books — in both the first and second languages — in the lives of students…." Adding first-language speakers, songs, and books to programs serving young children can help them prepare to take full advantage of our educational system.

For most programs, it's no problem to include first-language books and songs in any language spoken by enrolled families. But having adults who speak the family's first language can be a challenge, especially when there is wide diversity among enrolled families. Some ways that centers address this need:

- Hiring full- or part-time employees who speak the first language of families.

- Recruiting volunteers who speak the first language. This is a great way to get enrolled families involved. Filling the role of a respected volunteer who can share customs, stories, and songs with the children is a validating experience for parent and grandparent volunteers and their enrolled children.

- Contract with a first-language speaker to come to the center and do a special presentation, such as teaching a game or song from that language.

- Hire a first-language teacher to visit the center regularly and teach the children the language through age-appropriate activities and interactions.

Directors sometimes hear concerns from English-speaking families about their children being confused by the introduction of a second language. Reassuring families that this experience has been proven advantageous for language development is easier when the director has some written information ready for parents. For example, researchers at the Cornell Language Acquisition Lab found that learning a second language early leads more quickly to native-like proficiency — and also found that maintaining attention, despite distractions, is easier for children who learn a second language. Consider articles from *Exchange*, *Young Children*, and *ERIC Digest*, and other respected resources for this purpose.

In the Washington, DC area where I work, a constant turnover of residents from all over the world ensures that most programs have a minimum of three languages spoken by families — usually many more. Many children are multilingual, speaking three languages or more. For example, a three-year-old boy is fluent in Arabic, Urdu, and English. A pair of preschool sisters, ages three and five, speak Polish, Hindi, and English.

> In my role as Parenting Coach for America Online employees, I was asked in a seminar how many languages a child could learn. A Korean father raised his hand to tell us that his three-year-old son could communicate in six languages and was fluent in three! He explained that grandparents and great-grandparents who spoke only their own first languages and lived with the family made it necessary for his son to learn their languages if he wanted to communicate with them at all.

Cultural Challenges

At a recent conference held at George Washington University, researcher and consultant Annice van der Sluis (2010) explained that bicultural awareness involves understanding how families apply social rules and behavior. Confronting a different culture, with different norms, opportunities, and values comes into sharp focus as families prepare to send their children to schools in the United States. Basic assumptions about what children should be able to do as they enter schools often differ from the family's perspective. In the U.S., many children are expected to be independent and self-reliant. In other cultures, these traits may be seen as a disadvantage, even dangerous. For example, in cultures where food has been scarce in the past, children may be fed by an adult until the age of four or even later. In the U.S., this might be seen as coddling or holding the child back rather than preserving the food supply from spillage or waste. Early childhood educators need to understand the values and experiences that inform parents' thinking before assessing the child's development and needs. We must make an effort to understand and respect the family's perspective in order to truly understand and serve the child.

In addition, images in American culture sometimes can confuse parents new to this country. For example, as Dr. Maria Elena Martinez, Program Administrator of Provider Services in Fairfax County, Virginia, told me, "Families come to the U.S., and after having watched our television programs and seeing ads and shows promoting junk food, they get the idea that this is the American way." Early childhood educators can help families differentiate between good practices and marketing. Sharing information about good parenting practices, health, and development helps all parents.

At the same time they confront a new culture, families want to be sure their children are ready for school. Ongoing assessment, parent conferences, and cooperative planning with parents are the best ways to accomplish this goal.

> A 27-month-old child, when first assessed, showed none of the expected behaviors for his age. The family child care provider shared the results with his parents and learned that this child, the youngest of three, was not expected to do anything for himself at home. She helped the parents understand the difficulties their child would face in school if he had no self-care skills, and worked with the parents on a plan to help him learn to do things for himself, like taking his shoes off and picking up toys.

Parents also need help in navigating our school system. Networking with kindergarten teachers and administrators in our school districts, and linking them with parents, can help to meet this need. Jeannie Sponheim, Instructional Coach at Lincoln Elementary School in Loveland, Colorado, told me:

"We build trust by inviting and including our bilingual families at school events, offering materials, information, and liaisons in their language, and building awareness and understanding of their cultures. Through examining and being aware of our own privileges and biases, we can open ourselves to the perspectives of this special and important community, and listen more deeply to their unique and individual needs. Listening deeply and responding to individual needs helps families feel valued. Intentional inclusion narrows the achievement gap of 'minority' populations."

One important difference that bicultural/bilingual families often bring to our programs is the important role of the extended family in their children's development. In one local, small cul-de-sac community of eight homes, I recently counted six households that included at least three generations; three of them had four generations. When programs are enrolling children, it is wise to send the invitation for a tour, event, or conference to extended family members, if the parents consent. Parents are often relying on guidance and support from grandparents or great-grandparents, especially those in the home. These older relatives may be the decision-makers about schools, finances, and health care. Programs that practice respectful inclusion of these family members find that the child and family adjust much more easily.

How to Help

We can impact the future school success of bilingual, bicultural children by:

- educating parents about how their children can learn English.

- having first-language speakers, books, and songs in our programs.
- seeking to understand families' beliefs and values.
- regularly assessing children's development, and sharing that information with parents.
- working with parents to plan learning experiences while in care and at home.
- linking parents with the school system before their children enroll.
- including the extended family in our understanding of the family and their needs.

I told the parent who worried about her two-year-old's acceptance to an elite high school, "Speak often with your son, in Chinese. Read to him for a while every day. Take him outside for walks and activities. Encourage his interests. Limit how much television he watches. Enroll him in the best program you can find; they will help him to learn English. Learn more about the school system. No matter where your son goes to school, his best and most important influence will be his parents."

Hazel Osborn

Hazel Osborn, MA, is currently mentoring more than 50 programs serving bilingual, bicultural children. She is the author of numerous articles, curricula, and two books. She has lived in the Washington, DC area with her family since the early '90s.

References

Kinberg, M. (2001). *Perspectives on foreign language immersion programs.* Lewiston, NY: Edwin Mellen Press.

Krashen, S. (1997). Why bilingual education? *ERIC Digest.* Retrieved: www.ericdigests.org/1997-3/bilingual.html

Lang, S. (2009). "Learning a second language is good childhood mind medicine, studies find." *Cornell University Chronicle Online:* www.news.cornell.edu/stories/may09/bilingual.kids.sl.html

van der Sluis, A. (2010, May 24). "Bilingual/bicultural early childhood assessment." Presentation at Project ITAP Annual Networking Conference, Washington, DC, George Washington University.

A Journey towards Inclusion

by Kate Jordan-Downs

For as long as I can remember, I have been disturbed by how people tend to exclude others who look, speak, believe, or behave differently. I heard the jeers made by classmates about my father's physical disability; listened to my friend, Sarah, repeat back a joke that someone told at her expense, yet convinced her it was funny; and worked with countless families searching for an early childhood program that would welcome their child, rather than slam the door in their faces. All of these experiences, and countless more, have led me to work to bring about a spirit of inclusion rather than exclusion.

As early childhood educators and leaders, we hold immense power and responsibility in our hands. We have the ability to impact the earliest experiences of entire generations, which will set children on paths that influence how children view themselves, others, and the world around them. With this power, we must commit to creating equal opportunity for all children to grow and learn, so that they will be equipped to become engaged members of their communities. By welcoming children of all abilities and life experiences, we take the first step in changing the general belief that high-quality early learning settings are only available to certain children. We are sending a message that each child is not only welcome, but a valued member of his center family — a message that will positively influence his growing sense of self-worth.

The Evolution of Inclusion

For most professionals in early childhood education, the first thing that comes to mind when hearing 'inclusion' is supporting children with diagnosed disabilities in a classroom. And that's correct. Diagnosed disabilities, disorders, and developmental delays are at the heart of historical legislation such as the Americans with Disabilities Act (ADA) and the Individuals with Disabilities Education Act (IDEA). These laws were designed to protect adults and children with disabilities from discrimination so that they have access to equal educational and life opportunities. In September 2015, the U.S. Department of Health and Human Services and the U.S. Department of Education released their joint policy statement on the inclusion of children with disabilities in early childhood settings, in the hopes of increasing the number of infants, toddlers, and preschool-aged children with disabilities in high-quality programs.[1]

However, the concept of inclusion should not be solely reserved for those with disabilities. Sadly, data has shown and continues to show that preschool disciplinary practices (such as suspensions and expulsions) are fraught with racial, gender, and disability disparities and these disparities do not change in K-12 data. In fact, after the release of the 2011-2012 U.S. Department of Education Civil Rights Data Snapshot on early childhood disciplinary practices, the U.S. Department of Health and Human Services and the U.S. Department of Education issued a joint statement on expulsion and suspension policies in early childhood settings.[2]

Take a moment and let this reality sink in — the reality that our federal agencies have to issue statements about the policies early childhood programs should implement regarding the expulsion of… three-year-olds. In the words of Dr. Walter Gilliam, "what makes less sense than expelling a preschooler?"[3] Yet this is our reality and one that the early childhood field must face, not just out of compliance, but because we must do better. We must change the status quo, but how?

**Celeste Dills,
Inclusion Services Specialist:**

My daily conversations give me the opportunity to support our educators by providing them the tools needed to advance learning for children of all abilities. Many of the conversations we have come from children who exhibit challenging behavior. Guiding teachers through the journey from a child's perspective is a deep and heartfelt experience. There is a moment of understanding that connects the teacher to the reasoning behind why the tools work. That moment is when they begin to see results and you hear the joy in their voice as they share the magic of the child's success.

What are the Barriers?

Why is the practice of inclusion so difficult? For one thing, as many teachers and center directors will tell you, the training and resources about working with children who have unique needs are scarce. Although there are many state and local licensing regulations that require professional development opportunities for early childhood educators including training opportunities on how to support children with unique needs, not enough time is allotted to practice the implementation of this new knowledge in the classroom. In addition, many early childhood centers do not have access to the support from specialists such as therapists, mental-health consultants, or one-to-one special instructors in the classroom. Unlike our K-12 counterparts, we are rarely afforded the support services and personnel prescribed in a child's Individual Family Service Plan (IFSP) or Individualized Education Program (IEP), leaving teachers overwhelmed as they try to meet the goals outlined in these plans, and children without the proper support they need to be successful in the classroom.

As we continue to advocate for the necessary training and resources to support our teachers and children in early childhood settings, we must also put as much effort into shifting the attitudes and hearts of early childhood educators so that they will work harder to support all children in our programs. Even with the best training and resources available, if an educator's heart is not invested in supporting all children — in even the most challenging circumstances — then those trainings and resources will make little impact.

Teaching children with disabilities and those who have lived through adverse childhood experiences (ACE) is not easy. It challenges us to constantly adjust our teaching practices, to reframe our perception of a child's behavior, and to fight the constant thought that we cannot reach each child. However, working with children with unique needs also has rewards beyond measure. Our teaching practices improve, benefiting all children; we stay immersed in the latest research and strategies from our field; and we become champions for children in desperate need

> **Taunya Couch,
> Inclusion Services Specialist:**
>
> Every day, I have the opportunity to support our centers by finding workable options to meet the needs of the children in our care. These strategies span a wide spectrum of needs, such as determining the best way to introduce a child with limited mobility or adaptive equipment to her prekindergarten peers, reviewing behavior logs to help teachers further develop behavior support strategies, or training teachers on working with children with autism in the ECE classroom. At the heart of all our conversations are the needs of each unique child and the desire to partner with their families, schools, and service providers to determine the ways we can best meet those needs.

of an army of advocates. There is no better feeling than seeing a child walk or talk for the first time when all the odds were against her, or to see a child who struggled with self-regulation and challenging behaviors become a leader amongst his peers. Every child deserves to have a place that will encourage and support them as they encounter and struggle with obstacles.

Making Inclusion Happen

Centralized Inclusion Services Team

One way to approach inclusion is to develop what we call our centralized Inclusion Services team. Some of our early childhood education professionals have worked directly with children with unique needs, but many have not. The Inclusion Services team offers a helpline that directors and teachers can call anytime they have questions regarding the care and education of a child with unique needs or challenging behaviors. These questions are specific to the situation and can range from how to meet the needs of a newly-enrolled child with autism to how to successfully transition a child with cerebral palsy from a toddler to a preschool classroom.

Identify the Champions of Inclusive Practices

Kayte Lucas, the Center Director at a KinderCare in Vancouver, Washington, has created an inclusive community and culture in her center. Lucas says that her mantra to teachers and families is "we do not give up on children — no matter what." Her talent in supporting children of all abilities is something that we encourage other center directors to learn from. Having a colleague who can support our journey to inclusion is imperative — we cannot do it alone. Kayte's expertise is comprised of her passion for her work and the years of experience she has gained by fighting to create an environment where every child can be successful, and she graciously shares her knowledge with other educators. Here is a little about her story.

When she was just four years old, Center Director Kayte Lucas hit another child in the face — and broke his nose. "I was one of those kids," she says. She remembers how it felt to be misunderstood as a child: the 'problem kid' labels, the negative attention, how her family worried. But it's precisely those early experiences that make her so dedicated to helping children with challenging behaviors today. "Every child is valuable and every child is valued here," she says. Anger, aggression, furniture climbing, biting, chair throwing: this center has plenty of 'those kids.' But to Kayte, these are merely behaviors that children present in an effort to communicate something that is causing them distress. There are practical solutions to challenging behaviors once you know the root cause. "Behaviors do not define who a child is or his future potential," she says. She believes that these children deserve a great education and compassionate, kind teachers

Here are a few things Kayte shared about celebrating individual differences and the power of positivity to help children be successful in an inclusive environment.

- **Know the child and the family completely.** Once families know I am never going to dis-enroll their children, they open up. That gives me a lot of information about what might be happening at home.

- **Separate the challenge from the child.** There is always a reason for challenging or aggressive behavior. Some challenges are obvious because they are related to the child's diagnosis; however, some are not as easy to pinpoint. He may be hungry, tired, or having difficulty with transitions. Maybe there is a separation in the family. Looking for the 'why' helps you solve the issue compassionately.

- **Chart the challenges.** We use a chart that divides the day into several specific time frames: morning group, transitions to nap, nap time, afternoon time. This is a very powerful tool, because it helps us begin to notice patterns of behavior. Does the child begin to get overwhelmed at the end of the day? Is the transition to nap time when the child tends to throw toys and hit?

- **Anticipate and act.** Once you know the child and her patterns, you learn to be proactive. If fatigue sets in for a child with a mobility impairment right before lunch, make sure that child is settled at the table before the others. If a child with ADHD struggles with the transition to outdoor time, be prepared to redirect the child or intervene before the behavior occurs. Watch body language and facial expressions. There are always cues before a behavior happens; you just have to observe closely to catch them.

- **Focus on the positive.** The time-frame chart also helps prove to us that no child is always struggling — not even the most challenging child. By keeping this chart, we can see that every child has a period of time when they are actively engaged and successful in the classroom. When we talk to parents, we always start with something positive, such as "He had three good mornings in a row this week!"

- **Stay flexible and choose your battles.** No two children are the same. An individual rewards system may work with one child, while another may respond to jokes and humor. I have one child who has to move everywhere all the time. He cannot do circle time. But if you ask him a question, he can tell you the answer, proving that he is listening and learning. So we let him roam. Keep trying until you find the solution that works.

- **Communicate proactively with parents.** When there are challenges with a child successfully participating in the classroom, we are completely transparent with all parents about what happened, what we did about it, and what we're going to do to prevent this challenge in the future. That shows we're quickly resolving concerns, and it goes a long way.

- **Hire with heart.** I listen for two things in an interview. I want to hear prospective employees speak positively about differences, and I want to hear that a candidate handles discipline differently, depending on the child. I look for staff who share my spirit of inclusion: it's a must in my center.

just as much as other children do. Families whose children require accommodations or additional support, or who exhibit challenging or aggressive behaviors, can struggle to find early childhood education centers that will accept their children. This can be very stressful and discouraging for parents. These children often get dis-enrolled and families whose kids have been dis-enrolled elsewhere feel like they've won the lottery when they find Kayte and her staff. At last, here is a place that doesn't see their children as a 'problem!'

Conclusion

Each day our families give us the opportunity to help shape their children's lives. When children come to us, they're essentially a blank canvas and they fully soak in every relationship and experience. As they get older, it is more difficult to shape their perspective about themselves and others, so it's imperative that their earliest learning experiences provide them with the opportunity to be included; to learn about differences in a positive way; and to come from a place of love and respect, so that as they grow they will begin to positively participate and be involved within their community. Children have the power to shape our world into one that is more inclusive. If we want to see a more inclusive world come about, all we must do is give them the foundational inclusive experiences they need to achieve it.

Endnotes

1. U.S. Department of Health and Human Services and the U.S. Department of Education. Joint policy statement on the inclusion of children with disabilities in early childhood settings: www2.ed.gov/policy/speced/guid/earlylearning/joint-statement-full-text.pdf

2. U.S. Department of Health and Human Services and the U.S. Department of Education. Joint statement on expulsion and suspension policies in early childhood settings: www2.ed.gov/policy/gen/guid/school-discipline/policy-statement-ece-expulsions-suspensions.pdf

3. Gilliam, W.: http://psychologybenefits.org/2014/12/13/preschool-expulsions/

Kate Jordan-Downs

Kate Jordan-Downs is the Director of Inclusion at KinderCare Education. She has 15 years of professional experience in education and disability services. Her journey includes experience as a middle school inclusion teacher, working with adults with disabilities in their homes and communities, and leading as the program director for two non-profit, inclusive early childhood programs in Washington, DC. In her current position, she is redefining the vision for inclusive education. She is committed to ensuring that all children have a safe and respectful environment where they can build the self-confidence necessary to learn and grow, as well as celebrate the diversity they contribute to their school community.

**Stef Plebanek,
Inclusion Services Specialist:**

In my role advising our centers how to include children with disabilities and/or challenging behaviors, I have the opportunity to help teachers and directors value the diversity that children with a range of abilities bring to our centers, rather than seeing them as detracting from the orderly operations of their classrooms. When classrooms are set up to help children of all abilities succeed, it is so gratifying to hear from new families that they love that the center seems to 'get' their child's unique needs and how teachers respond with enthusiasm, creativity, and insight.

The Intangibles in the Early Childhood Classroom

by Carol B. Hillman

The early years are such formative years, when attitudes are being created, when habits are taking shape, when thoughts are being crystallized. This is when the very essence of each child is coming into being. These are the intangibles that we may look for within early childhood settings.

We must look towards the child care centers around the world, the nursery schools, the public schools, and in the home care settings. It is there, in these important places, where we want to create a place where each child wants to be. For without that physical and emotional comfort the possibility of learning is greatly diminished. So from the very beginning, from the first steps away from home, we, as educators, must take it upon ourselves to think in-depth, to plan for, organize, and thoughtfully build an environment that beckons the best both for and from the children.

What is it that we want young children to know beyond the alphabet and numbers, beyond the days of the week, the colors of the rainbow, beyond what testing is looking for? What are the goals we set for 'our' children during the year(s) that we share together?

An overarching belief for educators of young children is to foster a zest for learning, to cultivate an ongoing curiosity about the world we live in, that is both vibrant and self-sustaining. We feel the importance of fostering and establishing an inextinguishable enthusiasm about the joy and the process of gaining new knowledge, assuring that it engenders in young children a sustained interest and involvement.

The implications for teachers are vast. We are calling for all classrooms, no matter what their level of sophistication, to be vessels of interest and challenge in which young minds and bodies have the freedom to explore new areas of thought and experience; to seek the following intangibles. Here is where:

- training and skill of teachers come into play.

- importance of observation and understanding are the guiding forces in choosing what is offered to the children on a daily basis.

- teachers design curriculum based on their understanding of each child on a very personal level, along with his developmental needs.

- adults are aware of all the strengths, weaknesses, and dreams that each child holds.

These early years are a time for children to:

- learn about trust, about knowing that there are people in this world who children can look up to and count on to be there for them on a consistent basis.

- learn that an adult can keep a special secret if a child asks for that to happen.

- know, unequivocally, that an adult can also be a friend.

- think about who they are, to understand what gives them pleasure, and to understand what is difficult for them to do.

- learn how to be open and receptive to new ideas: changes in relation to old ideas, the way things always have been.

- learn to be flexible: for making adjustments with equilibrium, to understand how things can change, and life can still be all right.

- learn by watching others, and figuring out what is important.

- practice how to do things so that young children better understand who they are.

- look around, discover new ways, and become aware and attuned to other peoples' actions and reactions.

- do things for themselves: to begin to understand how to discipline their own actions, and further build their self-awareness.

- consider the needs of their peers and to establish relationships with other children and adults, and in the process recognize new aspects of their own identity.

So much of what happens in a given classroom is based upon work within small groups. Here children are given ample opportunity to express their own ideas, to be creative, to negotiate with others, and to work in a collaborative manner. It is a social scene filled with challenges, where emotions can run high, where give-and-take is always in play. It is real life at play at the preschool level.

Wherever young children are gathered as a group, their safety must be considered paramount. The room itself must be under constant scrutiny for danger spots. We must be watchful for sharp edges from broken toys and wet slippery floors. As educators it is a matter vigilance. This includes establishing ground rules, including that it is everyone's responsibility to see that each person remains safe: no running in the classroom and words, not fists, are used to settle disagreements. It is working together to create a social consciousness of caring for one another in a deep and meaningful way.

In order to make these things happen, young children need to be skilled in the art of communication. They need to:

- feel free to express themselves, their wishes, their frustrations, their fears, and their enjoyment of life.

- feel comfortable about asking questions over and over again and receive thoughtful responses from caring adults: "When can I do it?"; "Why can't I?"; "What makes the grass grow?"; "Why do robins sing?"

The preschool classroom is a microcosm of the world. So much that is meaningful can take place in this setting. It is imperative that all rooms where young children gather be places where experimentation is honored and children feel free to take chances. These are places to feel what work is all about, to be an architect and build a skyscraper with wooden blocks that may come tumbling down. Here, young children can find out that it is all right to get their hands dirty when they plant their first green bean in a small clay pot. Here, they can learn to take care of a living thing, and feel a sense of responsibility for its care. It is here, in this safe environment, that children can learn the pleasures of a deep work ethic and become stronger within themselves through the work that they have accomplished.

In this safe environment children have the opportunity to take risks, to see others take risks, to be successful — and sometimes fail. Here they can witness and be part of making raisin bread that doesn't rise, block buildings that come crashing down, or beans that never sprout. This is also the place to learn that the world doesn't stop when things don't work out: recipes can be tried again, new block buildings can be built, and beans can be replanted. Early childhood classrooms are places where young children are encouraged to practice their skills and feel good about having the time and opportunity to try again — and to know that this is okay. This is also a time to witness that adults are less than perfect people, that they too make mistakes: a teacher can forget that it was Jack's turn to pick out the story for Thursday, or that she was supposed to go to the lumberyard to get more wood for the workbench. Children get to see that Jack can pick out the story for Friday, and the teacher can pick up the new wood tomorrow. It is also a time when a teacher can tell the children, "I am really sorry that I forgot."

Through these many interactions, children learn about action and reaction. They are exposed to conflict and resolution. They see firsthand what cooperation and collaboration can yield. They can feel the impact of social action, and experience the pride that goes along with being a participant.

It is also essential for children to develop a conscience about caring for our Earth and things around us: learning not to be wasteful, not to use more than is necessary, and to be gentle with what we have so that it will last longer. It is recognizing that each of us can play a part in caring for our environment. A mini-recycling project can begin small in the classroom by collecting scraps of paper from art projects.

Developing children's aesthetic awareness starts with the teacher's choices about how the classroom is set up: the materials presented to the children, and the manner in which they are displayed. It is seeing that the paints are fresh each day and maintaining a sense of order by creating a separate space for each object. It is arranging and rearranging wall displays throughout the year and making the mainstay the work of the young artists in your classroom. Creating an aesthetic sense also has to do with simplicity: knowing that clutter is counter-productive. Blank spaces on the walls allow the eye to rest and the body to relax.

An aesthetic sense can also be heightened by having live plants and flowers growing in your classroom to look at and wonder about each day. These lend beauty, color, and fragrance in subtle but satisfying ways. Keeping an aesthetic sense alive calls for a great deal of thought and planning that is woven into the very fabric of who you are, how you think, and how you choose your actions. It is like an artist who mixes the colors from her palate, overlaying the colors, one atop another until the blending creates just the right shade of color she sought.

Part of what we, as teachers, hope every early childhood classroom would contain is a reverence for the written word. May there always be books in abundance: to look at and to read to children. And stories to tell. And opportunities for children to write their own stories. Storytelling has always been a remarkable way to engage young minds. Through the music of words we hear about new ideas, meet new people and animals, and thrill to the new adventure that awaits the turn of each page or the inflection of the voice. It is through the written word that we gain new insights that can enhance our thinking and shape our goals.

I have given a lot of thought to what it is I want each child to gain during the precious preschool time, to take with them for the rest of their lives. I call my list 'the intangibles.' What would you add?

I welcome an online dialogue with readers. Please send your ideas to cbhillman@gmail.com.

Carol B. Hillman

Carol B. Hillman is a member of The Professional Advisory Board of the Child Development Institute at Sarah Lawrence College, Co-Chair of The Westchester Bank Street Alumni Group, Vice President of The Teachers' Loft, and works online with early childhood students at Texas State University. Formerly, Carol served on the Board of Trustees and The Dean's Leadership Council at Bank Street College of Education. For 20 years Carol was the lead teacher of four-year-olds at The Nursery School in White Plains, New York. Her publications include: *Before The School Bell Rings*, *Mentoring Early Childhood Educators*, and *Teaching Four-Year-Olds: A Personal Journey*.

Universal Early Childhood Curriculum Principles

Searching Globally, Applying Locally

by Lawrence J. Schweinhart and Diane Trister Dodge, Initiative Coordinators, World Forum Foundation Early Childhood Curriculum Initiative

The topic of curriculum in early childhood programs has been of great interest at every World Forum on Early Care and Education since 1999 and has generated engaged and meaningful conversations among participants. The World Forum's Early Childhood Curriculum Initiative evolved from sessions that described specific curriculum models and how they were being implemented to an effort to identify and promote a list of early childhood curriculum principles that all early childhood educators can agree on.

This article reviews the history of how the topic of curriculum has been addressed at the World Forum over many years, describes the process of developing universal principles, and presents the 11 principles. The 2014 principles now focus on relationships, environment, play as children's work, respect, content, children's role in the curriculum, outcomes, the inter-relatedness of development, early childhood assessment, families and teachers as partners, and ongoing professional development. We suggest ways the principles can be used, and invite an ongoing dialogue that will continue to refine and extend the principles as needed.

Initial Focus on Well-known Models

At the first seven World Forum meetings, from 1999 in Honolulu, Hawaii, through 2007 in Kuala Lumpur, Malaysia, curriculum-related sessions focused on several well-regarded, widely-used curricula: *The Creative Curriculum*, HighScope, Montessori, and Reggio Emilia. These curricula are all committed to certain curriculum principles, particularly a respect for all aspects of children's development and a recognition that teachers are facilitators of children's development and learning. Recognized leaders of each curriculum served as spokespersons in these presentations, and spokespersons of programs using these curricula described how they had implemented and adapted the curriculum to their culture and settings. These sessions were always well-attended and generated lively discussions.

Ongoing interest in the topic of curriculum reflects its changing role in programs around the world that serve young children and their families. In recognition of the importance of the early childhood years in preparing young children for success in school and in life, there is a growing consensus that high-quality early learning experiences are too important to be left to chance. Teachers need to be purposeful and intentional about their work. A comprehensive curriculum can be an invaluable guide to help teachers and directors make thoughtful decisions about how and what to teach.

Learning More about how Programs Use a Curriculum

As a follow-up to the World Forum in Acapulco, México (2003), we cast a wider net to find out more about what, how, and why programs around the world use a curriculum to guide their decisions. A questionnaire was sent out to all World Forum participants and 80 enthusiastic and varied responses were received; we learned a lot from this process.

While the curriculum models featured at the World Forum sessions were the most widely used, in many countries early childhood educators develop their own curriculum or meld a variety of approaches. They may follow a country-specific framework, but teachers have a great deal of leeway in designing experiences that reflect their children and community. Those who responded to the questionnaire, like those who attended sessions at the World Forum, strongly believe that teachers have a vital role to play in designing curriculum that is responsive to the children they teach. There was universal agreement that prescriptive curriculum approaches that tell teachers what to teach and how and when to teach it, not allowing any flexibility to adapt instruction as needed, are not appropriate or respectful of teachers' and children's thinking and decision-making.

Whatever approach programs use, their curriculum becomes the focus of ongoing professional development, directors often provide training and coaching for their staff, send teachers to conferences and seminars, and maintain a resource library. Teachers are encouraged to observe the children, document what they are learning, use that information to plan experiences, communicate with families, and construct the curriculum.

Transition to Universal Principles

As plans were being made for the 2011 World Forum in Honolulu, our approach to the topic of curriculum in early childhood began to change. This was in part due to the emerging ethos of the World Forum to see early childhood educators from around the world coming together to learn from each other, rather than to hear from the experts on specific curriculum models. We shifted to the working group approach that characterized other topics examined at the World Forum. Our mission changed to developing and promoting a small number of clearly stated early childhood curriculum principles that would receive universal agreement.

We recruited early childhood curriculum developers, program administrators, trainers, and teachers to participate. For a year before the 2011 World Forum in Honolulu, we used email communication to develop a set of 11 principles that served as the focus for discussion at the World Forum in Honolulu. At that time, we finalized the list and wording of each principle at working group meetings and presented the statement to a larger group of Forum participants for their consideration and feedback.

Reflecting the diversity of World Forum participants, the curriculum working group included about 40 leading early childhood educators from around the world, including Africa, various parts of Asia, Europe, Australia, New Zealand, and North America. After defining early childhood, this group identified the most important early childhood education curriculum questions, then discussed them each at length. The 2012 Curriculum Principles can be found on the World Forum website: www.worldforum foundation.org/curriculum-report-2012/.

A few years later, we picked up where we left off as we prepared for the 2014 World Forum in San Juan, Puerto Rico. We invited former members of the curriculum working group to become active and recruited new members. Using an email listing of group members, a listserv, we reexamined the 2011 principles over several months. This generated rich exchanges of views and recommendations for revising the principles.

At the World Forum in Puerto Rico, we reexamined the list and revised it some more. We began by discussing and agreeing on a definition of early childhood as the period of human life from conception and birth through age 8 or 9. Our reasoning was that these are formative years in children's development and learning when a high-quality program can build a solid foundation for children's success and fulfillment in school and in life. We agreed that the purpose of an early childhood curriculum is to guide such programs in offering experiences that optimize children's well-being, development, and learning.

The working group decided that the first two principles were actually definitions rather than principles themselves. We made them a preface to the list of principles. We carefully reworded all the principles while retaining their core meaning and made the following revisions. We:

- renamed the care and education principle relationships.

- added principles about environment, play as children's work, outcomes, and curriculum content.

- combined principles about respect for children and respect for culture into one principle on respect.

- retained principles on children's role in the curriculum, inter-relatedness of development, early childhood assessment, families and teachers and partners, and professional development of staff, folding the principle of curriculum review into the latter.

It is our expectation and hope that the Early Childhood Curriculum Principles will remain a living and dynamic document. It can be the starting point for further refinement and adaptation to changing conditions or changing group consensus at future World Forum meetings and collaborative communications. We welcome ideas on how they are being used and their impact. Please stay up-to-date on the work of the Curriculum Initiative by visiting the World Forum website: worldforumfoundation.org/curriculum.

Lawrence J. Schweinhart

Larry Schweinhart is an early childhood program researcher and speaker throughout the U.S. and around the world. He has conducted research at HighScope Educational Research Foundation in Ypsilanti, Michigan, since 1975 and has served as its president since 2003. He has directed: *The landmark HighScope Perry Preschool Study through age 40*, establishing the great human and financial potential of high-quality early childhood programs; *The HighScope Preschool Curriculum Comparison Study*, which shows that child-initiated learning activities are critical to the success of early childhood programs; and studies of the effectiveness of Head Start training and of Michigan's Great Start Readiness Program. He received his PhD in Education from Indiana University in 1975 and has taught elementary school and college courses. He and his wife Sue have two children and five grandchildren.

Diane Trister Dodge

Diane Trister Dodge is the founder and president emerita of Teaching Strategies, LLC, a company dedicated to improving the quality of early childhood programs by providing the most effective resources in curriculum, assessment, professional development, and family connections. She is the lead author of *The Creative Curriculum®* and many other Teaching Strategies resources, which are widely used in Head Start, child care, and Pre-K programs in the United States and internationally.

Universal Early Childhood Curriculum Principles

The following Universal Early Childhood Curriculum Principles represent the best thinking of World Forum early childhood educators around the world on the most essential criteria for a curriculum that promotes children's optimal development and learning. Their primary purpose is to guide programs as they develop their own curriculum or review an existing curriculum model. They are meant to be a starting point, and can be adapted to local conditions in any of the diverse cultures, regions, and countries of the world.

Children's Role in the Curriculum Children's stages of development, needs, and interests are at the center of the curriculum. Children receive responsive care and have daily opportunities to make choices and explore topics that interest them.

Content The curriculum helps children develop a deeper appreciation and understanding of their community and the world around them and promotes curiosity about and responsibility for the natural and social world.

Early Childhood Assessment Ongoing observation and documentation of children's development and learning during everyday experience enable adults to support each child's learning and development and track each child's progress.

Environment Children learn from their interactions with people and their environment. The early care and education environment should be developmentally appropriate, allowing children to engage in positive and safe interactions. It may need to be adapted to ensure that children of all abilities can participate in experiences as fully as possible.

Families and Teachers as Partners Educators, families, and communities should work together in partnership for the benefit of children's well-being and development.

Inter-relatedness of Development All aspects of development and learning are inter-related and deserve attention.

Ongoing Professional Development for all staff members is essential to the successful implementation of any curriculum. A process for regularly reflecting on and evaluating the quality and effectiveness of the curriculum enables continuous program improvement.

Outcomes The curriculum fosters children's curiosity and life-long love of learning and helps them develop essential skills and knowledge in all areas of development and learning: social-emotional, physical, cognitive, language, literacy, mathematics, social studies, science and technology, health, spirituality, and the arts.

Play as Children's Work Play is integral to children's learning and development. The daily program includes ample opportunities for children to engage in open-ended as well as guided play experiences that enable them to take risks and gain a deeper understanding of themselves, others, and the world around them.

Relationships Care and education are inseparable. All young children learn and develop in the context of nurturing, responsive relationships with adults who provide them with stimulating, developmentally appropriate experiences, as well as positive relationships with other children.

Respect Family, gender, home language, culture, customs, and beliefs strongly influence children's development. Adults demonstrate respect for these influences and for young children as individuals and take a genuine interest in what they say and do.

Applying the Principles

The Universal Curriculum Principles of Early Childhood Education can be used in these ways:

They can be shared with other educators, professions, and the general public as a way to communicate the essential criteria of an effective early childhood curriculum. The principles can form the basis for an article in a professional journal or a workshop at a professional conference.

They can serve as the focus for discussion in teacher education programs and workshops. Each principle could serve as a jumping off point for a small-group discussion about what the principle means and how it can guide daily practice.

They can be a tool to examine and assess a variety of curriculum approaches. Programs seeking to select a curriculum can use the principles to decide whether a curriculum is appropriate for their program. The principles can also be used to determine what aspects of their current curriculum may need to be modified or added.

They can be used to help families understand and appreciate the value of the curriculum a program is using and how it supports their child's learning and development. The principles can be posted at a center or school, discussed at parent meetings, and used to develop a family handbook describing the program's approach and philosophy.

They can be adapted by early childhood educators to ensure that they apply to specific settings and cultures. Educators can elaborate on each principle, showing how they apply the principle in their programs, and the list can be expanded to include other shared beliefs about best practices.

CULTIVATING
AN EARLY CHILDHOOD CURRICULUM

CHAPTER 3
Designing the Space

The Physical Environment: A Powerful Regulator of Experience *by Elizabeth Prescott* 88

Places to Live: Important Dimensions of Child Care Settings *by Jim Greenman* 92

How to Create an Environment that Counteracts Stereotyping *by Alice Sterling Honig* 97

Places for ALL Children: Building Environments for Differing Needs
by Diane Trister Dodge 104

Children Need to Live in the Real World *by Jim Greenman* 110

Planning Intentionally for Children's Outdoor Environments
The Gift of Change *by Nancy Rosenow* 113

Are Your Children in Times Square?
Moving from Confinement to Engagement *by Sandra Duncan and Michelle Salcedo* 117

Creating Environments that Intrigue and Delight Children and Adults
by Wendy Shepherd and Jennifer Eaton 123

The Physical Environment
A Powerful Regulator of Experience

by Elizabeth Prescott

Anytime I encounter children who have been in a child care center, I ask them what they remember about it. Invariably their memories are about the agony of lying still at nap time, playing in the sand pile, having to eat beans, having one's back rubbed at nap time, or being outside on hot days. Apparently their memories are stored primarily as tactile sensory impressions.

This phenomenon suggests to me the importance of paying attention to the physical environment we create in a child care program. I would like to address five key dimensions of environment, which impact on the experiences of children. Then I will demonstrate how to consider these dimensions in solving some typical problems in child care settings.

Dimensions of the Environment

Softness/Hardness. Softness is provided for in a center's environment through the presence of objects, which are responsive to one's touch — which provide a variety of tactile sensory stimuli. Such objects include sand, water, grass, swings, rugs, pillows, soft furniture such as large pillows and couches, finger paints, play dough/clay, and laps to sit on.

A common characteristic of these soft materials is that they provide experiences where the environment responds to the child. You can use your body the way you want to on a rug. You push sand around or pound on clay, and each does what you want it to do. Hard surroundings (tiled floors, wooden furniture, asphalt playgrounds) provide a different experience. You just don't feel as comfortable sitting on a tiled floor, and you don't feel inclined to roll around on an asphalt play yard. In like manner, a straight hard chair tells your body what to do.

These hard materials give the message that "you better shape up and do what the environment requires" — it's not going to give in to you. I think young children are not developmentally ready for this message for very much of the day. Especially in a full-day program, inhabitants — big and little — of a hard environment will inevitably experience tension and fatigue.

Open/Closed. Play equipment that is open has no one right way of using it — it can be manipulated in a variety of ways. For example, sand, collage materials, and dress up clothes can be played with in a wide variety of ways — none of these ways is inherently incorrect.

Closed equipment, on the other hand, can only be played with in one way; it can only be manipulated one way to come out right. With a puzzle, for example, the pieces must be fitted the proper way to complete the puzzle. Lotto games and nearly all Montessori equipment exhibit this closed nature. Such equipment is useful and can give a sense of competence, but only if it is well matched to a child's growing edge — if a child has learned how to do the one operation, it is no longer interesting; and if he can't do it at all, it is often frustrating.

Then there is some equipment, which is in between. Legos® and Tinkertoys are good examples. They require you to pay attention to their qualities. They won't do everything you want them to do, but if used in the proper way, they permit some opportunity for creativity.

I feel that a center needs to provide all these kinds of experiences for children. But for preschool children it is especially important to have open equipment available. Sometimes centers believe they are well equipped if they have lots of puzzles and cognitive games. Often open equipment is considered less important and is provided in a haphazard, thoughtless way. The opportunities available in open equipment need to be taken seriously.

Simple/Complex. Play equipment can differ in its holding power, i.e., the capacity to sustain attention. We have called this dimension complexity and have rated play units according to the number of different materials, which are combined. A simple unit has one manipulatable aspect, a complex unit has two different kinds of materials combined, and a super unit has three different kinds of materials that go together.

For example, a sand pile with no equipment is a simple unit. Add digging equipment and it is a complex unit. If you add water as a third element, it becomes a super unit. Play dough by itself is a simple unit. With toothpicks it is a complex unit, and with toothpicks and cookie cutters it is a super unit.

The advantage of a super unit is that it is much more complex so that it holds children's interest for a much longer time. As you add more features or materials to a unit, you geometrically increase the number of things that can be done with it. The usefulness of this concept is that when you look at play that isn't working well, you can often get it to work better by making it more complex.

Intrusion/Seclusion. This dimension describes opportunities for privacy and control over one's own territory.

To me, this is an especially important issue in child care. It is one thing for a child to go to a morning nursery school, where the main goal is to give the child a social experience. But a child going to a child care center where he has to deal with many people for an entire day may get much more of a social experience than he needs.

For this reason, I think it is especially important to have the environment set up with places where children can be alone at times or alone with a best friend or adult so that they can feel secure that they are not going to be intruded upon. In child care, it is important for children to know there are times when they do not have to share and can use equipment without interruption and can have some individual adult attention.

High Mobility/Low Mobility. This aspect looks at the freedom a child has to move around. High mobility activities permit the child to use his whole body — running, climbing, or trike riding. Other activities, such as story time and puzzles, by their very nature require children to sit still. There are also activities that are in between — playing in the housekeeping area or the block corner.

One thing I've observed in cognitively-oriented child care centers is that children are sometimes sitting for long periods of time. I remember observing in a center once where children sat for a matching game at tables, then moved to a story time on a nearby rug, then back to a sitting down activity at the tables. In all, the children had to sit still for nearly two hours, which was very difficult for them. The teacher, who was moving about the entire time, apparently wasn't aware that she had provided three low-mobility activities in a row.

I've also noticed in centers where children are provided many choices there are a number of children who will never choose sitting down activities. One thing adults have to be more inventive about in such circumstances is in providing cognitive activities, which permit high mobility. There are many counting games that you can do while you're running or trike riding. Also with trike riding, building in stop signs, a trike-riding path, or inventing slalom games are all ways of making children pay attention to perceptual cues. In many centers, you only have to pay that kind of attention in sitting down activities.

Dealing with Problems Environmentally

Problem: Children not sharing. There are two spatial problems that are apt to be involved in sharing. One is that there often isn't enough to do. In our observations, we counted the number of things to do against the number of children in a center. We found that during a free choice period it actually takes about five things per child at any given time to make for a really well functioning program. If there were only two things, we would invariably see sharing problems.

The second spatial problem often associated with sharing is insufficient complexity. For example, if children are fighting over tricycles, often the answer is not to get more tricycles but to provide variety in the type of wheel toy and props to go with them.

If you have some tricycles with rear seats and some with wagons that hook on, if you have traffic signs and gasoline pumps, and perhaps some blocks that can be piled on the wagons, then this activity can absorb far more children without having them fight over the use of the trike itself. Some can be riding, some directing traffic, some hooking on wagons, and some piling on blocks. The resulting play will have a richness of theme seldom seen where only simple tricycles are provided.

Problem: Children not becoming involved. When children cannot find something to do or are bored with an activity, the problem often can be solved by increasing the complexity of play units, thus adding novelty and providing more focus. If you've had play dough out for a long time, bringing in buttons and toothpicks will add to its interest.

Non involvement may also be the result of poor organization of the play space resulting in excessive intrusion. If activities are arranged around the edges of a rectangular room with empty space in the middle, it is likely that children will be drawn out of the activities and into the open empty middle to run. Also a problem will arise if you have an activity area which is not well protected so that children moving from one activity to another move through it. This traffic will disrupt and discourage the children playing in this area.

It is crucial, therefore, to provide activity areas, which are well defined and well protected. I would recommend taking a look at your room and yard to determine if there are clear functional pathways between areas. It may be helpful to get down at the children's height to view the area as they see it. This perspective may reveal visual obstacles, which are not apparent from the adult's eye level.

Problem: A child keeps repeating one activity. If a child really seems to be stuck on an activity and is in clear need of having his activity level broadened, a look at the environment may suggest some alternatives which provide a secure way for the child to make a move.

First, you may want to introduce some novelty into the environment. If a child is stuck on puzzles at a certain table, it may help to simply move the puzzles away for a week and to experiment with placing a more open activity such as collage or drawing with felt pens on the table where puzzles have always been located.

Second, it may help to restructure the activity. If a child plays continually with play dough as a means of avoiding social contact, it may help to bring the social contact to the play dough and to protect the budding relationship from intrusions. This child is probably not ready for the complexity of social skills that comes with fast moving, high mobility dramatic play, but could handle a bit of interaction over a 'safe' activity.

Problem: Children coming unglued at the end of the morning. I've seen some interesting solutions to this problem. Usually the solutions provide for increasing softness. For example, having children take their shoes off before lunchtime is a way of letting them wind down and of letting them know there is a different part of the day coming. I also remember a center where children were really at loose ends after the usual end of the morning cleaning up and washing up. Each adult then took her children into a quiet, enclosed area that had a rug and pillows. They had a nice intimate time together — talking and reading stories. The children lounged on the pillows and were relaxed and calm for lunch and naptime.

Problem: Adults coming unglued at the end of the day. One thing that really surprised me in our observations was that it is the adults more than the children who have a difficult time coping with the final hours of the day. We started out assuming it was the children who fell apart. But we found that after the children got up from their naps, they were raring to go again.

When we coded their behavior, they did quite well. In center after center, we found it was the adults who appeared fatigued and less effective.

Child care programs will go to a great deal of trouble and expense to provide activities and equipment they think are good for children. But it wouldn't occur to them to get a really comfortable easy chair for an adult who has been there for eight hours. Likewise, I know of centers where adults may not sit down when children are outside. To me, this is not a wise policy — a yard ought to be safe enough so that an adult can sit down. Just as with the easy chair inside, once the adult sits down, she really becomes accessible to children. When an adult is sitting, she can snuggle and converse in a close way, which is impossible when she is standing up.

If you want an adult to nurture children, she's got to feel that she's nurtured too. I think providing comfortable furniture and encouraging the adults to be comfortable is one way that you get good things to happen for children.

Another way of saying this is to propose that the dimensions, which I have discussed can be applied to enhance the comfort and interest of the environment for adults in child care. They, too, need softness, complexity, variety, and freedom from too much intrusion.

Further Readings

Jones, E., & Prescott, E. (Out of print). "Dimensions of teaching — Learning environments II." *Focus on day care*. Washington, DC: NAEYC.

Kritchevsky, S., & Prescott, E. (Out of print). *Planning environments for young children: Physical space*. Washington, DC: NAEYC.

Elizabeth Prescott

Elizabeth Prescott retired as a professor of early childhood education at Pacific Oaks College in Pasadena, California. She resides in Bellingham, Washington.

Places to Live

Important Dimensions of Child Care Settings

by Jim Greenman

We have institutionalized childhood!
We have institutionalized our children!

Yikes! Shocking but true. Many young children spend all day, five days a week, 48 or more weeks a year in child care centers; up to 12,000 hours in the first decade of their life; about the same time they spend in school, kindergarten through grade 12.

Further, we are forcing children to get older, younger. When you look at what is expected of young children in early care and education, age 4 has become the new 6. (Interesting, this reverses itself for adults — 40 is the new 30!)

The hard edge shock value associated with the word institution is useful, not because institutions are bad, but because they can be bad, if we don't get them right. Institutions are valuable because they can represent order, stability, tradition, and the establishment of good practice.

Child care centers can be great institutions of learning and caring, if we pay attention to some important dimensions that also make them reasonable places to live.

Comfort and Softness

> It was a spotless classroom, gleaming tile floors, and shiny tables and chairs. It might have been a great playroom or school for a few hours, but a place for all day, all week, all year living? Something was missing, something important. When the children were gone, there was no imprint, none of the general residue or artifacts of lived lives. The care and the education were there, but it was a place devoid of feeling, character, or real warmth.

Comfort is not the enemy of serious early childhood education. Most of us want comfort from the places where we live. We need pliability, responsiveness in our furnishings and the people we are with, and some freedom. We may need to sprawl, slouch, or collapse for a while. The strains and tensions of everyday life may be made manageable by a stretch on a couch, cuddling with a child or lover, or simply a few moments of silence in an easy chair. The ability to make an imprint on a setting where one spends up to ten hours a day for a number of years is important in the development of self-esteem. Young children, more recent womb-dwellers than we are and native sensualists operate in a world dominated more by sensory impression than by mind and language — they sense the world.

Children need a place where they have full use of their bodies and senses and enough freedom to take advantage of the variety of life, where they can find or invent the spaces they need and have places and moments in time to pause and recharge.

But remember, comfort is subjective, and like everything else, culture bound. It has to do with our own sense of softness, responsiveness, familiarity, and a reasonable level of sensory stimulation — neither too much nor too little, that leads to a sense of calm.

Softness

In many schools, workplaces, and most other institutions (like hospitals, nursing homes, dormitories, prisons), many things are far too hard, cold, and unrelenting. Most of us usually like things rounded and cushioned and warm to the touch. A hard physical setting, combined with the inflexibility of institutional or group life, can harden us or put us on edge. We may be left with no way to make an imprint — to make our presence felt literally on anything (for a child, the best imprint may be on a lap). Over 30 years ago, Elizabeth Prescott and Betty Jones (Prescott, 1984, p. 52) identified softness as a key dimension in their research on child care settings:

"The dimension of softness was so named because it appeared to indicate a responsive quality of the environment to the child, especially on a sensual/tactile level. It was based on the presence or absence of 11 components:

1. Malleable materials, such as clay or play-dough

2. Sand that children can be in, either in a box or play area

3. Laps — teachers holding children

4. Single-sling swings

5. Grass that children can be on

6. Large rug or carpeting indoors

7. Water as an activity

8. Very messy materials, such as finger-paint, clay, or mud

9. Child/adult cozy furniture, such as rockers, couches, or lawn swings

10. Dirt to dig in

11. Animals that can be held, such as guinea pigs, dogs, and cats."

A soft, responsive, physical environment reaches out to children and creates a nest that helps children to feel more secure, enabling them to venture out and explore the world, much the way that homes provide adults with the haven from which they can face an often difficult and heartless world. The moments alone rocking in a chair or on a swing, or kneading dough allow children to recharge. But softness has an equally significant educational purpose, because so much of young children's learning is sensory-motor based and requires hands-on (more accurately, bodies-on) experience. Pounding on play dough or smearing paint is not only therapeutic and fun, but also the medium for a young scientist learning chemistry and physics in action. Handling animals and plants requires children to be gentle and sensitive to living things. Adult stomachs and laps and arms reassure with the intimacy of touch, smell, and body warmth, and at the same time provide the proximity necessary for quality language interactions and social learning. The younger the child and the longer the day, the more importance softness and comfort assume to create the conditions for learning.

But it isn't just about the kids. A six- to eight-hour day with children requires considerable giving of our adult physical and emotional selves. Just like children, we replenish our reservoirs of energy, patience, and goodwill through moments of relaxation free from the need to remain upright and erect. We can de-stress by working with pliable sensory materials like clay, bread dough, or water, and by having moments of relaxed physical contact with other human beings. The intimacy of snuggling with a young child or rubbing a baby's stomach or preschooler's back calms both human beings involved.

To say that comfort and softness are important is not to say that children's settings need to be pleasure based. They are work settings for children and adults, sites for some no-nonsense upright learning and performing. Activities that require concentration of mind and body, such as building, listening, writing, and stacking, benefit from a hard context with minimal distractions. There needs to be a balance. Comfort provides the security for fledgling scholars to tackle the demands of sustained concentration. It masks and mutes the necessary efficiency and order of institutional life. A physical environment that yields compensates somewhat for the imposing demands group living requires of individuals, yielding to the pace, interests, and sensibilities of the group.

Privacy and Semi-seclusion: Places to Pause

Life in the group was constant. Everyone could always see everyone else, always in earshot, life in a pack.

Good design in early childhood settings reflects the need for an active social environment, where positive social relationships are fostered; settings that facilitate play and encourage participation at different levels and at the same time allow non-participation. Early childhood programs are usually the first time a child submits to the judgment of peers. This is a serious business.

Being at our social best, at any age, requires private places that allow us to retreat. And lots of learning and play experiences require some seclusion. Reading a book, trading treasures with a best friend, or concentrating on a difficult task, such as playing with a stacking toy if you are 18 months or a model if you are eight, all require some seclusion. Away from the action and flow, off the beaten path, a preschool child can construct and sustain an imaginary world — a manageable world where he or she is at the center, working through the bewildering issues of growing up. School-age children can explore what it means to have best friends or exclusive, secret clubs.

Children (and adults) need simplified environments when they are feeling tired, unhappy, small, powerless, or out of control. Semi-private spaces to retreat to, removed from the stimulating hustle and bustle, allow for that. In all-day settings these feelings are more frequent. Withdrawal can be a healthy and necessary adaptation.

Unfortunately, in the United States we have almost entirely defined supervision as surveillance, rather than a combination of carefully planned environments, and established norms and expectations for behavior. Privacy and seclusion are considered not only unnecessary, but inappropriate.

However, there are degrees of privacy in a space. Physical boundaries may or may not provide separation of all sight and sound. Acoustic separation assumes great importance in a noisy setting, particularly if the noise is sharp and irregular or if we want privacy to wail and moan or explode with joy.

What we need most are 'places to pause for awhile,' enough separation and off the beaten path to stop: semi-enclosed spaces that allow a teacher to see in, enclosed spaces which allow children to see out, and spaces that may not be enclosed but that have a defined sense of place and allow lingering. Children need places to watch from and to hold back in, places in which to hide and seek things, and places, which enable them to pause and reflect. Children are attracted to "elements within the environment that have a quality of delight and constant change." Places to pause often reflect this — a window to the street, a view to another group, a fish tank, a mobile, or a teacher-designed surprise space. Low dividers, lattice or gauzy fabric screen, plants, or crates with openings can provide the illusion of privacy.

Unfortunately, these private spaces, retreats, and 'places to pause' are often absent in centers or limited to a single 'cozy corner.' The contrast with homes is dramatic. Imagine if our only alternative when you were feeling stress was to go to a cozy corner you shared with 15 other people!

When privacy is not available, people cocoon. We simply filter out or ignore unwanted contact; our behavior in elevators or crowded sidewalks provides a good example. Children do the same. Young babies simply shut down all their systems when the environmental load gets too high. Programs, however, don't always recognize or allow children to regulate this need to simplify the environment, and 'cocooning' or 'spacing out' may be seen as a disciplinary issue or a sign of child pathology.

Autonomy

I can do it myself (maybe, at least some of the time, when I want to, when I need to, if you give me a chance)!

Autonomy, the power to govern oneself, to be independent, is always a dual struggle for self-control and freedom from external restraints. Young children are struggling to gain control over their bodies, their emotions, and their impulses. At the same time they have to learn how to balance their desire to be independent with their adjustment to the demands of the larger world.

Issues of autonomy are present in all aspects of children's environments. How much are children allowed or encouraged to hold sway over their:

Bodily needs: hunger, thirst, access to the bathroom, sleep, body temperature, and so on? "Can I get a drink, take off my socks and scratch my foot, lie down and rest (or get up and play)?"

Mobility: to move around, to be still. "Can I hop, climb, or stay and rest on this pillow?"

Space: to adapt, define, personalize, or protect a space. "Can I pull up a chair, turn a light on or off, create my own order or clutter which may look simply like a mess to the unknowing eyes of others?"

Social life: to choose one's own company. "Can I be alone, choose my lunch date, or my loft associates?"

Time: to set one's own pace, to stop and start. "Can I take a break?"

Things: to be able to select, determine the use of, and put things away. "Can I go get the Legos® by myself? Can I use them to make a space gun?"

Activities: to choose activities and conduct them free from intrusion. "Do I have to listen?"

Children are not adults. For reasons of safety we don't grant them the autonomy that adults often have — in order to protect them from their own impulses and from failure, and to protect the entire group from the effects of egocentrism run amok. Yet, without ample, measured autonomy, how can children develop into independent, resourceful, confident people?

Autonomy does more than build children's self-esteem and add to life's quality; it helps the setting work better. Given freedom and the necessity to do so, children invent the spaces they need. If children are given the opportunity to remake and adapt spaces, they learn that conditions are not fixed. They squeeze behind furniture, climb on whatever is available, seclude themselves under blankets, and build forts or houses. Creating spaces that allow children to do these things safely regulates behaviors like climbing.

Autonomy contributes to the simple enjoyment of life. From an early age, we all pluck our own joys and delights. Nothing can take them away from our minds. Poet Michael Brownstein said, "Pause before anything ordinary and it becomes important." Yet, without the freedom to pause, to choose our objects of desire and wonder, life can become dreary and diminished, even at an early age.

Final Word

There are other interrelated important dimensions that determine the livability of the group settings we inhabit: competence, order, the routines and rituals, mobility, and the sense of security. Together, they determine whether our places feel like our places and allow us to be the best people we can be.

Reference

Prescott, E. (1984). "The physical setting in day care." In J. Greenman and R. Fuqua (eds.), *Making day care better: Training, evaluation, and the process of change.* New York: Teachers College Press.

Jim Greenman

Jim Greenman dedicated more than 30 years to the early childhood field as an educator, early childhood administrator, and author. Throughout his career, he worked with employer-sponsored, inner city, hospital, and university programs; early childhood and family education programs; Head Start; family child care; and public and private schools. Jim played a significant role in the facility and program design process for more than 100 early childhood projects, taught at the Institute on Child Care Design at the Harvard Graduate School of Design, and was senior vice president for education and program development at Bright Horizons Family Solutions. He held a master's degree from the University of California at Berkeley, where he also completed additional advanced graduate courses. Jim passed away in 2009 after a courageous battle with cancer. He inspired many people in the early childhood field through his dedication and work in the early childhood field; Jim's legacy leaves an everlasting gift to children and educators.

How to Create an Environment that Counteracts Stereotyping

by Alice Sterling Honig

'Stereotyping' means having fixed, unchanging ideas about the characteristics of individuals in different groups. The ideas could be about almost anything in a person's world, for example, that "boys should never play with dolls or they will become sissies," or that "girls are too delicate to climb a tree." Gender is biologically based, but gender roles are constantly constructed, and by about age 2 or 3 children's play reveals gender differences.

> A year-old baby looks up at the smiling, looming face of the stranger approaching and cries mightily, because all faces different from a parent's face seem alien and frightening. The baby's brain tries to make sense of the world by pigeonholing experiences as safe or unsafe, familiar or unfamiliar. People from some cultures are taught, for example, that the right hand is to be used for eating and the left hand for toilet functions. If they see someone from a different culture group using both hands freely for eating, they may become shocked and even revolted and disparage and shun that person. People of one particular religious persuasion may 'demonize' folks who have totally different beliefs as 'heathens' or 'pagans' and be willing even to torture and kill those who will not convert to what they consider the 'true' religion.

By stereotyping, some folks take a lazy way of knowing others rather than learning who that individual person 'really' is! Persons prone to stereotype are sure that they know the characteristics of every person in a group they approve of or in a group that they are scared of or repudiate. Stereotypes shape our thoughts and expectations. Research with a baby dressed in pink and labeled a 'girl' showed that adults characterized the baby as more delicate, more scared; if the baby was dressed in blue and labeled a boy, then adults used words to suggest the baby was bolder, and more interested in a toy football.

Stereotypes start early! They include ideas children have learned from families, television, and communities about what are 'appropriate' and what are 'expected' behaviors for persons who differ in culture, ethnicity, religion, dress, speech patterns, and gender.

Some teachers also promote stereotypes. Researchers note that teachers are more uncomfortable about preschool boys choosing to play with 'girl' toys than they are with girls choosing 'boy' toys. Seeing a preschooler approach the dress-up corner and take up a pocketbook with a handle, a caregiver called out, "That is for little girls, honey!" Teachers also give more attention to boy toddlers, who often express more neediness and 'rowdiness' (Wittmer & Honig, 1987; Chick, Heilman, Houser, & Hunter, 2002).

Early in life, stereotyping becomes a 'convenient' way for small children to make sense of the world. Indeed, Maccoby and colleagues suggest that the rigid sex-role stereotyping that characterizes the same-sex playgroups of preschool boys and girls arises, as young children try to understand their world and determine who and what fits into a cognitive category.

> The four-year-old girls came to complain to Ms. Genia that the boys were hogging the block corner, and they did not have a chance to play with blocks. At circle time, the teacher talked with the children about taking turns and how the girls wanted a chance to build with blocks, too. The boys assured her that girls do not like blocks! When she explained that they really did want to play and had come to her to complain about not having time in the block corner, the boys seemed genuinely puzzled and surprised. Then they brightened up and decided, "Okay. The girls can play with the blocks when we have outside playground time!" This solution, alas, did not resolve the girls' grievances.

Stereotyped gender role thinking about the appropriateness of certain toys is strongly visible beginning in preschool. The stereotyping of sex roles is sometimes aided by the boisterousness of boys' play as some little girls see it. "I am not inviting any boys to my five-year-old birthday party!" announced the child of a sociologist famous for sensitivity in cross-cultural research. "Boys play too rough!" she added. The father confided to me that he had always been so fair about beliefs, customs, and patterns of interactions of the peoples he studied. He was uncomfortable with his daughter's decision, but could not 'force' her to invite boys. Examination of sex role differences across many studies shows that indeed boys, as a group, have higher activity and aggression levels than girls. But the rigidity of stereotyped play behaviors and name calling in some preschool environments challenges us to become more thoughtful in creating classroom atmospheres that promote more flexible thinking and interacting.

Since categorizations begin very early as a cognitive 'shorthand' convenient way of thinking early in life, how can teachers and parents assist young children in changing their rigid concepts about groups of people, whether of different ethnicity, gender, or for example, those with special needs? In *Berenstain Bears, No Girls Allowed*, the boy cubs do not want Sister Bear around. She always beats them at baseball and other 'boy'-type games. The older boy cubs are upset because she boasts about being better, and they try to exclude her from their club. Should Papa Bear 'force' the boy cubs to let her in their club? Although she is hopping mad, Sister Bear learns how important it is to be a good winner. This book shows a good win-win manner to resolve this problem.

Becoming Aware of Our Own Stereotypes

Becoming aware of our own adult stereotypes is a first step in understanding how strong other people's stereotypes may be. Research shows that teachers interrupt preschool girls more than boys. Teachers have been found to praise little girls far more than boys for good looks. One study showed that children at a summer camp ridiculed and rejected a fat child even more than they acted mean toward children with any other bodily condition, such as hearing loss or lack of mobility.

Some adults also unconsciously behave in more negative ways toward others who look too fat or too short. Sometimes a caregiver may be more impatient with a child dressed more ragged than other children or one who speaks with a 'funny' drawl. Interviews in high schools reveal widespread use of cruel jibes and bullying when a peer is timid, physically weak, pimply, or 'too' smart. Youths described their anguish, despair, and belief that teachers do not notice bullying and harassment of those ostracized as 'different' (Garbarino & DeLara, 2002).

So our first line of defense to help create a classroom climate of acceptance for all the children is to think deeply about our own stereotypes and to keep our eyes open! Do we assume that a child who slurs speech or still wets his pants in preschool comes from a 'bad' family in some way or 'must' be a slower learner than other children? Do we give a lot more attention (although often negative!) to boys than to girls in the classroom, as many researchers show? As we increase our own awareness, we can become more attuned to unkind categorizations occurring in the classroom and can plan out helpful actions.

Some parents may simply be overwhelmed by daily tasks and not notice needs that teachers see clearly. A Head Start teacher working in a state with a warm climate told me quietly about a boy whom the children would not sit near because he 'smelled' so bad. The rejection and isolation so saddened the little boy. A home visit revealed that mom was single and alcoholic. She did not have the strength to address this problem. The teacher bought a bar of soap for the boy and taught him how to wash and clean his clothes.

A teacher needs to be clear when a classroom problem of aversion or bullying is due to a personal difficulty or to stereotyping. It may take some sleuthing to figure out what is actually going on in the classroom. Observation is a teacher's first tool in gaining insights and information about social difficulties any children are having in the classroom. Many social interactions that are negative, for example, may be due to cultural differences or to interpersonal patterns of relating learned in the first years of life.

Work Valiantly to Lessen the Power of Stereotyped Cultural Beliefs and Taboos

Some culture groups stigmatize women strongly. A child care director called me with a problem. A child from a culture where males dominate very strongly was attending the University preschool. He hit little girls in the preschool class whenever he wanted a toy or felt contradicted. The teachers explained firmly and kindly that little girls and boys have equal rights in the class. He could not hit a girl, despite the cultural norm he had learned earlier. When cultural stereotypes are powerful yet inimical to fairness, a teacher needs to reaffirm gently and enforce firmly the idea that all persons deserve to be treated fairly and kindly, whether the person is male or female.

The Importance of Attachment History

Bowlby and Ainsworth's pioneer work on Attachment Theory has resulted in dozens of studies that confirm how important secure attachment is for creating harmonious, cooperative relationships in the preschool classroom. Children who are insecurely attached to their primary caregivers in the first year of life often end up either as 'bullies' or as 'victims' in preschool (Sroufe & Fleeson, 1986). If caregivers want to create less stereotyping of some kids as 'bad' and others as 'good' in classrooms, the challenge may well be to create loving, warm, nurturing relationships with all the children. Once these intimate bonds have been developed, the child labeled as 'bad' by peers can use a newly developing secure attachment to the teacher to behave in more cooperative ways that lessen the chances for stigmatization. The teacher will also work creatively with the whole class to lessen the stereotype that peers have conjured. Creating nurturing, intimate interactions that lure little ones into secure attachments is a technique to decrease stereotyping of certain children as the 'bad kids' in the classroom (Honig, 2002).

Modeling

How we talk about others impacts young children. We need to find the positives (and note them out loud) about every child in the classroom. Using the technique of the "Kindness Jar" is one way. Talk out loud each day as you note a kindly, thoughtful, or empathic response; hurry to write it down on a piece of paper and add that paper to others in your "Kindness Jar." The kids catch on quickly!

Integrated Classrooms

Children who experience many different kinds of playmates in their nursery environment will find differences in accent, ethnicity, skin color, clothing much less important than the wonderful experience of having play partners they enjoy. An integrated classroom, where teachers have enough support staff to help children with special needs, provides a natural milieu for youngsters to become comfortable with a variety of others (Neugebauer & Wolf, 2004).

Bibliotherapy

Storybooks can assist a teacher in promoting peer acceptance rather than stereotyping and rejection of 'different' others. The book *Nick Joins In* tells the story of a wheelchair-bound child who saves the day in the gym when the ball gets stuck on some ceiling bars. He quickly wheels his chair to where the janitor keeps the long pole for opening high gym windows. With the pole, the children are able to get down the ball and the play goes on, thanks to Nick. In the story *Crow Boy*, a poor farmer's child walks miles to the Japanese village school, where the other children ostracize him for his 'different' ways. When the teacher learns that the boy has the special ability to use a bird call to call down crows from the sky, the teacher realizes that he, too, misjudged this child and is then able to get the other children to admire the boy's special skill. Some picture books incite more compassion for those who are ridiculed for being different. Dr. Seuss's books featuring Horton the Elephant are admirable examples. In the book *Otto's Trunk*, an elephant with a trunk much smaller than the other preschooler elephants is jeered at and called "little squirt." Their scorn turns to admiration when Otto discovers a talent of his own — he can snort in different ways to create a menagerie.

The high-spirited badger in *Best Friends for Frances* is grumpy that Albert and Harold, who are playing ball, say that "she is not much good" at baseball and "besides this is a no-girls game." Frances realizes that earlier in the day she had snubbed her little sister Gloria in much the same way, saying that she was "not much good" with a ball. So Frances goes home and offers to play as an accepting and helpful older sister with little Gloria. Next day, both sisters go off on a picnic. They carry a sign that says: "Best friends outing. NO BOYS." When Albert sees the sign AND the lusciously filled picnic hamper, he begins to realize there surely is a down side to excluding girls from games! Little sister Gloria urges Frances to accept him (if he promises to catch a snake for her at the pond!). Once Albert promises that there will no longer be 'no-girls' baseball games, Frances crosses off the words "NO BOYS" on her sign. Off the friends go to have a splendid adventurous afternoon on the hill by the pond. And Albert does catch a snake for Gloria! Reading picture books that increase empathy and decrease ostracizing others will increase class sensitivity to and acceptance of differences as a natural part of our wondrous human family.

Reinforce Children's Interest in a Variety of Toys and Activities

Teachers who encourage little girls who assert that they want to grow up to become doctors or soccer players are helping to decrease the stereotype that little girls mostly want to be ballerinas. Teachers can become participants in activities where both boys and girls share a variety of roles. Rather than passively standing by and watching while boys play 'fire chief' and girls dress up as 'brides,' teachers need actively to enter into the spirit of a pretend game. Personally involve both boys and girls to don the yellow dress-up clothes of fire fighters so that all the kids can 'help put out a fire' and 'save the kids in the burning house.' Teachers can create group games that involve lots of activity (that preschool boys often do prefer) that require group helpfulness to keep the game going. Holding on the fringes of a parachute and running in a great circle, and then running inward to collapse the parachute and then out again to re-create the billowing circle, is one such game.

On the playground, it is helpful to have a large group swing. There, several children, boys and girls, need to pump energetically to keep the swing in motion as they all hang on firmly and work together as a 'team' to keep the swing in motion. These cooperative activities are another way to ensure that the children will not always be playing in sex-stereotyped ways, but can cooperate in games together. A three-legged race, where two children side by side have their inner legs in one burlap sack, is a good game to pair a boy and girl together. The game becomes even more exciting, and cooperative, when each partner must help steady a large spoon with an egg on it while they hobble along as fast as they can in the race of three-legged partners. When teachers take preschoolers on a trip to a park or wooded area, then boys and girls together can search for leaves of different trees, catch grasshoppers gently, and try to spy frogs in a pond. On a trip to a supermarket, all the children can chime in to decide which peppers have the smoothest skin and which apples the teacher should buy so that they can make applesauce together back at their center.

Cooking is another activity where a boy or girl can be 'chef' and help the team get ingredients together and make cookies or shred lettuce leaves for a salad or prepare peanut butter sandwiches for snack time for all. Caregivers can ask children at circle time what they want to be when they grow up, and then offer encouraging affirmation when children mention non-stereotypic vocations.

Some children think of older women as 'witches' and stereotype all older folks as incompetent and scary. A program that builds in regular visits to retirement homes can help decrease this stereotype. Planning helps. When the children draw pictures, make collages, learn a group song to sing for the elderly; the smiles and appreciation they receive will help decrease stereotypes about 'scary old people.'

Cross-age Tutoring

Sometimes children show intolerance of children who are slower or younger or still in diapers in a preschool classroom. Set up buddy systems that involve children working together or teaching each other something one knows but the other child does not. Working together often creates a familiar comfortable feeling, and the child who stereotyped another as a 'baby' for still sucking a thumb, for example, may forget the pejorative feeling while working together on a group project, such as drawing a wall mural with a sea theme that includes fishes, boats, swimmers, whales, and big waves.

Use Videos to Decrease Stereotypes

Many television programs reinforce sex-role and other stereotypes. Videos shown to preschoolers should be chosen carefully to counteract stereotyping. For example, "Finding Nemo" shows a father fish in a nurturing, caring role with his son, rather than as a macho male figure. If you tape television shows, select shows such as "Dragon Tales," which evenly treat the girl and boy protagonists as competent and friendly, rather than showing a predominant male figure.

Invite Moral Mentors as Visitors to the Classroom

Invite people from different walks of society and different ethnic groups to visit the classroom. They may dress in different clothes from their own country and explain different customs, such as a piñata at parties. They may play an instrument, such as a samisen, that the children have never seen. Although children may at first seem wary of folks who look different from themselves, their fascination with the visitor's stories, songs, and special offerings can dispel stereotypes the children may have had about another culture group.

Invite helpers, such as folks who fight fires or deliver mail. Children are very curious about jobs. An older teen who coaches kids with special needs in swimming would make a great moral mentor to invite to the classroom. Try to invite persons who defy ordinary stereotypes. Some preschoolers believe that only men can be doctors and only women can be nurses. Invite a female doctor and a male nurse to come talk about their jobs in the classroom.

Talk with the children about the difference between actions that are 'morally' not okay such as deliberately hurting another person, or things that are socially not approved of, such as wearing socks on top of the head! Research shows that children whose parents hold more rigid views in confounding moral and social 'rightness' show more stereotyping.

Lure Children to Use a Variety of Toys

Arrange toys so that boys and girls find them attractive. Cheerfully and creatively engage groups in play with the toys despite the children's stereotypic belief that certain toys are only for boys or only for girls. During ongoing housekeeping play use ingenuity to suggest roles and responsibilities that cut across gender stereotypes (Honig, 2000).

Talk with Parents

During parent meetings, teachers will want to clarify the goal of having a classroom that accepts many different kinds of persons and abilities. Some parents may believe that it is 'shameful' for a boy to wash dishes or clean up. Stay calm and gentle in describing the ways in which your classroom is trying to promote acceptance of others and acceptance of the many rich roles we can all play to make life happier and more peaceful with each other. Be sure to ask parents to share with you times they have observed their child being kind and playing well with children from different groups and express your admiration of parents' values. Share your insights and techniques that have helped the children in your group to become more accepting and able to treat with respect and care peers who are different from them.

Although research shows that young boys do prefer more rough and tumble games and games with high activity level, and are often less verbal than little girls, teachers can use ingenuity to create many opportunities for enjoyable group games and imaginative pretend scenarios where the skills and active participation of both boys and girls enrich play for all. Sex role stereotyping is much less likely when children have had a good time playing together, regardless of ethnicity, gender, or typicality.

References

Berenstain, S., & Berenstain, J. (1986). *The Berenstain Bears, No girls allowed.* New York: Random House.

Chick, K. A., Heilman-Houser, R. A., & Hunter, M. W. (2002). The impact of child care on gender role development and gender stereotypes. *Early Childhood Education Journal, 29*(3), 149–154.

Garbarino, J., & DeLara, E. (Eds). (2002). *And words can hurt forever. How to protect adolescents from bullying, harassment, and emotional violence.* New York: Free Press.

Honig, A. S. (2000). Psychosexual development in infants and young children: Implications for caregivers. *Young Children, 55*(5), 70–77.

Honig, A. S. (2002). *Secure relationships: Nurturing infant/toddler attachment in early care settings.* Washington, DC: National Association for the Education of Young Children.

Neugebauer, B., & Wolf, D. P. (eds.) (2004). *Connecting: Friendship in the lives of young children and their teachers.* Redmond, WA: Exchange Press.

Sroufe, L. A., & Fleeson, J. (1986). "Attachment and the construction of relationships." In W. W. Hartup & Z. Rubin (eds.) *Relationships and development* (pp. 51–71). Hillsdale, NJ: Erlbaum.

Wittmer, A. S. A., & Honig, A. S. (1987). Do boy toddlers bug teachers more? *Canadian Children, 12*(1), 21–27.

Alice Sterling Honig

Alice Sterling Honig, PhD, professor emerita in the Syracuse University department of child and family studies, has devoted her career to discovering ways to best nurture and support the development of infants and toddlers. For 36 years, she directed Syracuse University's National Quality Infant/Toddler Caregiving Workshop. Additionally, she has taught courses in parenting, prosocial development, observation and assessment, cross-cultural and language development, and research methods in studying children.

Dr. Honig is the author of over 600 articles and chapters and regularly presents training sessions and delivers keynote addresses to promote high-quality child care all over the United States and in several other countries. For a decade, Dr. Honig was program director of the Children's Center, a pioneer enrichment project serving teen parents and children. As a licensed psychologist in the state of New York, Dr. Honig carries out assessments of infants', preschoolers', and school-age children's cognitive and emotional development as well as helping families with problems.

Places for ALL Children

Building Environments for Differing Needs

by Diane Trister Dodge

Increasing inclusion of children with differing abilities in early childhood classrooms is one of the most exciting developments in education today. It reflects the coming together of two professions, each of which has a strong tradition to contribute. What early childhood education has to offer is developmentally appropriate practice: how to design curriculum and implement a program based on child development theory that promotes child-initiated and active learning. What special education brings is a strong focus on individualizing: identifying each child's strengths, interests, and needs in order to adapt the curriculum to promote individual growth.

While the move to inclusion may have begun as an issue of simple justice, we are now beginning to understand and appreciate the far-ranging benefits of inclusion for everyone involved. All children learn best in an environment appropriate for their individual stage of development, an environment that emphasizes initiative and active exploration. Studies have shown that children with special needs, in particular, thrive in situations where adults encourage them to select their own play materials and initiate their own actions, and when adults respond to children's actions and encourage verbal and nonverbal communication.

The opportunities for all children to develop socially and cognitively are greatly enhanced in a classroom that acknowledges and builds respect for diversity. And for teachers, inclusion of children with special needs offers opportunities to enrich the curriculum by helping children to learn about and accept differences.

The Need for Thoughtful Planning

Successful inclusion, however, doesn't just happen. Careful thought and planning are required to ensure that the physical and social environments in the child care setting make all children feel accepted and competent.

The arrangement of furniture and the organization of materials have a profound effect on children's behavior and learning. A well-organized classroom, adapted where needed to address special needs, can make it possible for all children to function with increasing independence and self-control.

Equally important as a strategy for successful inclusion is the social environment of the classroom — how teachers and children interact and how children relate to each other. Children will be naturally curious about each other's differences and may not know how to respond to one another. The *Anti-bias Curriculum* states: "Contact by itself does not necessarily reduce non-disabled children's misconceptions or fears — it may even intensify them — unless adults take active steps to promote children's learning about each other" (Derman-Sparks and ABC Task Force).

Attention to the physical and social environments of the classroom to ensure the successful inclusion of children with differing abilities addresses several important goals: helping children develop a sense of trust and belonging, developing the ability to accept and work cooperatively with others, enhancing children's independence, and increasing children's ability to stay involved in their work. The strategies for building an environment to meet these goals apply equally to all children. However, some specific adaptations may be needed to address specific needs. Each of these goals and some strategies for achieving them are described in this article (based in part on *The New Room Arrangement as a Teaching Strategy*, see references).

Promoting a Sense of Trust and Belonging

Children are more likely to trust and feel they belong in a new environment if it includes familiar objects and images. The greater the difference between the child's environment outside the child care setting and the classroom environment, the more important it is to ensure that children see themselves, and images of persons like themselves, in the classroom.

A prominent bulletin board display might feature a photograph of each child in the class and each staff member, thus graphically conveying the message that each person is an equally important member of the classroom community. Teachers can help children to locate their own pictures and to identify other members of the class. A good discussion for circle time might be to have children identify all the ways that we are the same, and all the ways that we are different.

In selecting books, toys, pictures to display, and props for dramatic play, it's important to include relevant objects and pictures of people with different needs, just as you would to reflect cultural differences. For example, stories about and including people with differing abilities should be included in the book area, and adaptive equipment such as braces or hearing devices might be placed in the classroom so that children can try them out in their play.

For children who have limited control over many aspects of their lives, predictability and consistency is especially important for developing a sense of trust. A consistent schedule and set of routines helps children feel secure and in control. When children can refer to the schedule, they know what to expect throughout the day. Illustrating the schedule can be helpful for most children.

A classroom environment that is neat and well organized reassures children that they can find things in the same place each day. This is especially important for children with visual problems who will function more independently when the space and materials are arranged predictably. Having a place to keep their personal belongings that they can reach on their own conveys to children that their belongings will be safe and protected.

Circle time activities can help children function as a member of the group and experience a sense of belonging. Meetings should be short, no more than 10 to 15 minutes in the beginning of the year. Arranging everyone in a circle ensures that children and adults can see and be seen by all members of the group. The designated area for circle time must be large enough to avoid crowding the children, but not so large that they will find it hard to participate or feel a part of the action. A rug or carpet squares in the meeting area make sitting more comfortable. If children need guidance on where and how to sit, the carpet squares can be arranged prior to the meeting, or tape can be placed on the floor to indicate the seating arrangement.

Helping Children Learn to Work Cooperatively with Others

An important goal of inclusion is helping children of all backgrounds and abilities to live and work together. To achieve this goal, organize the environment so that children can work successfully in small groups, and actively teach children social skills.

Arranging the classroom into attractive and clearly defined interest areas with sufficient space to accommodate two to four children invites children to work with their peers. A soft rug makes a comfortable place to spread out, and it absorbs sounds that can be distracting for children with hearing impairments. To accommodate non-ambulatory children in wheelchairs, bolsters may be needed on the floor, and table heights may need to be adjusted for wheelchairs and other equipment.

Providing duplicates of materials minimizes the demands on children to share, thus avoiding potential fights and disagreements. Ample supplies of materials such as markers and table blocks encourage children to share materials and use them cooperatively. Materials that can be used in many ways such as play dough, sand, water, blocks, and art supplies are soothing and relaxing for children, thereby naturally encouraging them to work together.

Teachers set a tone of acceptance and, when necessary, provide specific guidance to children to promote positive relationships in the classroom. Key strategies to keep in mind include:

- **Establish rules for the classroom.** Decide on your most important rules and share them with the children. For example: "It's not okay to say, 'You can't play.'" (See *You Can't Say You Can't Play* by Vivian Gussin Paley, under references.)

- **Address misconceptions and hurtful statements immediately.** If children mock or make fun of a child with a special need, teachers cannot ignore the situation. "Josie isn't making those noises to annoy you. People who can't hear make unusual noises sometimes. We can all learn to talk with Josie by signing words with our hands."

- **Hold discussions on the topic of making friends.** Circle time is ideal for discussing a topic related to making and keeping friends. A picture book on the topic is a good way to introduce the subject.

- **Pair children to work on a task.** Partnering or pairing is one way to give children opportunities to work with peers they wouldn't normally seek out. Having a child work with a differently-abled peer to complete a task can make both children feel competent.

- **Interpret children's actions.** Children sometimes are not conscious of what they are doing to alienate their peers. By verbalizing what is happening, you can help them become aware and then change their behavior. "Bobbie pulled on the book because he wanted to look at it with you. He didn't mean to take it away. He wants to be friendly." "Bobbie, if you sit next to Jose and tell him what you want, he may be happy to look at the book with you."

Enhancing Children's Independence

All young children have a strong drive to establish a sense of independence. Children who may be dependent on others for many of the basic functions of life have a particular need to do as much as possible for themselves.

Selecting an activity is one way in which children demonstrate their independence. Limiting the number of choices in the beginning is especially

Strategies for Successfully Including Children with Differing Abilities

Language delay	Expand on what child says; talk about what you are doing; model the correct usage and pronunciation instead of correcting. Provide frequent visual or concrete reinforcement. Keep directions simple; encourage child to repeat them for reinforcement. Explain new concepts or vocabulary.
Attention problems	Start with short group sessions and activities. Provide visual clues (e.g. define floor space with tape). Offer a limited number of choices. Provide positive reinforcement for sustained attention. Help child quiet down after vigorous play. Plan for transition times, including arrival and departure.
Developmental delays and learning disabilities	Allow for extra demonstrations and practice sessions. Keep all directions simple, sequenced, and organized. Offer extra help in developing fine and gross motor skills, if needed.
Emotional/social problems	Provide extra structure by limiting toys and defining physical space for activities. Allow shy child to observe group activities until ready to participate. Help aggressive child control behavior through consistent enforcement of rules. Observe dramatic play for important clues about feelings and concerns. Help child learn how to express feelings in appropriate ways.
Mental retardation	Establish realistic goals for each child. Provide frequent positive feedback. Sequence learning activities into small steps. Allow adequate time for performance and learning. Encourage cooperative play and help the child move from independent to parallel to group interaction.
Impaired hearing	Obtain child's attention when speaking; seat child close to voice or music. Repeat, rephrase as needed; alert other children to use same technique. Learn some sign language and teach signing to the entire class. Provide visual clues (e.g. pictures or . . — . . — to represent rhythm). Demonstrate new activities or tasks.
Impaired vision	Ensure child's safety at all times without being overprotective. Provide verbal clues for activities. Introduce child to equipment and space verbally and through touch. Use a 'buddy' system.

Physical disability or poor coordination	*Accessibility*
	    Organize physical space to accommodate child in wheelchair.
	    Use tables that accommodate wheelchairs or provide trays on wheelchairs.
	    Use bolsters or other supports for floor activities.
	    Provide adaptive equipment for standing.
	    Learn about the availability of assistive technology and devices.
	Manual dexterity
	    Use magnetic toys to facilitate small muscle activities.
	    Attach bells to wrist or ankles for musical activities.
	    Use adaptive scissors or spoons as needed.

Reprinted from *The Creative Curriculum® for Early Childhood* (3rd edition). Teaching Strategies, Inc., Washington, DC ©1992.

critical for children who may be overwhelmed by too many choices. Teachers can gradually add new choices when they feel children can handle them.

Remember that children have individual learning styles and will approach activities in their own ways. Some will want to watch what other children are doing before they make their own choices. Others will need assistance and encouragement to move into an interest area or join a small group.

Traffic patterns must be considered carefully, especially if there are children with physical disabilities in the classroom. Make an assessment of each interest area to ensure that children can move in and out easily and have access to the shelves.

When everything in the classroom has a place, children can see what options are available, select the materials they need, and return them to the appropriate place. Materials should be organized on low shelves in the areas in which they will be used — blocks and props in the block area, art materials on the art shelf, and so on. Picture labels show that everything has a place and indicate where materials should be returned. It may be helpful to also use tactile labels (e.g. taping a pattern block piece on the shelf where the pattern blocks go), if there are children with visual disabilities in the classroom.

Helping Children Stay Involved in Their Work

Young children are easily distracted by activities and noise in the room. Some children may find it particularly difficult to sustain their involvement in an activity. Both classroom arrangement and choice of materials can be used to promote sustained involvement.

To minimize distractions, organize the classroom so that shelves and furniture used to define interest areas block the children's view of other areas. For example, move the sand and water table against a wall so children engaged in play will have their backs to potential distractions.

Children are more likely to sustain their play if the materials offer lots of options for exploration and investigation. Materials like play dough or water are especially appealing. Adding different kinds of props and utensils increases the complexity of the activity and extends the opportunities for children to remain involved.

Adaptations or the addition of new materials can promote children's involvement in activities while minimizing frustrations. For example, puzzles with knobs on the pieces make it easier for children to grasp, magnetic toys can help a child with limited small muscle control, inserting a rubber ball on the paint brush handles and markers will make it easier for a child to grasp and control them, taping a piece of paper to the table will make the paper more stable, and placing drawing paper or pieces of a game on a cafeteria tray may help a child with a visual impairment stay focused on the activity.

Children with special needs, like all children, thrive in an environment that supports their independence and encourages them to pursue their own interests. When adults create an atmosphere of acceptance and are responsive to what children say and do, competence and self-esteem grow. Including children with differing abilities in the classroom allows teachers to enrich the curriculum by promoting acceptance and greater understanding of others. What is now required by law has far-ranging benefits for everyone involved.

References

Derman-Sparks, L., & ABC Task Force. (1989). *Anti-bias curriculum: Tools for empowering young children* (p. 40). Washington, DC: National Association for the Education of Young Children.

The new room arrangement as a teaching strategy (a slide/videotape). (1992). Washington, DC: Teaching Strategies, Inc.

Paley, V. G. (1992). *You can't say you can't play*. Cambridge, MA: Harvard University Press.

Diane Trister Dodge

Diane Trister Dodge, author of *The Creative Curriculum for Early Childhood*, is the president of Teaching Strategies, Inc., a Washington, DC-based company that designs practical curriculum and training materials to support quality early childhood programs. She wishes to acknowledge the work of Shizuko Akasaki and Whit Hayslip in the Los Angeles Unified School District who first taught her the value of developmentally appropriate practice for children with special needs. They have assisted with successfully implementing the *Creative Curriculum* in over 700 classrooms serving pre-kindergarten children.

Children Need to Live in the Real World

by Jim Greenman

"...he not busy being born
Is busy dying."
Bob Dylan, "It's Alright Ma" (I'm Only Bleeding)

Being born is a messy thing, the first time and every time. There's always a lot of screaming and crying and bodily fluids. But there are also hoots of laughter and tears of pure pleasure. It doesn't take long to get cleaned up and there are lots of smiles and touching. But we are never too far away from the screaming and the crying and the bodily fluids.

At what point did caution become dominant? When did we surrender our children's lives to tabloid-induced fear and the sacred order of risk managers? "The purpose of life, after all, is to live it, to taste experience to the utmost, to reach out eagerly and without fear for newer richer experience," said Eleanor Roosevelt, who overcame crippling shyness and a love-starved childhood.

At what point did childhood become so driven? Children have a lot to learn. We can fill them up, busy their days, keep them occupied and industrious in all manner of ways. There can be singing and dancing, books, and computers. It can all look good — it can even be good. But unless we can connect them to the real world of nature and people outside the walls of our children's world, unless within our walls we can give them time and place to simply be and find themselves, it is not enough.

There are melodies in the waves and poetry in the wind that blows the leaves off trees. There is art in the anthills and the strands of seaweed on the beach. Thoughts lay dormant without stillness and solitude. Reality is difficult. It is messy and loud and profane. There are people with warts and frowns, and decidedly mixed virtues.

But childhood is a time when we help children begin to live in the world and love the world, and we can't do that fenced off from it in a world of two-dimensional glowing screens and plastic balls and slides.

Nature was there before the Nature Company, before playgrounds, before parks. An infinite laboratory, a stage and concert hall, the natural world is a school for young children.

Nature is unpredictable. It is the uneven, the changing and evolving, the glorious untidiness of it all that provides such contrast with life inside. The ground under our feet may slope or buckle. The air may be heavy and weigh us down or be so light that time has fallen asleep in the sunshine. Nothing falls from the sky inside — but outside there are leaves and snowflakes, rain and hail. Inside, nothing flies (except flies) or burrows or leaps from tree to tree. Many of us age and forget the joy of the small, unstaged event — the sudden dark cloud, the bird at the feeder, the toad in the garden.

Nature is bountiful. There are shapes and sizes, colors and textures, smells and tastes — an enormous variety of substances. In a world of catalogs and consumable objects, designed spaces, and programmed areas, sometimes it helps to remember that the natural world is full of multi-dimensional, unassailing educational experiences for children. Nature is hard, soft, fragile, heavy, light, smooth, and rough. Armed with our five senses, we explore the world and call the adventure science — or, if you prefer, cognitive development, classification, sensory development, or perceptual-motor learning.

Nature is beautiful. The rainbow in the oily water or the rainbow in the sky, the dandelion or the apple blossom; there is so much loveliness we grow slack and leave the awe to artists. But *look* at those towering cliffs of clouds and the light streaking through the pine needles. *See* the silvery birch leaves and the swirls in the bark, the rain dripping from the roof, and delicate, lace-like etchings in the leaf.

Nature is alive with sounds. It is not only Maxwell House coffeemakers that make music, so do the wind and rain, and, of course, birds and crickets; even dogs make music. The world is full of natural and man-made rhythms that children experience and imitate.

Nature creates a multitude of places. Lie out in the open on that hill, or under that willow. Sit on that rock or in that high grass. Squeeze under the hedge or march through that puddle. A small strand of trees makes a forest if you are small.

Nature is real. Everything dies — the ant, the baby bird that fell from the nest, the flower, the leaf. Thistles have stickers, and roots trip unsuspecting feet. It is our world, not Gilligan's Island.

Nature lives inside and out. Any room is enlivened by plants and animals, birds and reptiles, flowers and dried plants, stone and wood. Open a window, turn off a light.

Let Them Be — Sometimes

Anne was having a long conversation with her best friend Kassie, trying to find a time to get together for a 'play date.' The two six-year-olds kept running into conflicts of swim/gym, soccer, music lessons, and other play dates as they checked the calendars kept by their mothers. Listening to them, I fully expected the conversation to end with: "Well, Kassie, I'll have my people call your people and we'll take lunch real soon." I wonder if there are any six-year-olds with beepers or their own cellular phones?

It's not just that most children don't have the lives of Tom Sawyer or Opie in Mayberry anymore, they don't even have the freedom of the Brady Bunch. Many lead scheduled week-at-a-glance lives, managed by parents and punctuated by television. The neighborhood, the park, even the yard plays less of a role in the lives of many children.

Children need time to mess around, literally, without direction of any kind; and with stuff of their choosing, in places of their making, making their weird sounds and faces. Between idleness and industry lie other states — of experimentation (alias play), reflection, or joy.

It's Not Just What You Do, It's Who You Are

"What's that yucky stuff on the water?"
I don't know. Don't touch it.

"What is that flower?"
I don't know. But don't eat it.

"Why doesn't the vacuum work?"
"I don't know, it's broken," said the teacher.

There are few things more depressing than to be in the classroom of the incurious (except the classroom of the uncaring) — rooms staffed with people who fail to ask "why" and "how," not to stimulate the children's thinking and answer their questions, but to answer their own. Not knowing is certainly no sin in the classroom. Not being interested, not having questions, not seeking answers, not showing an enthusiasm for discovery is a sin, because intellectual lethargy is contagious. The *failure to wonder* shrinks the universe and begins to dampen the child's marvelous spirit of inquiry.

One does not have to be interested in everything, or in a constant state of childlike awe. However, a passionate interest in something, as well as delight and appreciation for a child's sense of wonder, brings a classroom to life.

Just Do It!

"It's all right, dad, I'm only crying."
Emma Greenman, age 4
(when life was a little too real)

The drive to protect our children is profound and easily can extend to scotch-guarding their lives. Scrubbing and polishing every raw experience in the name of health and safety or protecting innocence scapes away from the natural luster of childhood. Some of the wonders and joys of childhood that fuel the best in our adult selves are unavoidably birthed in bumps and bruises and tears.

Jim Greenman

Jim Greenman dedicated more than 30 years to the early childhood field as an educator, early childhood administrator, and author. Throughout his career, he worked with employer-sponsored, inner city, hospital, and university programs; early childhood and family education programs; Head Start; family child care; and public and private schools. Jim played a significant role in the facility and program design process for more than 100 early childhood projects, taught at the Institute on Child Care Design at the Harvard Graduate School of Design, and was senior vice president for education and program development at Bright Horizons Family Solutions. He held a master's degree from the University of California at Berkeley, where he also completed additional advanced graduate courses. Jim passed away in 2009 after a courageous battle with cancer. He inspired many people in the early childhood field through his dedication and work in the early childhood field; Jim's legacy leaves an everlasting gift to children and educators.

Planning Intentionally for Children's Outdoor Environments

The Gift of Change

by Nancy Rosenow

When I was a child 50 years ago, nobody planned my outdoor environment. My home was close to flower-filled meadows that I could explore freely, and my preschool and elementary school classrooms opened onto beautiful woodlands that we children used as an important part of our day-to-day learning. The last time I visited my old school, I noticed with dismay that the meadows and woods were gone, replaced by high-rise apartment buildings and other signs of 'progress.' The outdoor spaces were now made of asphalt and plastic.

How easy it would be to fall into the trap of thinking that "everything was better back then." Certainly many things have changed for children since I was young, and undoubtedly some of the changes have been difficult ones. However, over the past ten years, as I've worked with people around the world who are interested in children's outdoor environments, I've come to understand that even the upsetting changes have pushed us in ways that have helped us discover new gifts. More on this in a moment.

First, the bad news. No doubt today's children are facing a host of daunting challenges that will take hard work to fix:

- In 1995, Marion Wright Edelman described some of these challenges in her book, *Guide My Feet*:

"Never have we exposed children so early and relentlessly to cultural messages glamorizing violence, sex, possessions, alcohol and tobacco, with so few mediating influences from responsible adults."

She goes on to describe her sadness at the erosion of cultural values:

"No value has been left uncommercialized in a culture where planned obsolescence of consumer products keeps cash registers ringing, and plastic smiles, plastic cards, and plastic souls have lost touch with the genuine."

Many would say that things have only gotten worse since these words were written. The world today's children face has grown increasingly more commercialized than it was even when the first edition of *Exchange* was published.

- British Broadcasting Company correspondent John Berger (1990) writes:

"In the cities in which we live, all of us see hundreds of publicity images every day of our lives. In no other form of society in history has there been such a concentration of images."

- Po Bronson and Ashley Merriman, in their recent book, *NurtureShock* (2009), talk about the harmful effect that this over-abundance of media is having on children's health. They present new research that today's child sleeps at least an hour less every night than a generation ago. They write:

"There are many causes for this lost hour of sleep… lax bedtimes, televisions and cell phones in the bedroom." They assert that lost sleep contributes to "the international obesity epidemic and the rise of ADHD."

- Richard Louv, in his groundbreaking work, *Last Child in the Woods* (2005), describes the adverse effect electronic media is having on children's relationships with the natural world:

"For a new generation, nature is more abstraction than reality. Increasingly, nature is something to watch, to consume, to wear — to ignore. A recent television ad depicts a four-wheel-drive SUV racing along a breathtakingly beautiful mountain stream — while in the backseat two children watch a movie on a flip-down video screen, oblivious to the landscape and water beyond the windows."

So, yes, life has changed in the last 50 years. Our family had no television set when I was five years old, and my relationship with the natural world was a close and nurturing one. Today's five-year-old is likely to have a personal television set (and perhaps video games and a cell phone) in her bedroom, but a dearth of nearby natural spaces to explore. It might be tempting to throw up our hands, despairing at the impossibility of changing things back to the way they were. However, some additional words from Marion Wright Edelman (1995) might show a better way: "So often we dwell on the things that seem impossible rather than on the things that are possible."

Now for some good news: many things are possible. It may be impossible to go back to the 'good old days,' but there are many opportunities — gifts, really — that we adults can find as we work to address our children's challenges and usher in the 'good new days.'

One opportunity is to change the way we think about our relationship with the natural world, and about the way we plan for our children's outdoor environments. An unintended consequence for those of us who grew up with 'free-range childhoods' (where nature was ever-present and accessible) was that it became all too easy to take nature for granted. Why not change a woodland into a high-rise apartment? Aren't natural spaces a dime a dozen? Sadly, we've learned that the answer is no. We are beginning to realize that progress often comes with a steep price, and that not all new plans are good ones. This is a valuable lesson that will stand us in good stead moving forward, and one that's worth passing on to our children.

Playground designer Rusty Keeler (2008) wrote that his realization of what was changing in the world caused him to make a major career shift:

"I thought about the children growing up today and how they, too, need the opportunity to play in the natural world. It was then I decided to break away from the play equipment industry and work on my own to create children's environments filled with nature and art, built with the love and support of families and communities."

Others around the world were coming to similar realizations. Adults began raising awareness of the importance of making sure connections with the natural world were again part of our children's daily lives:

- Claire Warden in Scotland began writing about her Forest Kindergartens.

- Toni and Robin Christie in New Zealand began speaking about their work to create nature-filled outdoor spaces that honor individual cultures and settings.

- Landscape architect Helle Nebelong's work in Denmark began demonstrating the exciting possibilities for designing nature-based play spaces in community playgrounds and parks.

- In the United States, many others, such as designer Robin Moore and educators Stephen Kellert and Ruth Wilson, were also making their voices heard.

- Landscape architect, Jim Wike, sold his traditional practice to work with the Nature Explore program, a collaboration between an environmental organization and a research foundation that brings natural space designs and educator workshops to diverse settings where children spend their days. In his book, *Learning with Nature* (Cuppens, Rosenow, & Wike, 2007), Jim writes:

  "The most wonderfully designed natural outdoor classroom will only be as effective for children as the adults who explore it with them…. Educators and families who encourage children to master new challenges, develop increasingly complex skills, and closely observe and appreciate the natural world will give children gifts that will last for a lifetime."

- Child Educational Center near Pasadena, California, began holding state-wide workshops to encourage educators to embrace the idea of the outdoor classroom as a place for daily learning and discovery.

- The staff at Boulder Journey School in Colorado were reviving the ideas of David and Frances Hawkins, who encouraged 'environmental education' in the most holistic sense of the word. In the 1970s, noted educator Frances Hawkins (1997), who along with her husband, mathematician, philosopher and educator, David, founded the Mountain View Center for Environmental Education, wrote these wise words:

  "We must provide for children those kinds of environments which elicit their interests and talents and which deepen their engagement in practice and thought. An environment of 'loving' adults who are themselves alienated from the world around them is an educational vacuum."

Many others, far too numerous to mention here, but all important to the effort, began to voice the need for nature-child connections. And, this is what is remarkable: People from all over the world and from multiple professions began talking to each other — face to face — and through email (one of the gifts of change) about our children's future. No longer were individual, isolated geographic areas making separate, disconnected decisions and discoveries about what our children's outside spaces in our schools and communities might look like. Conversations were happening and information was being shared. A comprehensive and collaborative effort from the World Forum Foundation's Nature Action Collaborative for Children's international leadership team resulted in a set of "Universal Principles for Connecting the World's Children with Nature" (www.worldforumfoundation.org/nature). These ideas will help guide designers and educators for years to come. The cooperation it took to find common ground on this effort is an example of what human beings can accomplish when individual egos are set aside in pursuit of a transcendent goal.

So, with a nod to Marion Wright Edelman, let's focus not on what we can't do, but on what we've learned we can do to make the world a better place for children through their outdoor environments. Listed are some of these 'can do' steps:

- We can work to ensure that every outdoor environment used by children will become a nature-filled, joyful space.

- We can help children truly notice and appreciate the wonders of the natural world.

- We can create and use outdoor spaces in ways that are right for each unique setting.

- We can encourage children to experience managed risk and challenge.

- We can spread the word that children learn in valuable ways in nature-filled outdoor spaces just as much as they do indoors.

The changes in our world have caused us to stop and think more intentionally about what children's relationship with outdoor environments can and should be. Along the way, we've made some valuable discoveries. In her article, "The Seeds of Learning," researcher Dana Miller (2007) writes:

"The outdoors provides an arena where children can communicate what they know in a very different way than they might in a traditional classroom…. With teacher support, the outdoors becomes a safe place to express positive emotions and learn to process and manage negative emotions. Children learn courage and confidence and how to successfully interact with others as they explore the wonders of nature together."

Environmental writer Gary Paul Nabhan (2003), in an article called "Listening to the Other," says that teaching children to love the natural world where they live, and helping them understand the interconnectedness of all living systems, might be a powerful motivator for avoiding the ravages of wars that displace humans and disrupt nature. He asserts that:

"Every war we avoid allows millions to remain in place, and keeps the vibrant places of the Earth from being dismembered. It is the healing power of the land and our shared history with it that offers hope of a brighter future."

Scientist and therapist Joan Borysenko (1990), who writes about the connection between emotions and health, describes what happens when children (and adults) spend time in nature: "The peaceful, loving quality of life's source floods through our connection to the moment…. And when we connect to this inner wellspring, we feel all of life so much more strongly."

Our children's growing disconnection from the wisdom of nature has been a wake-up call for all of us. If it has caused us to stop and remember to honor our relationship with the Earth and never take it for granted again, then that is a powerful, life-enhancing gift indeed.

References

Berger, J. (1990). *Ways of seeing.* London: Penguin Books.

Borysenko, J. (1990). *Guilt is the teacher, love is the lesson.* New York: Warner Books.

Bronson, P., & Merryman, A. (2009). *NurtureShock: New thinking about children.* New York: Hachette Book Group.

Cuppens, V., Rosenow, N., & Wike, J. (2007). *Learning with nature idea book: Creating nurturing outdoor spaces for children.* Lincoln, NE: Arbor Day Foundation.

Edelman, M. W. (1995). *Guide my feet: Prayers and meditations on loving and working for children.* Boston: Beacon Press.

Hawkins, F. (1997). *Journey with children: The autobiography of a teacher.* Niwot, CO: The University Press of Colorado.

Keeler, R. (2008). *Natural playscapes.* Redmond, WA: Exchange Press.

Lopez, B. (2007). *The future of nature: Writings on a human ecology from Orion Magazine.* Minneapolis: Orion Society.

Louv, R. (2005). *Last child in the woods: Saving our children from nature-deficit disorder.* New York: Algonquin Books of Chapel Hill.

Miller, D. L. (2007). The seeds of learning. *Applied Environmental Education and Communication,* 6(2).

Nabhan, G. P. (2003, May/June). Listening to the other: Can a sense of place help the peace-making process? *Onion Magazine.* Available: www.orionmagazine.org/index.php/articles/article/139

Nancy Rosenow

Nancy Rosenow is the executive director of Dimensions Educational Research Foundation/Nature Explore and a founding member of World Forum Foundation's Nature Action Collaborative for Children.

Are Your Children in Times Square?

Moving from Confinement to Engagement

by Sandra Duncan and Michelle Salcedo

> **Editor's Note:** In the November/December 2012 issue of *Exchange*, Sandra Duncan and Michelle Salcedo made an analogy between the chaotic environment of Times Square and the environments of many early childhood classrooms. In this related article, the authors continue to look at how teachers can move from the overwhelming nature of Times Square to appropriate and engaging classrooms.

Like the colossally tall, cold steel buildings and the confining spaces that make up New York's Times Square, we often configure early childhood classrooms in ways that create a sense of confinement for young children. Some of these environmental configurations are physical — and lead to confinement of the body — while others are less tangible and result in confinement of the mind and spirit. As we seek to effectively educate and care for young children, it is important to identify and tear down these classroom structures in order to move from confining spaces to active and engaging environments.

Confinement of the Body

Early childhood teachers typically use shelving units and other types of furniture to define learning areas in their classrooms. In some cases, this practice leads to enclosed spaces in which children cannot easily move, and leaves them without adequate space to explore and investigate.

Young children are just learning to move in space. When early childhood teachers design spaces completely surrounded or enclosed by furnishings, children's ability to move about freely is limited. Because these environmental structures (i.e., cabinets, shelving units) do not allow children's freedom of movement, they may result in physical challenges such as being unable to avoid a classmate's block tower or accidentally bumping into others playing in the same space.

Effective design of classroom spaces and structures takes into account children's ages and stages of physical development. Appropriate infant and toddler spaces, for example, include a balance of hard and soft surfaces for children to practice rolling, scooting, crawling, and toddling. Since baby walkers, jumpers, and activity centers confine children's bodies and could possibly thwart physical development, they should not be used.

Regardless of age or stage, all children need non-confining and ample space to promote not only physical development but cognitive and social development as well. Children are sensory-motor learners, so it is important to create environments where they can experiment and learn with their physical being as they move their bodies through the classroom space.

Confinement of the Mind

Children's minds are confined when they are not allowed to make choices, think on their own, or consider the many ways a problem could be solved. When children are limited to mundane tasks or experiences (i.e., project art, flash cards, or letters of the week), they are cheated out of opportunities to truly engage their minds. Likewise, educational materials with limited outcomes also underestimate children's unlimited capacity to learn (Curtis, Brown, Baird & Coughlin, 2013). While puzzles, for instance, have educational value, most limit children's capacities for imagination and creativity. Because there is usually only one way to put a puzzle together, children's creative minds may be limited.

For decades, the great thinkers in our field have denounced confinement of children's minds:

"We overestimate children academically but underestimate them cognitively." — Lilian G. Katz

"You don't teach children to think by telling them the answers." — Leah Adams

"A child's brain is a fire to be ignited, not a pot to be filled." — John Locke

These educators understand that if children's minds are confined, we deprive our society of a valuable gift. While the future cannot be completely or accurately predicted, most would agree that the 21st

---

4 Confinement-busting Strategies Creating Spaces to Enable Children's Movements

- Define learning areas with rugs, light, or color as opposed to always using shelves or cabinets. 'Float' centers in the middle of the classroom by positioning furniture and equipment away from the walls and using a rug to anchor the space.

- Provide many ways to enter and exit learning centers rather than having just one passageway into and out of the space.

- Eliminate confining apparatus or equipment such as baby walkers or jumpers.

- Design spaces to be flexible and easily reconfigured. Change the size and layout of learning centers based on children's current usage and interest.

---

century skills essential for success are the ability to think critically, solve complex problems, and live in an increasingly interconnected society.

Many workforce trend experts (i.e., Department of Labor, FutureWork, and Career Development International) identify a new group of skills that a child will need to successfully navigate a career of the future. These emerging skills include innovation (through problem solving and critical thinking) and creativity (through flexibility and adaptability). According to Phil McKinney, Vice President and Chief Technology Officer of Hewlett-Packard, these skills are known as the creative economy. In order to effectively prepare young children, it is important for children to receive care and education in environments where outcomes are not controlled and prescribed. Rather than teaching the 'right answers' or exclusively teaching to the learning standards and academic achievement tests, young children need to be learning how to think creatively in play-based classrooms.

It is the responsibility, therefore, of today's teachers to cultivate these important skills for the creative economy through the tenets of active, engaging learning. If you are not sure how to identify active learning, remember the acronym HOMES:

H = Hands-on — Children need to actively manipulate authentic objects.

O = Open-ended — There is no right answer or expected outcome.

M = Meaningful — Children can connect the classroom experience to their lives.

E = Engaging — Planned activities intentionally involve and engage children's bodies and minds.

S = Sensory-oriented — Learning experiences include interesting things to smell, touch, listen to, taste, and/or see (Salcedo, 2013).

---

3 Confinement-busting Strategies Creating Expectations to Enable Children's Individuality

- Reflect children's interests in the classroom by planning experiences, which mirror their conversations and play.

- Tear down the behavior chart.

- Question your rules. Are classroom rules for your convenience or to support children's growth and development?

---

3 Confinement-busting Strategies Creating Experiences to Enable Children's Thinking

- Ask questions to which you don't know the answer. Ask open-ended questions (i.e., who, what, why) rather than questions that can be answered with a yes or no response.

- Add interesting materials to learning centers to provoke children's thinking. Include loose parts, collections of natural materials, items with a variety of textures, and recyclables to provoke divergent exploration (see sidebar on next page for provocation ideas).

- Eliminate product art.

When teachers infuse learning spaces with interesting and unique materials that do not confine children's minds but rather are intentionally designed to promote active learning, children's minds and spirits ascend to new heights.

In many early childhood classrooms, cutesy art projects decorate the walls. This reliance on product art also confines children's minds. Product art focuses on the thing being produced, while process art focuses on how children express their creativity and their ideas. When teachers define an end product, they confine children's creations to what must be instead of what could be. Even when children are allowed to put pre-cut pieces wherever they want, their creativity to express their own understanding is hampered.

More than 100 years ago Elbert Hubbard, American artist, writer, and philosopher said, "Art is not a thing — it is a way." He was speaking about the difference between product and process art. True art

Unique Materials for Provocation				
Thin Wire	Foil Papers	Florist's Green Tape	Sea Glass	Cellophane
Charcoal	Pickling Spices	Driftwood	Gauze	Tree Bark
Flashlights	Bushel Baskets	Doilies	Fresh/Dried Flowers	Fossils
Holograms	Gemstones	Grapevines	Prisms	Jewelry/Bangles/Bracelet
LED Lights	Color Paddles	Faux Fur/Textiles	Dental Floss	Moss/Ferns/Greens
Corks	Queen Anne's Lace	PVC Pipes	Pinecones/Pine Needles	Seedlings
Wheels/Hubcaps	Spools	Sunflowers	Sandpaper	Textured Tile Squares
Nuts/Bolts	Tree Cookies	Bricks/Pavers	Recyclables	Polished Stones
Wildflowers/Herb Sprigs	Tree Roots/Vine Systems	Acorns	Seedpods	Pulleys
Marble Pieces	Ziploc/Twist Ties	River Rock		

is about science, wonder, and discovery. As an early childhood teacher, your goal is to provide materials, inspiration, time, and space for children to engage in the process of art so their inherently creative minds can soar.

Confinement of Spirit

Children enter our classrooms with myriad spirits. Some have the spirit of an adventurer who is ready for any new experience that comes her way. Another child may enter with the spirit of a flower, shyly waiting to bloom where the soil is right. At times, instead of encouraging each child's unique spirit, there is a tendency to confine them into cookie-cutter versions of what we feel children should be. Often teachers distill young children's inherent passions for life with silly phrases like 'criss-cross applesauce' and with inappropriate child management strategies such as behavior charts. These rigid structures seek to confine children's spirits into predetermined molds.

Rather than confine children's spirits, consider focusing on what makes each child an amazing individual. Design classroom environments and routines around how children grow and thrive as opposed to insisting they conform to a prescribed list of behavioral standards. Before establishing a classroom rule, ask yourself the reasoning behind the rule: Is the rule about health and safety? Is it about respecting others or classroom materials? Or, is it about controlling children's spirits?

I found I could say things with color and shapes that I couldn't say any other way — things I had no words for. — Georgia O'Keeffe		
	Product Art	Process Art
1. There is an end product in mind. (Let's all make . . .)		
2. Final products all look similar.		
3. The teacher predetermines the answer to the question: "What is it?"		
4. Teacher provides materials; children use them in many different ways.		
5. The goal is for children's work to reflect a set theme or a teacher's idea.		
6. The goal is for children to express themselves, think critically, and explore the world.		
7. Teacher spends a lot of time cutting out and preparing pieces for upcoming art experience.		
Rules and models destroy genius and art. — William Hazlitt		
Key: Product Art: 1, 2, 3, 5, 7	Process Art: 4, 6	
Art enables us to find ourselves and lose ourselves at the same time. — Thomas Merton		

- Why must every child sit with their legs crossed, exactly the same?

- Why do all children have to stand in a straight line, with toes on the masking tape line, before the class goes outside?

- Why do children have to wait before everyone is finished to clean up after snack?

If the answer is because children will have to conform next year when they enter elementary school, or because it is just what you think children should be doing, perhaps the rule needs revising… or is the rule worth having in the first place?

Another way to release, rather than confine, children's spirits is create classrooms reflective of those who learn and grow within the space. Seek out ways to incorporate children's interests into the classroom. Nothing says that you care and know a child who loves horses more than putting a book about horses in the library — even if the weekly theme is pumpkins. Or, better yet, eliminate themes and units of study and instead plan engaging projects or experiences around topics children discuss in their everyday conversations with each other.

Conclusion

To set children on a path of creativity, critical thinking, constructive problem solving, and positive growth and development, teachers must first look at how to modify or eliminate the structures that confine children's minds, bodies, and spirits in the classroom. Only then can children soar into the future they deserve.

References

Curtis, D., Brown, K., Baird, L., & Coughlin, M. (2013, September). Planning environments and materials that respond to young children's lively minds. *Young Children*, 68(4), 26–31.

Salcedo, M. (2013). "Active learning: Exercise for the brain." *Sunshine House Family Newsletter*.

Sandra Duncan

As adjunct faculty, Sandra Duncan works with doctoral candidates at Nova Southeastern University Fischler Graduate School of Education and teaches early childhood education at Ivy Tech Community College. She is the co-author of *Inspiring Spaces for Young Children and Rating Observation Scale for Young Children*. Proud grandma of Sierra Elizabeth, she can be reached at sandrdun@aol.com.

Michelle Salcedo

As the Chief Academic Officer for The Sunshine House, Michelle Salcedo has the honor and privilege of developing curricular programs to meet the learning and developmental needs of thousands of children across the country. In this role, Ms. Salcedo oversees the education team in the creation of curriculum and curricular-related resources, as well as training and support for the multiple locations. Michelle holds a Bachelor of Arts from University of Detroit Mercy in Detroit in Developmental Psychology with an emphasis in Family Life Education. She also holds a Masters of Arts in Early Childhood Education from Concordia College.

Creating Environments that Intrigue and Delight Children and Adults

by Wendy Shepherd and Jennifer Eaton

Attention to the design, organization, presentation, and atmosphere of the learning environment is crucial. Creating an enriched environment that is a space for wonder and delight, a place for the stimulation and exchange of ideas, is an essential component of an early childhood program. The arrangement of the physical space should invite children to explore, inquire, hypothesize, solve problems, and to marvel at the wonders of nature. Children should have the opportunity to make choices, to play or work with others or alone, to be quiet or busy, or to settle into cozy spaces, which they have constructed or imagined.

Greenman synthesizes and validates the teacher's intuitive knowledge. He affirms the effect of the environment in shaping children's behavior. He inspires reflection on the organization of the learning environment within early childhood settings when he states, "An environment is a living, changing system. More than physical space, it includes the way time is structured and the roles we are expected to play. It conditions how we feel, think, and behave; and it dramatically affects the quality of our lives." (Greenman, 1988, p. 5)

Through reflection, the environment can be viewed as a dynamic and key element of teaching and learning. The principles of enriching an environment to promote wonder and delight should underpin each statement within the center philosophy. This requires a shift away from traditional and non-specific terms such as *caring* and *nurturing* to statements, which reflect a more complex understanding of the integral role of the environment in the learning process. Reflecting on and evaluating the environment enables an understanding of the environment as 'the third teacher' to emerge. The family is the child's primary teacher, ideally the early childhood professional shares this responsibility in a mutually respectful partnership. The environment is the third teacher.

The center *culture* or *climate* conveys messages to children and adults. Elements such as time, space, and resources affect the quality of the interactions between staff and children and families. Thus the center culture and climate must respect, honor, and value children, families, and staff.

In preparation, therefore, the process requires:

- reflection, discussion, and collaboration on philosophy and practice.

- observing, collecting, and recalling insights into what intrigues children and adults.

- respecting, valuing, and including cultural diversity within the program and the environment.

- organizing time so that routines do not dominate the program and allowing for large blocks of time for children and adults to be involved in observation, exploration, investigations, and engaging interactions.

- valuing rather than diminishing children's imagination and creativity by avoiding furnishings and displays that promote a commercial image of childhood.

- respecting and valuing children's thinking and doing regardless of learning style and preferences.

Begin by:

- planning environments to 'afford' the preferred activities of children.

- de-cluttering the environment (this requires great strength as most early childhood people are bower birds or are acquisitive!).

- de-institutionalizing the environment.

- taking stock of equipment and resources — if adults think equipment and resources are shabby, what is the message conveyed to children?

- organizing fundraising events to replace old shabby items, or simply going without — chances are, the items or equipment are well past their use by date, although it is hard parting with 'old' favorites.

- maintaining resources, equipment, and the environment is an ongoing task requiring diligence and hard work by everyone.

- considering the presentation of the environment, learning centers, and activities — giving attention to color, design, shape, form, and function.

- using cultural objects and containers — for example, wall hangings and fabrics, cushions, rugs, baskets, masks.

- arranging items, objects, and resources in an enticing, thought-provoking, inviting, special, or imaginative way.

Places of Wonder and Delight

Aesthetically pleasing objects, arrangements, and displays are often undervalued or overlooked in early childhood settings. "Aesthetics is a worthy but often unconsidered goal when designing a visual environment for infants and toddlers (and preschoolers). Children are more likely to grow up with an eye for beauty if the adults around them demonstrate that they value aesthetics." (Gonzalez-Mena & Eyer, 1997, p. 94)

> A toddler was observed playing with a 'family' of cone shaped mother of pearl spiral shells in the block corner and had returned them to their cardboard square on top of a shelving unit. The shells were not replaced in order of size and, on seeing this, another toddler very deliberately organized them from small to big, lining them up in a neat row. And in another group, an infant/toddler at the lunch table had a daily ritual of picking up the bud vase and smelling the flowers and carefully replacing it.

The arrangement of the environment, or objects in it, should move children to a higher, more complex order of thinking, to make links and connections. In other words, making "ordinary things look extraordinary" (Kolbe, 1994, p. 11).

These observations are the rewards for staff that takes the time and effort in enhancing children's experiences.

Enriching environments is not costly. In fact, it makes for more thoughtful decisions about equipment purchases in the light of tight budgets. *Found objects* or 'gifts' from families add intriguing qualities to room arrangements. Home-like furnishings and furniture add an unexpected and comfortable dimension, so that both adults and children feel at home and valued.

Research indicates children prefer enclosed spaces and may often modify open arrangements to create 'refuges' for their play (Kirby, 1989). Therefore, to delight children and to extend their play, arrange each play space into a designated play enclosure. Low shelving units are useful as dividers and have the utilitarian facility of providing storage as well as a surface for display.

Once the room is organized into designated play spaces, adding the wonder and delight is the next step. It is important to consider that children should be trusted to value the special and interesting additions to their classroom. The following is an example of adults doubting children's ability to do so:

> The teacher wanted to place five specimen vases on the writing table to contain a variety of unusual spring flowers. The teaching team brainstormed ways of securing the vases — ranging from making a wooden plinth, blue tac, masking tape, and plaster. It was decided that all of the ideas would be ugly and defeating the purpose of creating a beautiful display. It was cautiously decided to just place them on the table. They are still there to this day!

Some ideas to think about:

- **Mirrors:** on walls, in front of work stations, in learning centers, inside alcoves, in home corner, and in the outdoor environment. Mirrors to reflect light, to place behind objects, to provide another perspective.
- **Lighting:** soft lighting from lamps, directed/spot lighting to focus on objects or children's work, light tables, lava lamps, torches and shadow play, fairy lights with festoons of muslin or in branches of twisted willow or accenting displays or children's constructions.
- **Natural elements:** flowers, foliage, sturdy vegetables, seed pods, shells, birds' nests, feathers — displayed in real vases or arranged in shadow boxes or baskets of all shapes, sizes, and types.
- **Clear containers or spaghetti jars** filled with water and lemons or leaves or shells. The water magnifies and intensifies color, texture, pattern, and shape.
- **Snails, worms, ants, tadpoles, fish, hermit crabs, milkweed, caterpillars** housed in containers simulating their habitat.
- **'Families' of pumpkins, or leaves, or pinecones to display in size order from large to small** (manufactured items such as teddy bears, shapes are more usual but still fascinating for children).

Made objects:

- Gallery prints
- Sculptures
- Pottery
- Interesting and precious ornaments (children can learn to be so careful when handling precious items)
- Clothing, costumes, soft furnishings, masks, wall hangings that represent the diversity of cultures represented in the center and others in the wider community
- Multicultural cooking implements in home corner, the center kitchen, and for use by children at meal times

The resources:

- Colored paper arranged in rainbow order on shelves

- Collage materials that reflect a common attribute — e.g. paper, fabric, yarn, or cardboard in different shades of a color or type or transparent

- Writing implements stored in small baskets or beautiful boxes

The lists above only offer a few suggestions. The materials or objects themselves often suggest the method and context for their display. Through taking care of the environment and thoughtfully planning the room arrangement as a team, the people who work and play in the room gain a sense of community and a sense of belonging.

Sense of Belonging

By weaving in resources donated by families, the families will gain a sense of belonging and ownership. Photographs also communicate messages of valuing and membership within a group. Photographs of children and staff and families can be grouped together, displayed on a low shelf or in frames on the wall, which are at child height.

Photographs can be used in documentation to capture moments in time that highlight the processes of learning. The notion that the process is important is imparted to children and their families. Children can refer to the documentation to reflect on their past work and progress forward.

Photographs used in cubbies or lockers instead of symbols provide each child with a sense of ownership or place. The use of video cameras and other technological devices will no doubt be the tools of the future to reproduce images of children and adults within a setting.

Designated Play Spaces

Children in early childhood settings need familiarity and stability in their environment. They need the comfort and certainty of knowing where to find materials and resources and to know that they can return each day to an environment in which they feel valued and respected. Young children also need a sense of order. Gonzalez-Mena and Eyer (1997) state, "Room arrangement should contribute to the sense of order" (p. 202). Indeed, what messages do we send to children when their play environment is constantly rearranged, altered, or packed away?

- In many centers, it is common practice to pack away large areas of the room. This places an unnecessary physical burden and time constraint on staff. It can also prove very unsettling for children as they watch this take place around them.

- Children's interests are likely to be sustained when they are able to return to a play space or learning center regularly, assured that the equipment they need or wish to use is available and accessible.

- Children are far less likely to invest their time and effort in a project if they know it has to be packed away at the end of a play session or the end of a day. For example: Enable children who are building with blocks, especially on a large scale, to keep their structures intact, ready to be extended upon over days and even weeks (let the cleaners vacuum around it!).

It has been fascinating to observe children, as young as two and three years of age, decorating their elaborate block structures with found objects from the room resources, some of which have remained standing for more than three weeks. It can provide a wonderful opportunity for enriched play, encouraging collaborative work amongst peers, challenge and extension of their problem solving skills, and more complex use of materials.

- Children are likely to become more self-directed rather than teacher-directed if they can make choices and decisions about materials to use. Open shelving and open storage spaces filled with a range, for example, of art media or construction toys or games, and puzzles can be empowering for a child, rather than waiting for a teacher to make their choice about what resources will be provided on any given day. When children are given real choices, they are more likely to remain at an experience or a task for an extended period of time.

- A playroom with open shelving and designated spaces allows children to take some responsibility for maintaining the environment as they quickly become familiar with where items belong and how they are to be arranged. Children tend to take a lot more care of the materials and objects on display if they are given some responsibility for this.

- In a stable and orderly environment, children are secure in their knowledge of where things are and aimless wandering is therefore reduced.

- When there is a sense of order about an environment, it helps to organize and support children's rituals. This can be especially important for infants in their attempts to navigate their way around a room. One example of this was observed when a 12-month-old infant, on arrival each morning, would toddle over to the cozy book area, select a book from the shelf, and plunk himself down on the cushions to 'read.'

The Teacher's Role

The teacher plays a crucial role in designing and maintaining an enriched environment with thoughtful consideration given to room arrangements and the aesthetic presentation of equipment, documentation, children's artwork, and objects of interest. There is an assumption that the organization of space, time, and resources requires more staff; but, in reality, through the processes put in place by effective organization and simple yet enticing room arrangements, staff has more time and energy to give to meaningful interactions with children and colleagues. The following is a list of other considerations for the teacher:

- **Creating an environment that supports peer collaboration.** In the organization of the environment, we need to ensure the establishment of spaces where children can work together in collaboration. Such opportunities for children to work in pairs and shared small group experiences enhance their social construction of knowledge. Staff should assess their playroom and surrounding areas for spaces in which children can work in an uninterrupted and relaxed mode that is conducive to observation, discussion, active participation, and reflection.

  Meanwhile, staff needs to recognize that some children will want to observe others from a distance until they feel confident to become involved, and this space or area should be factored into the organization of the learning environment. As Katz (1991) advocates, "Data from child development research suggests that, in principle, an appropriate pedagogy for young children is one that provides ample opportunity for them to be engaged in activities in which cooperation and coordination of effort are functional and consequential" (p. 63).

- **Providing long, uninterrupted periods of time.** Too often, we timetable in constant changes to the daily schedule, which prevent children from becoming engaged for extended periods of time. Instead, children should be able to work with the understanding that they are not going to be required to finish a game, project, construction, or painting within a 30-minute time frame. We need to ensure, then, that spaces are available for children to continue uninterrupted. It is also important that routines do not rule the program, but rather they should be part of the rhythm of the day.

- **The rhythm of the day should be unhurried.** This is more likely to occur when staff is not engaged in unnecessary packing away and resetting of play areas. Therefore, they have more time to establish calm and enjoyable routines for meals, sleep, and toileting.

De-institutionalizing the Environment

Why is this important?

- Children can spend up to 12,500 hours within a long day care setting, more hours than the child will spend at school — an institution (Wangmann, 1995).
- Most institutions require conformity and compliance.
- The trappings of an institution act as barriers to the development of warm, trusting relationships, a sense of community, and feelings of ownership and belonging.

What are the trappings of an institution?

- Notice boards bristling with notices for everyone and no one in particular, which are never noticed, never culled or tidied.
- Colored footprints or fluorescent arrows leading to notices are condescending and demeaning, and are not usually removed at the end of the event.
- Anonymous 'washing lines' of children's paintings strung across classrooms or hallways.
- Cubbies with locker symbols that remind the current 'key' holder that when they move on, the symbol remains.
- Boxes overflowing with lost property that no one appears to have lost.
- Forlorn, weary, worn equipment that is shunted around in haphazard room arrangements, which indicates the adults hold the power.
- Displays of commercial images from books and cartoon characters, posters and charts, birthday, alphabet, number, color, shape posters, and charts displayed in layers on every spare inch of wall space adding to the visual chaos.
- Bright fluorescent-tube lighting.
- Utilitarian institutional furniture and soft furnishings.
- Institution color schemes and the use of primary colors — the obligatory early childhood color scheme, harsh and bright.
- Stacks of beds and chairs in children's playrooms.
- Heavy-duty dustbins in classrooms, passageways, and at the front door.
- Shelving units covered with curtains to prevent children from accessing the equipment.
- Furniture and equipment pushed to one side for eating and sleeping routines.
- Incomplete puzzles, tattered books, eyeless and/or armless dolls.
- Potted plants and garden beds with plants struggling to survive.
- Outdoor play environments that have become safe havens for the equipment and resources that have become too forlorn to remain inside.
- The lack of soft spaces for children or adults.
- The lack of visible traces of children and families and staff.
- Inflexible routines that dominate the program.

Early childhood environments should be early learning places, not a 'pre-institution.' The early childhood environment should honor and respect the community to nurture a cohesive and civil micro society.

In Summary

It is so satisfying to observe children, families, and staff communicating meaningfully and working purposefully. When children respond to the environment and investigate, invent, ask questions, collaborate with their peers, learn from one another, stay on task, choose, decide, negotiate, and demonstrate their care for the environment, the role of the teacher has been exemplified as facilitator and guide.

Adding elements to promote wonder and delight is only a part of the process. All aspects of the program must be considered to ensure that what has been added is not simply 'window dressing.' There is a need to re-look at the daily practice of the teacher, the environment, and how to organize it to support peer collaboration. The planning of the day should support children's need to dream and think and play and to grow and learn in an environment that nurtures all of the senses.

"The years between two and seven seem to be crucial in how children deal with mysteries. Within these years, they form beliefs, biases, artistry, curiosity, and a sense of self that carries them forward into adulthood. If allowed and encouraged, all children can remain active and curious philosophers and scientists throughout their lives." (Latham, 1997, p. 12)

References

Gonzalez-Mena, J., & Eyer, D. W. (1997). *Infants, toddlers, and caregivers* (4th edition). Mountain View, CA: Mayfield Publishing Company.

Greenman, J. (2007). *Caring spaces, learning places.* Redmond, WA: Exchange Press.

Katz, L. (1991). "Pedagogical Issues in Early Childhood Education." In S. Kagan (editor), *The care and education of America's young children: Obstacles and opportunities. 90th Yearbook of the National Society for the Study of Education, Part 1.* Chicago: The University of Chicago Press.

Kirby, M. (1989, Spring). Nature as refuge in children's environments. *Children's Environments Quarterly, 6*(1).

Kolbe, U., Shepherd, W., & Eaton, J. (1994). Mia-Mia Child and Family Study Centre, Centre Handbook. Sydney, Australia: Macquarie University.

Latham, G. (1997). Fostering and Preserving Wonderment. *Australian Journal of Early Childhood. Collected Titles on Early Childhood, 21*(1).

Wangmann, J. (1995). *Towards integration and quality assurance in children's services.* Melbourne: Australian Institute of Family Studies.

Reading List

Alloway, N. (1995). *Foundation stones: The construction of gender in early childhood.* Victoria, Australia: Curriculum Corporation.

Dau, E. (1991). "Let's Pretend: Socio-Dramatic Play in Early Childhood." In S. Wright, *The arts in early childhood.* Sydney, Australia: Prentice Hall of Australia.

Edwards, C., Gandini, L., & Forman, G. (editors). (1993). *The hundred languages of children: The Reggio Emilia Approach to early childhood education.* New Jersey: Ablex Publishing Corporation.

Feeney, S., & Moravcik, E. (1988). A thing of beauty: Aesthetic development in young children. *Young Children, 42*(6), 1987.

Thorpe, R. G., & Gallimore, R. (1988). "A Theory of Teaching As Assisted Performance." In *Rousing minds to life.* Cambridge: C. U. Press.

Wood, D. (1986). "Aspects of Teaching and Learning." In M. Richards and P. Light (editors), *Children of social minds.* Cambridge: Harvard University Press.

Wendy Shepherd

Wendy Shepherd is the Director of Mia Mia Child and Family Study Centre and an academic in the Institute of Early Childhood Teacher Education Program. Mia Mia is a lighthouse, long-day early childhood school and study centre at the leading edge in Australia and internationally in its approach to early childhood education and care. Shepherd and her teaching colleagues were instrumental in Mia Mia's development as the Institute of Early Childhood's demonstration program, which provides opportunities for educational training, mentoring, observation, and research. They have also scripted and edited several DVDs and contributed to books and journals to assist early childhood educators in their work.

Jennifer Eaton

Jennifer Eaton is Assistant Director/lecturer at Mia-Mia Child and Family Study Centre. She has had experience in both preschool and long-day care settings. She also works with the Institute students in the academic program, and her particular interests in early childhood education are relaxation, movement, and play. Lecturing in the academic program has provided an opportunity to link practice to theory, and this is an aspect that the students find most valuable.

the Art of LEADERSHIP
CULTIVATING AN EARLY CHILDHOOD CURRICULUM

CHAPTER 4
Evaluating the Program

Looking at the Quality of Early Childhood Programs *by Lilian G. Katz* 132

Measuring the Quality of Early Childhood Organizations
Guidelines for Effective Evaluation Tools *by Ann S. Epstein* 134

Learning to See… Seeing to Learn
The Role of Observation in Early Childhood Development *by Diane C. MacLean* 139

Are We Doing Things Just Because We've Always Done Them this Way?
by Kim Turner 144

Questions to Guide Our Work *by Margie Carter* 147

Conducting a Realistic Self-assessment with the *Environmental Rating Scale*
by Thelma Harms 152

Seeing Children's Lively Minds at Work *by Deb Curtis* 155

Be the Change You Wish to See in Your Program *by Elizabeth Beavers and Donna Kirkwood* 162

Looking at the Quality of Early Childhood Programs

by Lilian G. Katz

There are many ways to assess the quality of a program for young children. One is to look at it from the top down; another is from the bottom up. Both views are important.

A Top-down View of the Quality of a Program

When we enter an early childhood setting as adults and attempt to assess its quality, we look at such characteristics as:

- quality and quantity of space per child.
- quality and type of equipment and materials.
- adult/child ratio.
- number of toilets, fire safety provisions.

In addition, we should also consider the quality of teacher-parent relations and ask such questions as: Are they usually respectful? Supportive? Open? Inclusive? Tolerant? These positive attributes are relatively easy when teacher and parents like each other; come from the same background; share culture, values, language, and goals for children. Almost anyone can do that. But to build such positive respectful and supportive relations with parents who are different from us in these ways requires professionalism, which requires training and experience.

To be professional means to respond gracefully rather than defensively in moments of disagreement. It means also to develop relationships not on the basis of personal preferences and impulses, but on the basis of professional knowledge and judgment, and to make them problem-centered, rather than personal.

Furthermore, the top-down view should include an examination of staff relationships. We could ask:

- are they supportive rather than contentious?
- are they cooperative rather than competitive?
- are they accepting rather than antagonistic or even hostile?
- are they trusting rather than suspicious?
- are they respectful rather than bossy?

Dissension among the staff of the program can drain energy away from the main focus on children, their families, and their needs. Again, to relate well to colleagues we like — with whom we agree — who share the same goals, background, culture, language, and values is relatively easy. But to be respectful of those with whom we disagree or from whom we are different requires professionalism, and that usually requires knowledge, judgment, and training.

A Bottom-up View of the Quality of a Program

The characteristics of a program that really predict its outcome are the answers to the bottom-up question, which is: What does it feel like to be a child in this environment? Obtaining answers to this question is not easy! It requires making the very best guess one can about how each individual child in this group experiences the program. We can proceed by asking about the environment on behalf of each child:

- Is it welcoming rather than merely captivating?

- Do I belong in the group rather than merely have a good time?

- Am I usually accepted by adults rather than scolded?

- Am I taken seriously rather than just precious or cute?

- Am I usually accepted by some peers rather than isolated, neglected, or rejected?

- Is this environment usually involving rather than entertaining?

- Are the activities meaningful rather than mindless?

- Are the activities engaging rather than amusing?

- Are the activities interesting rather than boring?

- Do I usually come here willingly rather than reluctantly?

It seems to me that only when answers to most of these questions are positive can we assume that the quality of the program is worthy of our children.

This article is based on the address given at the Annual Conference of the Washington Association for the Education of Young Children, Bellevue, Washington, October 1991.

Lilian G. Katz

Lilian G. Katz, PhD, Professor Emerita, University of Illinois, Urbana-Champaign, is Co-Director of the Clearinghouse on Early Education and Parenting and Editor of Early Childhood Education and Parenting.

Measuring the Quality of Early Childhood Programs

Guidelines for Effective Evaluation Tools

by Ann S. Epstein

Every dedicated early childhood practitioner cares about program quality. Decades of research have consistently shown that the better the quality of the program, the more it supports the development of young children (e.g. Cost, Quality, and Child Outcome Study Team, 1995). Research reviews and policy statements such as those issued by the Carnegie Corporation of New York (1994) emphasize that the cognitive and social development outcomes desired for children cannot be achieved without services of sufficient quality. Moreover, high-quality programs encourage parent involvement and promote the retention of skilled staff. These findings are now commonly accepted — not only by professionals but also by the general public. Constituencies from all backgrounds now demand early childhood services that are not only available and accessible, but high quality as well.

But how do you define program quality? How do you take an honest look at your program so you can recognize what is good and know what to improve? How can you accurately communicate this information to parents, educators, administrators, researchers, and funders? Although we all have our own ideas about what constitutes a high-quality program, it is not enough to say "I know a high-quality program when I see one."

We need a common language so we can look at programs objectively and articulate our highest goals for children, parents, and staff. A good program evaluation tool is essential to promote this communication and help us work together to improve program quality. Creating an objective and multifaceted tool to measure program quality has always been a goal of the HighScope Educational Research Foundation, a private non-profit organization conducting curriculum development, staff training, and research. Our aim is to help all programs, not just those using the HighScope approach, take an honest look at the learning opportunities they are providing to all their participants.

In developing such a measure, HighScope staff looked at many existing program quality assessments such as the *Early Childhood Environment Rating Scale* (Harms & Clifford, 1980) and the program-monitoring tools used by Head Start and state-funded pre-kindergarten programs. There were many strengths in these instruments but also areas that we felt could be further expanded in an assessment tool.

This article summarizes what HighScope discovered to be the critical characteristics of a comprehensive and valid measure of program quality. It presents the many ways such a tool can be used to effectively evaluate and improve program quality. These points are highlighted with examples from the *HighScope Program Quality Assessment* (PQA, HighScope Educational Research Foundation, 1998), an instrument developed with these specific criteria in mind. By following the guidelines presented here, early childhood programs can more effectively assess their ongoing efforts to foster children's development, involve families, promote staff development, and engage in sound management practices.

The Characteristics of Effective Program Quality Measures

The most effective program assessment tools define quality along a continuum. In talking to practitioners and researchers, we found that many were frustrated by assessment instruments that permitted only "yes-no" responses to each item. Such measures were often focused on whether programs were in compliance with a set of regulations or standards, but they did not acknowledge that quality unfolds gradually and is achieved in stages. By using a continuum to rate quality, an assessment tool helps programs identify where they are on the path to achieving quality and the successive steps they must take as they continue their progress. For that reason, each item on the PQA was developed using a five-point scale describing a broad array of program characteristics from preliminary efforts to advanced understanding. Programs using an assessment tool of this type can see where they are and where they are headed as they continually strive to improve their services. In that way, evaluation provides encouragement for moving forward.

Program assessments are most helpful if they provide users with many examples. To ensure that people are using the assessment tool fairly and objectively, the instrument should be explicit about the behaviors that define low, medium, and high levels of quality. There should be many illustrative examples to guide raters and guarantee that different assessors will interpret and score the same behavior in the same way. In other words, assessment tools should be designed to produce a high level of agreement or inter-rater reliability. (See the discussion on testing program assessments for reliability and validity.) Multiple examples also allow staff to anchor themselves at recognizable points along the continuum and envision the changes they are striving to achieve as they advance their level. To meet these criteria, developers of the PQA provided many specific examples at levels 1, 3, and 5 of the five-point scale. The illustration below, from an item

---

Item III-F. Adults participate as partners in children's play.

1	2	3	4	5
Adults do not participate in children's play. Or, adults attempt to dominate children's play (e.g. by redirecting play around adult ideas, telling children what to play with or how to play).		Adults sometimes participate in children's play, using a limited number of strategies. Adults' participation in play is sometimes guided by their own agendas. Adults sometimes interrupt and attempt to redirect or take control of children's play.		Adults use a variety of strategies as co-players in children's play (e.g. adults observe and listen before and after entering children's play; assume roles as suggested by children; follow the children's cues about the content and direction of play; imitate children; match the complexity of their play; offer suggestions for extending play, staying within the children's play theme).

in the adult-child interaction section, shows how using concrete examples can help both outside observers and classroom practitioners reliably differentiate levels of behavior.

Program assessments are most informative if they are comprehensive. We identified two types of comprehensiveness. First, assessment tools should look at the dynamic or interactive features of a program as well as its static or structural elements. Most instruments do a detailed job of looking at the structural qualities of a program such as the safety of the physical facilities or the diversity of materials and equipment. However, many tools fail to pay equal, if not more, attention to the nature of the interactions between and among adults and children. Yet we know that these interpersonal characteristics are crucial to defining program quality and promoting child development and adult collaboration.

The second aspect of comprehensiveness refers to looking at the program from multiple perspectives. While our first concern as caregivers and educators is the child's experience of the setting, we should also pay attention to how a program serves families and staff members. A complete program assessment tool should therefore look at how teachers interact with parents, how staff interacts with one another to plan for the children, how supervisors support staff development, and how management secures adequate resources. In other words, a program quality assessment should focus on the classroom, the agency, the home, and the community — and the activities and experiences of all the participants.

Program assessments make the greatest contribution to the field if they have been tested and validated. Because we each want to capture the uniqueness of our program, it is tempting to create our own assessment tools. The problem with this approach is that we end up talking only to our immediate colleagues. We cannot communicate findings or replicate proven approaches outside our own agencies. Moreover, by reinventing the wheel, we fail to apply decades of research on how to define and measure the most important components of program quality. Of course,

we need to use assessment tools that are consistent with the values and curriculum models that are being implemented in our individual programs. But within these guidelines, the more we can build our assessments on agreed-upon best practices and measurement approaches, the more we will advance the field of early childhood programs as a whole. For that reason, we concluded that the most effective assessment tools also have the widest applicability across program settings.

To meet HighScope's commitment to strengthening the early childhood field as a whole, the PQA was developed by a diverse team of researchers, training consultants, and teachers. It was validated in a series of studies in diverse early childhood settings (Epstein, 1993; HighScope, 1997; Schweinhart, et al., 1998). We invited the review and comments of respected colleagues outside the Foundation. As a result of opening the process, the PQA conscientiously reflects best practices in all center-based settings, not just those using the HighScope educational approach. The instrument is consistent with NAEYC accreditation criteria, Head Start Performance Standards, and various state guidelines for developmental appropriateness. By collaborating with colleagues in both public and private agencies, HighScope hoped the PQA would be of value in a wide variety of program settings.

The Uses of Effective Program Quality Measures

An effective program quality assessment should also serve as a training tool. The best evaluation instruments reveal staff training needs. Assessing a program's quality should highlight its strengths and identify areas for improvement. Moreover, it should do so in a concrete way. Global quality ratings do not help staff identify specific training concerns. But comprehensive tools based on systematic observation can help teachers and administrators decide what areas they want to emphasize in pre-service and inservice training. A good measurement tool can define developmentally appropriate practice for novice teachers and help experienced teachers reflect on their practices from a new and more detailed perspective. These insights, translated into practice, are the goals of training. Creative assessment facilitates articulating and reaching these goals.

Effective assessment tools allow supervisors to observe individual staff members and provide them with constructive feedback. Assessment can be anxiety provoking if the rules are arbitrary and the intention is judgment rather than development. But a well-constructed tool can provide the person being assessed with clear expectations and opportunities for growth. Properly used, a good assessment tool allows a supervisor and a teacher to work as a team. Together, they can identify one or more areas for the supervisor to observe. Following the observation, the supervisor and the teacher can meet to review and discuss the ratings, acknowledge areas of strength, and identify specific strategies for professional growth. If designed with this use in mind, a program quality measure can contribute significantly to staff development.

Valid program quality measures are essential for research and program evaluation. At the agency level, we often need to document the quality of our programs to secure administrative support and funding. Beyond that, all practitioners share a responsibility to contribute to the knowledge of the field as a whole. A vital assessment tool can meet both local and broad interests. To meet rigorous scientific standards, the instrument must define its terminology and decision-making criteria, achieve high inter-rater reliability, demonstrate its validity in relation to other program quality measures and child outcomes, and provide a system for communicating results clearly and concisely.

Effective program assessment tools communicate to many audiences. A good assessment tool avoids jargon. It speaks to both professional and lay audiences in straightforward language. In addition to researchers and practitioners, the information gathered with a well-designed assessment tool can be easily communicated to administrators and policy makers, prospective funders, parents, and program support staff. If all these audiences speak the language used in the assessment tool, they are in a better position to collaborate on guaranteeing program quality.

Conclusion

An effective assessment tool consolidates what current theory, decades of practice, and ongoing research tell us about the components of high quality early childhood programs. It is important to regularly and systematically evaluate the structural and dynamic features of your program. Only in this way can we as practitioners, researchers, and policy makers guarantee that the services we deliver are of sufficient quality to promote the development of young children, encourage the involvement of families, and create supportive working environments for staff.

References

Carnegie Corporation of New York. (1994). *Starting points: Meeting the needs of our youngest children.* New York: Author.

Cost, Quality, and Child Outcomes Study Team. (1995). *Cost, quality, and child outcomes in child care centers.* Denver: University of Colorado at Denver Economics Department.

Epstein, A. S. (1993). *Training for quality: Improving early childhood programs through systematic inservice training.* Ypsilanti, MI: HighScope Press.

Harms, T., & Clifford, R. M. (1980). *The early childhood environment rating scale.* New York: Teachers College Press.

HighScope Educational Research Foundation. (1992). *HighScope Child Observation Record (COR) for Ages 2½–6.* Ypsilanti, MI: HighScope Press.

HighScope Educational Research Foundation. (1997). *Early returns: First-year report of the Michigan school readiness program evaluation.* Ypsilanti, MI: HighScope Research Division.

HighScope Educational Research Foundation. (1998). *HighScope Program Quality Assessment (PQA)*. Ypsilanti, MI: HighScope Press.

Schweinhart, L., Epstein, A., Okoloko, V., & Oden, S. (1998, April). "Assessing the quality of Head Start programs: The quality research consortium." Paper presented at the American Educational Research Association, San Diego.

For more information: To obtain copies of the *HighScope Program Quality Assessment (PQA)*, please contact the HighScope Press at (800) 407-7377 or (800) 442-4329 (fax). To learn more about the curriculum, training, and research activities of the HighScope Educational Research Foundation, please visit our website at www.highscope.org or email the Foundation: info@highscope.org.

Ann S. Epstein

Ann Epstein, PhD, is an assistant professor and coordinator of the Early Childhood Education Program at the University of Wisconsin–La Crosse. She taught preschool-age children for 15 years before turning her attention to her current pride and joy: Early childhood majors.

Learning to See... Seeing to Learn

The Role of Observation in Early Childhood Development

by Diane C. MacLean

Through a Child's Eyes: From the Inside, Out

> Eighteen-month-old Maggie had been pushed all morning. Mom pushed her into clean diapers, clothes, and shoes. Dad pushed her into her highchair and fed her oatmeal. She fussed and pushed at her bowl and spoon. Dad got fed up trying to feed her and put her in her car seat. He had to get moving. She'd had two bites of breakfast.
>
> Maggie arrived at child care hungry, just as breakfast was being cleared from the tables. On top of that her teacher, Ms. Hugs & Kisses, wasn't there yet. Instead, Ms. Substitute was trying to clean up the waffles the other kids had been served as she talked to Maggie's father. Maggie found some waffles on the floor and reached for them. "Oh no you don't, Maggie," her Dad told her as he pushed her into a chair and gave her a puzzle. Maggie cried loudly to convey her frustration. Her Dad told Ms. Substitute that Maggie had been in a bad mood all morning and wished her luck. He kissed a screaming Maggie goodbye and rushed off to work.
>
> Ms. Substitute went back to cleaning. Maggie sat and sniffled and watched breakfast go away. Another child came over to her table, reaching across Maggie to grab her puzzle. Maggie smelled the waffle syrup still stuck on her friend's arm. She leaned forward and bit down on the sweet smelling forearm of her friend. "No, Maggie! Not nice!" Ms. Substitute yelled in her face. Her crying friend was quickly scooped away and hugged and kissed. Ms. Substitute paged the front desk. "No one told me I had a biter in here. Please call Maggie's father and let him know that he will have to come and take her out of this class if she continues to bite the other children."

It happens so often. Miscues compound, and events spiral out of control. All too often we create the misbehaviors we are trying so hard to prevent. We inadvertently condition children to express negative behavior because it seems to be the only way they can get their point across. It is so hard for children to be really heard and understood. We do not ask them what they want or need because they do not speak our language. Or do they? Studies show that non-verbal children have already developed an extensive understanding of their home language. It's their developmental age that restricts them from conveying effective responses. Early Childhood Development Professionals have a unique opportunity to observe and uncover these behavior patterns. By documenting unbiased, objective observations of children's actions and reactions, teachers can reveal the clear body language that children use to convey their responses. This information can be used to create family partnerships, which guide and support children as they learn to communicate, and we learn to understand their needs.

The Parents' View: From the Outside, In

> Here's how the problems started: Both Mom and Dad had a rough night. Maggie was up three times. To top off a tough night, the morning alarm didn't go off and it was Maggie's crying that finally woke them up again, 20 minutes late. It was Dad's turn to get Maggie to child care and Mom rushed out the door, after rushing Maggie into her clean diapers and clothes.
>
> Maggie hadn't eaten well the night before, and Dad chose a hearty oatmeal breakfast for Maggie in an effort to get something substantial into her before sending her off to the center. Maggie's refusal to cooperate and eat really frustrated him. Dad checked his watch and realized he needed to get going. He had a staff meeting to attend and budget cuts to defend. Maggie obviously wasn't hungry again. He cleaned his daughter up and put her into her car seat. Maggie's class was just finishing breakfast when they arrived, and a substitute teacher was working to clean up quickly when Maggie arrived. Dad put Maggie at the puzzle table in an effort to distract her from the mess under the table. Her screams just topped off a beautiful morning; he apologized to Ms. Substitute and left as quickly as possible.

Miscommunication happens all the time. There is no one at fault here. We do the best we can. The question is how can we, in the course of our busy lives, take the time to translate our children's needs to others? Just when we think we have figured out their cues, their needs change. Our children develop so quickly, it's hard to keep up. Where do we begin?

Figuring Out What Went Wrong: Systematic Observation and Patterning

Systematic observation and patterning is a strategy for identifying patterns in children's responses that can prevent further miscues and resulting negative and uncontrollable behavior. Regular documentation of objective observations and behavior pattern reviews offer opportunities for promoting positive change and healthy development in young children.

When partnered with parent feedback, systematic observation and patterning provides invaluable insight into the unique expressive patterns of each child. In addition, documented observations throughout a child's day and over the years assist with assessment.

This is a complicated way of describing something that most of us do naturally. Unfortunately, our observations are often tainted with our own bias and personal experience. In addition, we often fail to take the time necessary to document what we see. Documented unbiased observations of children's actions and reactions over time serve as a priceless tool of discovery into the communicative attempts and motives of childhood expression. The following guidelines are helpful in documenting unbiased observations.

Guidelines for Objective Observation: See through the Eyes of the Child

Get down on the child's level and look at life from his or her eyes. Most of the time children see adults from the knees down, or, from the shoulders up. Which view would you prefer? Infants can be over-stimulated by the visual, auditory, and tactile information that they encounter in their environments. Their sense of smell is highly sensitive in infancy. Children's digestive tracts are learning to move in sync, and all too often there are a few kickbacks in the system. This causes a lot of physical pain.

Pre-toddlers can understand their home language more fluently than they can express it. This sets the stage for frustration and misinterpretation of intent.

Record Only What You See, Feel, Hear, and Smell

You cannot see 'angry'; you can see frowning and hear screaming. You cannot see 'loves,' you can see smiling and hear giggling. When you record the specific body language and sounds the child expresses, you maintain objectivity. This provides a more accurate view of what is happening with that child; it is a more accurate translation of the child's intent for multiple caregivers. For example, stating that *"Reggie (15 months) picked up the sensory tube and angrily threw it at the caregiver"* invites a whole set of misinterpretations depending on how the reader views what 'anger' looks like. Does it look like screaming and throwing with force and intent? Does it look like frowning and crying? The actual observation of this incident, written with objectivity, provided a completely different scenario. *"Reggie (15 months) picked up the sensory tube, made eye contact with the caregiver, and waved the tube back and forth. The caregiver held out her hand, palm up, toward Reggie. Reggie looked back down at the tube and released his hand. The tube flew past the caregiver and rolled across the floor. Reggie frowned and crawled away. He began banging on a piano with the palm of his hand."* This observation provides a non-judgmental documentation of a set of events free of subjective and often inaccurate conclusions.

Look at the Big Picture

Documenting observations on a regular basis is critical to piecing the 'syllables' of the child's body language together. From these observations you will be able to better understand intentions. Accurately translating a child's intent to communicate his or her need provides opportunities for positive interactions between caregiver and child and the development of trustworthy relationships, which is our goal.

Analyze Behavior Patterns

Look for patterns to environmental triggers. Is the infant's crying response regularly triggered by his inability to move in the direction intended, or do you see a regular crying response that is triggered after eating a meal? Having a number of documented observations can bring to light the triggers behind some often confusing behaviors. Understanding the intension behind these non-verbal response patterns allows the caregiver to enter into a 'teachable moment' with that child, providing support through the development process.

Lack of response to environmental triggers should also be noted. An infant normally goes through a period of insecurity and frustration before moving forward developmentally. Becoming aware of these patterns of insecurity and frustration and matching them to their environmental triggers can better alert caregivers toward developmental readiness. When we analyze these behavior patterns, we are better prepared to respond appropriately to the child's intent and foster a rich and rewarding relationship with both parent and child.

Trade, Share, and Combine Your Observations

We all view things from different perspectives. When we share our observations, our insights can be used to highlight critical developmental milestones and challenges for young children in our care. As the child grows, his or her needs change. Regular, informal conferences with parents regarding your observations of their child during the day, partnered with the parents' insight into their own observations, routines, and cultural patterns at home can greatly enrich the child's developmental experience. Consistent support and guidance is crucial to healthy development. Sudden changes in behavior patterns can alert adults to possible health and developmental concerns. Documented observations can be submitted to appropriate professionals for more effective and timely intervention opportunities.

A View from All Angles
Putting it All Together

> Maggie had a desire to eat, but wouldn't. She went to bed hungry; this could have caused the broken sleep pattern she experienced the night before. Both Maggie and her parents woke up without having much sleep and were rushed and cranky.

Ms. Hugs & Kisses arrived in her classroom at 11:00, just in time for lunch. She and Ms. Substitute sat down to a family-style lunch with the children. Maggie was tired and hungry. She grabbed her chicken nugget and bit down hard and yelped, throwing it back down on the plate. She fussed and picked up her milk, sucking the cool liquid down quickly. "Maggie, are you alright? You love chicken nuggets," Ms. Hugs & Kisses asked Maggie.

"I'm not surprised," interrupted Ms. Substitute. "Maggie has been trouble all morning. She started out by biting Andrew on the arm and has been fussy and angry with everyone all morning. She just doesn't want to be here."

"That's not usual for Maggie. What exactly happened this morning?" asked Ms. Hugs & Kisses. Ms. Hugs & Kisses wrote down Maggie's actions from the time she grabbed the waffle pieces, to the bite on Andrew's arm after breakfast, and then documented the fussy and pushy behavior of the last three hours.

Maggie had wandered from center to center until Ms. Substitute had filled the water table. There, Maggie splashed around in the water and did not want to give up her turn. She kept putting the washcloth and sponge they were using to wash the babies with into her mouth and sucking the water. Ms. Substitute finally lost patience trying to control Maggie's behavior and closed the activity center.

After settling Maggie and the other children down for nap, Ms. Hugs and Kisses excused herself to make a phone call to Maggie's father. She asked about Maggie's evening and sleep patterns the night before. She tracked Maggie's eating pattern and found attempts to eat, but resistance to the specific foods offered. Ms. Hugs & Kisses reviewed her notes and the pattern appeared.

Meeting Children's Needs

> Ms. Hugs & Kisses called up to the kitchen to see if they had any chicken nuggets left. She had a plate put aside, asked that they be stored in the freezer, and went back to class. As she suspected, Maggie woke early from her nap fussing and crying. Ms. Hugs & Kisses scooped Maggie up and hugged and held her as she paged the front desk for the chilled nuggets to be brought down. She sat with Maggie and offered her a cold spongy nugget, and Maggie sucked and chewed one down. As Maggie reached for another, Ms. Hugs & Kisses asked her to open wide and Maggie showed her swollen gums and an erupting tooth.
>
> That afternoon at pick-up time Maggie was sucking away at a frozen washcloth and playing in the kitchen. Ms. Hugs & Kisses explained to Dad about Maggie's sore mouth and suggested soft and cool foods for her, combined with a little extra TLC. Dad was relieved to have an explanation for his daughter's behavior and thanked her teacher for her suggestions. He hoped they would all get a good night's sleep.

This simple scenario illustrates investigative observation in action. Documenting patterns of child behavior for caregivers promotes consistency in responsiveness. Individualized observation portfolios, like those described in *The Creative Curriculum® for Infants and Toddlers*, travel with the children as they develop and provide behavior pattern summaries, which teachers can refer to in an effort to support the changing needs of the children in their care. Use of observation and assessment tools such as these are built on the belief that relationships are central.

References

Dombro, A. L., Colker, L. J., & Dodge, D. T. (1999). *The creative curriculum for infants and toddlers*. Washington, DC: Teaching Strategies, Inc. www.teachingstrategies.com.

Davis Goldman, B., & Bube Nychka, H. (1991). *Series of 6 training videotapes: Small talk — Creating conversations with young children*. Chapel Hill, NC: Riverside Publishing Company (a Houghton Mifflin Company).

Diane C. MacLean

Diane C. MacLean graduated with a BS in Education at Indiana University in 1983. She currently serves as a Training and Curriculum Specialist with the Department of Defense, United States Marine Corps in Camp Lejeune, North Carolina.

Are We Doing Things Just because We've Always Done Them this Way?

by Kim Turner

At one of the first preschools I taught at after graduating from college, every classroom environment stayed the same from year to year. Whatever furniture was in the classroom when a new teacher moved in stayed there, and the furniture never moved around the classroom. The classroom materials rarely changed. The table stayed by the wall because that is where it had always stood. The toddler classroom had the animal puzzle in it because it had always had the animal puzzle. Change was not valued. Further, uniqueness and variety in classrooms materials were not a priority. Individual classrooms were not particularly suited to the children in them.

Then I came to work at Boulder Journey School, where I currently teach. Boulder Journey School is a preschool in Boulder, Colorado, that welcomes children ages 6 weeks to 6 years. The learning community at Boulder Journey School has been studying the pedagogy of the schools for young children in Reggio Emilia, Italy, since 1995. Inspired by the schools in Reggio Emilia, the environments at Boulder Journey School change all the time — not just when we switch classrooms each summer or fall, but throughout the school year. Teachers move furniture around the classrooms and from one classroom to another, depending on the requirements of both the children and adults who spend their days there. Educators constantly add new materials and move existing materials to other areas of the classroom. The children help redesign classrooms, offering suggestions on where to move pieces of furniture and, oftentimes, moving furniture and materials themselves.

Our school's culture supports fluid classroom design that encourages teachers to tailor the classrooms to the children. Avoiding the monotony of having the same classroom set-up from year to year ensures that every classroom of children feels at home in an environment organized specifically for them. In the schools in Reggio Emilia, the environment is often seen as the 'third educator,' along with the teachers. "In order to act as an educator for the child, the environment has to be flexible: It must undergo frequent modification by the children and the teachers in order to remain up-to-date and responsive to their needs to be protagonists in constructing their knowledge" (Gandini, 1998, p. 148).

Thinking about the classroom environment in this new way didn't come easily for me. It took a lot of discussion, experimentation, and hard work. It takes discipline to get out of the mindset of doing the same thing year after year. It also takes a great deal of thought to change an environment, not just for the sake of change, but to better support children's work.

When I first started working at the school, this was not clear to me.

Then in fall 2008, I joined several of my colleagues in a newly-formed research group focused on studying the environment. The formation of this group was inspired by a June visit by Amelia Gambetti, Reggio Children International Network Coordinator and Liaison for Consultancy in Schools. During this visit, Amelia challenged educators at Boulder Journey School to continue our analysis of our environment. Our research group was enthusiastic about this challenge because it resonated with our desire to keep learning and thinking in deeper ways. Based on Amelia's challenge, we posed the following overarching questions to ourselves:

- Can we document all the things children need adult help with in the school? How can the environment support the children's autonomy?

- Can we research cutting-edge ways that technology has been used in schools? What new ideas can we develop?

- Can we work with parents to analyze each space in the environment and our style of communication/visibility/documentation? What are our positive and negative impressions?

- Can we rethink the organization of each space in the classroom? Can we research every decision made in the environment regarding materials, spaces, documentation?

- Can we research the connections between architecture/design of space and quality of life? What research is available on architecture and on classroom environments, both traditional and progressive?

- Can we better connect indoor and outdoor spaces? Can we compare the quality of experiences inside versus outside?

- Can we design more eco-friendly classrooms that contribute to sustainability?

- As a faculty, can we discover our biggest challenges during the day? How does the environment relate to these challenges?

- How can we better communicate through our documentation? How does documentation help children better understand the organization of the classroom and the school? How can documentation be used to make a strong statement about children's competence?

- Can we commit to considering the fundamental principles of the purpose of education in an ongoing manner and how that can influence the organization of the environment?

Reflecting on these questions led to discussions about what things we were doing out of habit — because we had always done them this way — and what things were based on clear intentions that were well thought out. At the same time, we looked to the Reggio publication, *Children, Spaces, and Relations: Metaproject for an Environment for Young Children*, as a resource (Ceppi & Zini, 1998). One passage in particular stood out: "A space that is responsive and transformable, that enables different ways of inhabitance and use during the course of the day and with the passing of time" (p. 17).

Based on our discussions surrounding habit versus responsiveness, transform-ability and multi-functionality, it became evident that each piece of furniture and each material in our classrooms, though fluid in terms of placement, held a teacher-imposed identity. For example, a couch was for sitting. But could the couch be replaced with a bench for sitting, with a tunnel underneath for hiding and crawling?

In our classroom, the block platform was for building. But in our documentation of children in the 'block area,' we observed the children jumping. A variety of blocks could be found in the block area, but the children brought other materials to this place for building. What would happen if we added a second, lower block platform in this area? This addition provoked children to dance and to continue jumping, but from a safer height. It was safer to build in this larger space, without competition from jumpers, or even dancers. To further increase the functions of this space, we introduced studio materials, such as paint, paper, brushes, and markers. The children found the platform to be a wonderful place to work together on big creations. The children also transformed the 'block platform' into a stage, on which to play house and hospital.

Creating a classroom environment is an ongoing process. We are still observing and documenting the children working in the block area so we can make changes as needed to better support them. And our questioning, observation, and documentation continue in other areas of the classroom, as well. My co-teacher and I are currently discussing how to redesign our dramatic play space to better support the children's work there.

Even when the classroom environment seems ideal, I have found it helpful to continue analyzing it. There is always the possibility that after reflection and reorganization, the environment will support the children's work even better. I have learned that I can give myself permission to experiment within the environment. If a new idea doesn't work, I can keep changing things until I find something that does work.

Designing a classroom can be a difficult process. Looking back at when I first started teaching, I realize I was doing the same things year after year because I hadn't yet been provoked to question or think even more deeply about my classroom design choices, as Amelia Gambetti provoked my colleagues and me to do at Boulder Journey School. Sometimes, I still find myself doing things just because that's how I've always done them. The challenge is to catch myself when I do this and to have the courage to question my decisions.

References

Ceppi, G., & Zini, M. (eds.). (1998). *Children, spaces, relations: Metaproject for an environment for young children*. Reggio Emilia, Italy: Reggio Children.

Gandini, L. (1998). "Educational and caring spaces." In C. Edwards, L. Gandini, & G. Forman (eds.), *The hundred languages of children: The Reggio Emilia approach to early childhood education* (pp. 135–149). Greenwich, CT: Ablex Publishing Company..

Kim Turner

Kim Turner is currently a mentor teacher at Boulder Journey School in Boulder, Colorado. She has taught at the school for seven years and has worked in the early childhood education field for 11 years. She holds a bachelor's degree in Journalism from the University of Colorado at Boulder and a master's degree in Educational Psychology from the University of Colorado at Denver.

Questions to Guide Our Work

by Margie Carter

Among the summer treasures of living in Seattle are the buckets full of blackberries that can be had in nearly any neighborhood, including our city center. Our annual harvest prompted me to create a back-to-school tradition with my grandchildren. Before Labor Day, our family gathers around my just-out-of-the-oven pie. As the ice cream gets scooped up, I offer the question, "What do you hope to learn in this coming year?" We each take a turn sharing our thoughts. Coe, about to enter fourth grade, once again, rocked me with his response. "This year I've been thinking I should learn how to make use of what they teach us in school, but it isn't that easy to figure out."

My, my, he's got that right! As is often the case with gems children offer us, we would do well, as educators, to ponder what Coe is wrestling with here. What are we teaching and why is it so difficult for children to discern its meaning for their lives? Does the problem lie with them or with our teaching?

Coe's younger brother, Jesse, starting first grade, tried to help his older brother out of this quandary. "When you learn math, you'll get a better job, Coe, and that means more money. (He chuckled, pleased to offer his next thought.) And, you'll be able to count all that money with bigger numbers." Jesse not only shows us his sense of humor, but the sense he makes of math, and our culture's emphasis for schooling: Education is to get you ready for economic function. This impoverished idea of education makes me flinch, just as I do with the notion that our country's economic security is dependent on continually buying more things. You might see me tearing my hair as I roar, "What is happening to our humanity? How did our imaginations get hijacked?" Jonathan Kozol (2000) captures my sentiments nicely:

"There is more to life, and ought to be much more to childhood, than readiness for economic function. Childhood ought to have at least a few entitlements that aren't entangled with utilitarian considerations. One of them should be the right to a degree of unencumbered satisfaction in the sheer delight and goodness of existence itself. Another ought to be the confidence of knowing that one's presence on this earth is taken as an unconditioned blessing that is not contaminated by the economic uses that a nation does or does not have for you."

Asking the Big Questions

In my view there has never been a more important time for us to ask ourselves what we believe the purpose of education to be. The future of American democracy may well be at stake here. Do schools and early childhood programs primarily exist to produce compliant workers for economic function? Or, is the goal to help children grow into their full potential as informed, engaged citizens eager to make a contribution to their communities? We must ask ourselves, "Do educational goals narrowed to test scores prepare children to be successful in an ever more complex world? Should early education focus solely on children's futures or does providing enriched childhood experiences give them a better future?"

The answers to these questions determine the approach to our early care and education programs. Should teachers design curriculum to remediate children's needs and deficits, or should they focus on children's inherent competencies, ideas, and questions? Can stronger policies and curriculum mandates really improve learning outcomes? Or should the emphasis be on improved working conditions, salaries, and teacher education to support the role of teachers in children's learning? What are your views on these questions? What questions are you raising as you undertake your work, attend meetings, and champion a care and education system with meaningful outcomes?

Strategy:
What outcomes do you want for children?

Inspired by Tom Drummond and colleagues he has joined with across the country (visit www.earlyeducationadvocates.org), I've been challenging directors and teachers to clarify the outcomes they want for children. Prompting some considerations with starting phrases yields a provocative discussion. We are reminded that whatever mandates others have for us, we should be planning for the objectives we think are important for children.

Crafting the Daily Questions

When I first entered our profession I generally thought the job of teachers was to be creative in giving children the information and answers they would need to be successful in school. With more experience and clarity on the philosophical and theoretical frameworks I wanted to work with, my pedagogical approach shifted to an emphasis on processes and questions that would open up the world for children and engage them in a quest for life-long learning. Now as a teacher educator I pursue a parallel pedagogy, provoking teachers to listen

When they leave our program, we want children to:	*Cuando se van de nuestro programa, queremos que los niños:*
Trust in…	*Tengan confianza en…*
Believe that…	*Crean que…*
Know that…	*Sepan que…*
Know how to…	*Sepan como…*
Question…	*Pregunten como…*

Used with permission from *The Visionary Director* (Redleaf Press, 2010).

carefully to children, offering questions to use as a thinking lens as they reflect on actions to take with them. While we continually raise the big questions about education, we should also craft the daily questions that will help us learn how to help children learn.

Strategy:
Use questions as a 'thinking lens'

Thinking further about my grandson, Coe's, musings on how to make use of what he's taught in school, I realize that a primary goal I have in my adult education work is helping teachers learn how to make use of what we teach them. In many cases I'm sure they resonate with Coe: "It isn't that easy to figure out."

Rather than guidance techniques or curriculum activities, I'm convinced teachers need a method for thinking about the complexities of their work. Reading *The Power of Protocols* (2007) has reaffirmed my belief that teachers benefit from a structure that provides 'a thinking culture.' I've found it useful to offer a set of questions for teachers to regularly cycle through when trying to make meaning out of what has unfolded and choosing what to do next.

For example, try consistently using questions such as the following when you discuss child observations with teachers. After a few months of steady practice with these questions, teachers will internalize them as a thinking lens for their work.

■ What specific details will paint a picture for us of what you saw?

Assessment from the Child's Perspective

The New Zealand approach to assessment asks teachers to consider questions from the child's voice as centres begin their journey of ensuring accountability through evaluation and assessment. These questions are built on the principles of their *Te Whaariki curriculum*, which provides the framework for defining learning and what is to be learned. Their goals are based on clearly defined values and reflect the following strands.

Belonging	Do you appreciate and understand my interests and abilities and those of my family?	Do you know me?
Well-being	Do you meet my daily needs with care and sensitive consideration?	Can I trust you?
Exploration	Do you engage my mind, offer challenges, and extend my world?	Do you let me fly?
Communication	Do you invite me to communicate and respond to my own articular efforts?	Do you hear me?
Contribution	Do you encourage and facilitate my endeavours to be part of the wider group?	Is this place fair for us?

Excerpted from *Learning Together with Young Children*, with permission from Podmore, V., May, H., & Carr, M. (2001). "The Child's Questions," Programme Evaluation with *Te Whaariki Using Teaching Stories*. Wellington: Institute for Early Childhood Studies, Victoria University of Wellington, NZ.

Practice Using the Thinking Lens® with this Story

Inventing a Game

The children are immediately drawn to this interesting architectural structure in the park. They have invented a game of peek-a-boo using the structure as the setting. Every day now for a few weeks they play the same game. They run up to the structure and peek through the various openings to look out. When they see one of the other children or their caregivers, they make eye contact and laugh uproariously. Then they move to another part of the structure and peek out of another opening and repeat the same looking and laughing behavior.

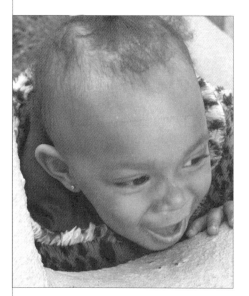

They all have adopted the same 'rules' for this game. They visit the openings from the lower concrete area and then up higher on the grassy area. Sometimes they hide away from the hole and then peek around the corner, surprising the person there. Other times they reach through the openings to touch hands with the person on the other side.

PHOTOGRAPHS BY THE AUTHOR

- How might different perspectives enhance our understandings of what this means? (e.g. the child's point of view, the family's cultural values, professional knowledge, desired outcomes)

- How can we find out more?

- What opportunities and possibilities do we see for taking action?

- What can we do to further our learning and that of the children?

Strategy:
Consider questions from the child's perspective

This summer I participated in a gathering to hear about the New Zealand system of early childhood education and, in particular, their approach to assessment referred to as "Learning Stories." Chris Bayes captivated us when she suggested we consider thinking of assessment from the child's point of view.

Drawing on the work of Podmore, May, and Carr (2001), she gave us these possible questions in the voice of a child in our center.

- Do you appreciate and understand my interests and abilities and those of my family? Do you know me?

- Do you meet my daily needs with care and sensitive consideration? Can I trust you?

- Do you engage my mind, offer challenges, and extend my world? Do you let me fly?

- Do you invite me to communicate and respond to my own particular efforts? Do you hear me?

- Do you encourage and facilitate my endeavors to be part of the wider group? Is this place fair for us?

I find it particularly helpful to think of these children's questions as offering us benchmarks to strive for. What might we see in a program as we try to assess, "Do you let me fly?" This takes me back to Jonathan Kozol, who so eloquently speaks to the heart of what I see as our work:

"I urge you to be teachers so that you can join with children as the co-collaborators in a plot to build a little place of ecstasy and poetry and gentle joy."

References

Curtis, D., & Carter, M. (2007). *Learning together with young children*. St Paul: Redleaf Press.

Kozol, J. (2000). *Ordinary resurrections: Children in the years of hope*. New York: Crown Publishers.

McDonald, J., Mohr, N., Dichter, A., & McDonald, E. (2007). *Power of protocols*. New York: Teachers College Press.

Podmore, V., May, H., & Carr, M. (2001). "The Child's Questions," *Programme Evaluation with Te Whaariki Using Teaching Stories*. Wellington: Institute for Early Childhood Studies, Victoria University of Wellington, NZ.

Margie Carter

Margie Carter is the co-founder of Harvest Resources Associates (www.ecetrainers.com) and the co-author of numerous books and early childhood videos. As she moves towards retirement years, her professional work is focused on highlighting and supporting the inspiring work of new leaders and uplifting the voices and leadership of teachers in the field.

Conducting a Realistic Self-assessment with the *Environment Rating Scales*

by Thelma Harms

Having staff complete a self-assessment of their own early childhood program using a quality rating instrument is a well-established practice included in national early childhood accreditation programs, as well as in state Quality Rating and Improvement Systems (QRIS). It is assumed that by conducting a self-assessment before the official assessment occurs, front-line staff will become aware of the requirements of the assessment instrument and be able to follow through with needed improvements in their classroom as they prepare for an official assessment. No doubt it is essential for the director and the early childhood teaching staff or the family child care provider to become knowledgeable about the requirements of the assessment instrument that will be used to assess their program. However, in order for the self-assessment process to make a significant and appropriate contribution to the improvement of program quality, several factors need to be considered.

Self-assessment vs. Objective Observation

First and foremost, we have to understand the different roles played by the self-assessment and the official agency assessment. Self-assessment is primarily useful to help staff understand, plan for, and make as many improvements as they possibly can in the quality of their program in accordance with the official agency requirements. Since the director and staff have a deep emotional and philosophical commitment to what they are doing, it is very difficult for them to assume the role of objective observer. Therefore, only the scores from official agency assessments completed by objective observers who are free of conflicts of interest, and have been trained to a high level of accuracy in using the scales and whose reliability is checked periodically, should be used as evidence of program quality level to fulfill the requirements for tiered reimbursement or other quality recognitions. If the sponsoring agency offering the quality improvement program wants to see how accurate the scores from self-assessments are, this can be done by selecting a sample of self-assessed programs, having these programs evaluated by a reliable observer, and comparing the results of both assessments for individual classrooms.

Accurate Use of the Assessment Instrument

Another challenge that must be met if self-assessment is to do any good, is that the assessment instrument itself must be used accurately by staff.

The first thing staff needs to check is whether the most current spiral-bound version of the age-appropriate *Environment Rating Scale* is available for use in the self-assessment:

- The *ECERS-R* is used for group programs where the children are 2½ through 5 years of age (preschoolers and kindergartners).

- The *ITERS-R* is for groups of infants and toddlers, from birth to 30 months of age.

- The *FCCERS-R* is for family child care homes, both large and small, where children of different ages may be enrolled.

The authors of the *Environment Rating Scales* have written resource books that give detailed explanations in words and photographs to help illustrate the many different ways that each requirement in the scales can be met. Currently, *All About ECERS-R* (Cryer, Harms, & Riley, 2003) and *All About ITERS-R* (Cryer, Harms, & Riley, 2004), and *All About the FCCERS-R* (Harms, Cryer, & Clifford, 2007) are available. These resource books are very helpful as staff try to learn to use the instruments accurately. It is also advisable to access our website (see Resources) to see whether additional notes for any of the scales or other supplementary materials are available. The authors continue to post new materials to add helpful information for scale users. In addition, questions can be submitted at any time to our website for us to answer.

The need for training. Most important for accuracy of self-assessment is recognizing that it takes considerable training on the specific requirements of the scale in order for classroom staff to produce a valid picture of the ongoing quality in the program. When completing an assessment with one of the *Environment Rating Scales*, not only will the staff members have to evaluate the indoor and outdoor space, the room arrangement, the materials and activities accessible for learning, and the health and safety practices, but also their teaching practices, and, most challenging, the quality of their interactions with the children, parents, and other staff members. Accurate self-assessment is a difficult task.

Currently a number of programs require self-assessments as a first step in establishing a Quality Rating and Improvement System (QRIS), before requiring a formal, official assessment based on an observation of classroom practices by observers who are trained to reliability. However, if self-assessment is to be effective at all, training on the instrument being used should be required, before staff conduct a self-assessment.

Preparatory training is so important that affordable, easily accessible courses should be offered and course credit or continuing education units (CEUs) should be given to those who complete such a course. To be most effective, locally available courses provided through Child Care Resource and Referral agencies (R&Rs) or community colleges should be given by professional early childhood educators who themselves have been trained on the *Environment Rating Scales*. The training for self-assessment needs to be of sufficient duration and intensity so that a working knowledge of the selected scale can be achieved.

Staff need time to absorb the new information they gain and to try doing an assessment in manageable steps. For example, instead of providing 8 hours of training all on one day, it is preferable to break an 8-hour course into 2-hour segments given on a weekly basis, each segment covering several subscales. This format gives the trainees time to try, in their own classrooms, the segment of the scale they have learned. When they return the following week they can ask questions based on their experience, before being trained on a new segment of the scale.

Support from a 'buddy,' another staff member participating in the course, also helps in both the learning and application processes. If possible, several staff members working in the same room should take the course together as a team. Then, if each one conducts an independent assessment on the segment they learned that week, the team can meet to compare and discuss their results before the next class meeting. This approach builds competence in using the scale and stimulates ideas for classroom changes.

It is also helpful to get an 'outsider's' assessment by a person well-trained on the scale, to compare with the staff self-assessment. Mentoring programs, technical assistance providers from Resource and Referral agencies, and state agency staff working for Quality Rating and Improvement Systems are available in some communities to conduct an assessment as part of preparation for the official assessment.

If possible, the 'outsider's' assessment and the staff self-assessment should be done at relatively the same time, so that they can be compared and discussed within a common context. Having a copy of the appropriate *All About* book available for reference during such comparisons helps to increase knowledge of the scale requirements and improve scoring accuracy.

Conclusion

The main value of self-assessment is to increase awareness of the actual environment and practices in one's own classroom. The assessment must, therefore, present a realistic picture of what the children are experiencing on a daily basis. Significant changes will be possible only if the staff have had sufficient training to produce accurate scores, the personal resilience to face the challenges of working towards improved quality, and the support of the administration and the community. It is important for all stakeholders, the early childhood program directors and front-line staff, the official quality rating program, as well as parents and the public to realize that, although many significant changes can be made in the short term, long-range goals will also be needed. An accurate self-assessment will help early childhood program directors and staff distinguish between the short- and long-range improvements needed, and to plan effectively for both.

Resources

Environment Rating Scales:
www.fpg.unc.edu/~ecers

For Further Information

Cryer, D., Harms, T., & Clifford, R. M. (2007). *All About the FCCERS-R*. Lewisville, NC: Kaplan PACT House Publishing.

Cryer, D., Harms, T., & Riley. C. (2004). *All About the ITERS-R*. Lewisville, NC: Kaplan PACT House Publishing.

Cryer, D., Harms, T., & Riley. C. (2003). *All About the ECERS-R*. Lewisville, NC: Kaplan PACT House Publishing.

Thelma Harms

Thelma Harms is Director of Curriculum Development at the Frank Porter Graham Child Development Institute and Research Professor Emeritus in the School of Education at the University of North Carolina at Chapel Hill. She earned an MA in Child Development and a PhD in Early Childhood Education at the University of California at Berkeley, where she was Head Teacher of their Harold E. Jones Child Study Center demonstration program for 15 years. Thelma has lectured and conducted training throughout the U.S., as well as in Canada, Germany, Portugal, Sweden, Hong Kong, South Korea, Singapore, Australia, and Russia. Dr. Harms is the lead author of four widely used program evaluation instruments: the *Early Childhood Environment Rating Scale-Revised* (Harms, Clifford & Cryer, 1998, 2004); the *Infant/Toddler Environment Rating Scale-Revised* (Harms, Cryer & Clifford, 2003, 2006); the *School-Age Care Environment Rating Scale* (Harms, Jacobs & White, 1996); and the *Family Child Care Environment Rating Scale-Revised* (Harms, Cryer & Clifford, 2007). As extensions of this work there are two newly published resource books, *All About the ECERS-R* and *All About the ITERS-R* (Cryer, Harms & Riley, 2003 & 2004). Thelma Harms has co-authored a number of curriculum materials including: the 7-volume *Active Learning Series*; the *Cook and Learn Series*; *Nutrition Education for Preschoolers*; and the 10-part educational television series, "Raising America's Children." She has also co-edited a book on working with preschool children in shelters who are homeless, and a book on infants and toddlers in out-of-home care. In addition to consulting and conducting training, Dr. Harms continues to be involved at the FPG Institute with several scales related research and development projects.

Seeing Children's Lively Minds at Work

by Deb Curtis

We overestimate children academically and underestimate them intellectually.
— Lilian G. Katz

One of my worries about the growing focus on academics and school readiness in programs for young children is it keeps many teachers from seeing children's innate, lively minds at work. When teachers are overly concerned about teaching the alphabet and other isolated skills and facts, they may miss children's serious approaches to tasks and voracious quests to understand the world around them. As Lilian Katz's quote above suggests, children are more apt to be interested in intellectual pursuits than academic lessons. I think clarifying the difference between the two can help teachers see and appreciate children's thinking, and in turn offer meaningful experiences that engage their lively minds.

Webster's dictionary defines *academic* as "very learned but inexperienced in practical matters," "conforming to the tradition or rules of a school," and "a body of established opinion widely accepted as authoritative in a particular field." And intellectual is defined as "given to study, reflection, and speculation," and "engaged activity requiring the creative use of the intellect."

Obviously it is important for children to learn appropriate academic skills and tasks, but rather than overly focusing on these goals, I strongly claim and enjoy my responsibility to help children become engaged thinkers, excited about the wonders around them. Young children bring an eager disposition to learn all of the time, so it's my job to find ways to really see, appreciate, and further their intellectual pursuits.

Take Children's Actions Seriously

It's easy to dismiss children's explorations because they move quickly, make messes, and put themselves in seemingly risky situations. I have developed the practice of waiting before jumping into a situation to determine what the thinking might be underneath a child's behavior. I have come to see that with most everything children do, they have something in mind; a purpose or question they are pursuing. When I take even their smallest actions seriously, I am astonished at children's deep engagement with the simple wonders around them; I notice they are studying and speculating, engrossed in the moment. Notice nine-month-old Maddie's lively mind at work in the following photos and story.

Sounds and Sparkles

Maddie was captivated with the shiny, crinkly paper that she found in a basket. She grabbed the paper and began to shake it with excitement as it made a loud, crackling noise. Then she pinched it with her fingers and explored it with her mouth. She quickly began to shake the paper again. I was curious as she put the paper up to her eyes and then went back to shaking it. Was she noticing the light reflecting off the surface of the paper? Did she see the transparency of the paper?

Maddie's joy in her investigation was obvious as she smiled and laughed with me as she tried each new action. Her favorite activity was shaking the paper. I think she loved the sound she was able to produce and my reaction to her, and she may have been delighting in the sparkles she could see coming from the paper as it moved. Next, Maddie clasped the paper with both her hands and began to stretch and pull it, watching the paper intently as she did this. I wondered if she had discovered something about the paper when she was shaking it and was exploring it further with this new action. What noise will it make if I pull it? Does it still sparkle when I stretch it this way? I loved seeing the paper from her point of view and watching her joy and intense engagement with the magic of this unusual material.

Use a *Thinking Lens*®

I use questions from a *Thinking Lens*® that I developed with Margie Carter and Ann Pelo to help me to remember to slow down, look for the details of what is unfolding, suspend my teacher agenda, and try to see children's perspectives. This one-page chart was part of a Beginnings Workshop article I wrote for the November/December 2008 issue of *Exchange*. The chart is included at the end of this article. As I participate with children in these daily quests for understanding, I document what I am seeing to tell the stories of their rich intellectual pursuits. I study my photos and notes carefully to capture the significance of the children's work. These stories show how children bring their whole selves — body, mind, and emotions — to every task. Notice the details and children's perspectives in the following photos and stories.

Immersed in Bubbles

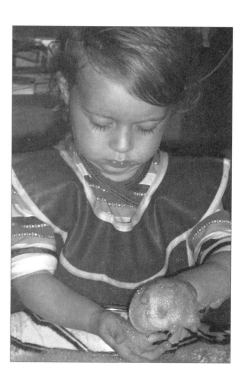

Two-year-old Mackenzie was totally absorbed in an intense study of bubbles today. I watched her purposefully fill a small cup and then pour the sudsy, wet substance onto her hand. She studied her wet and soapy hand for a long while and then poured some more water and bubbles on her hand again. I was surprised when, after investigating the bubbles this way for several minutes, Mackenzie leaned over and totally immersed her arms into the water, stretching her hands and fingers

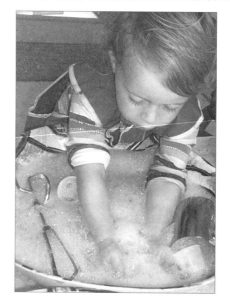

under the surface and again looking closely at the bubbles on her skin. She spent about 30 minutes playing in the water tub this way.

I delighted in Mackenzie's rapt attention for this investigation. It was such a simple set of materials, but she found so much to investigate. Seeing Mackenzie's lively mind at work certainly counters the idea that two-year-olds don't have a very long attention span. I wonder what she was noticing as she gazed at the bubbles. Did she feel tiny sensations of bubbles popping on her skin and then try to see what she was feeling? Was she noticing light and color shining through the bubbles? Was she interested in the textures, sheen, and shapes of her hands and arms in the water? Whatever was on her mind, the intention and focus she brought to this work was obviously a serious intellectual pursuit

Offer More to See More

When I've seen children exploring objects and materials with such concentration, I want to offer them expanded possibilities with similar experiences to deepen their investigations. I also want the opportunity myself to see more of what is on their minds and their growing understandings. Seeing toddlers' fascination with this magical substance called water, I decided to offer more ways for the group to continue with this intellectual pursuit.

The Magic of a Sponge

To build on the children's investigation of water, I offered them dry sponges at the water table. My hunch about their interest in this new material with the water was right on. The children approached the hard, dry sponges with great curiosity and intense exploration began. I loved the serious looks on their faces as they examined the sponges closely while they were

still dry, and then quickly put them in the water. They manipulated the sponges, intently watching as the sponges absorbed the water. The children discovered and then delighted in squeezing the water out of the sponges. They repeated the soaking and squeezing actions over and over again. Next, they became interested in filling the containers in the tub with water and the sponges. Oscar was determined to put every sponge in the water into the container. Then he covered the sponges with water and watched the water and sponges spill over the top. He repeated this several times. I think these experiences related to physics concepts, such as float and sink, absorption and displacement. I am excited to learn more about the specifics of this learning domain, so I can offer the children more possibilities.

The children easily discovered how their actions had an impact on the sponges and the water. They eagerly learned from the materials, their own actions, and from watching each other. I was amazed at the children's attention and ability to take in so much information so quickly. They were just like the sponges, soaking everything up. And seeing the world through their eyes, I gained a new appreciation of just how amazing sponges can be!

Seek Multiple Perspectives

My interest in children's lively minds and intellectual pursuits led me to the book *What is a Scientist?* by Barbara Lehn (1999). It portrays the elements of inquiry for young children that are identified by the National Science Foundation. One of the elements of our *Thinking Lens®* suggests considering multiple perspectives to describe and understand the many ways I observe children naturally using these elements of inquiry in their explorations. This book helped me to see the children's actions more complexly as I adapted the elements from it to use in analyzing and planning from my observations. Re-reading the observation stories above, can you see that even very young children are thinking and learning like scientists from the following list?

When young children think and learn like scientists they…

- wonder and ask questions.
- learn through their senses.
- observe closely and notice details.
- describe, draw, and write what they see and think.
- compare and sort by looking carefully.
- count and measure to make comparisons.
- experiment through trial and error and test predictions.
- keep trying over and over.
- work together with others and have fun!

These outcomes are also helpful when responding to concerns from parents and other professionals about what children are learning as they play. In the following story of four-year-old Joshua playing with colorful, translucent blocks you can see the lively mind of a scientist at work. Which of the science outcomes is he working on in his play?

Thinking and Learning Like a Scientist

One of Joshua's favorite places to work in the room is the Light and Color Table. Today he spent more than 35 minutes building, stacking, and knocking over the colorful, transparent blocks. He thoughtfully examined each piece before he added it to the line of blocks that he was creating. He lined each one, end to end in a row and then using his finger, he carefully knocked the blocks down one by one without disrupting the other blocks in the line. I was amazed at this difficult task he set for himself because it required much concentration and a steady hand.

It surprised me that Joshua didn't seem to be paying attention to the color or mirrored reflection, but instead to the size of the blocks. He put 2 long ones together and then 2 short ones, making this pattern each time. He chose the blocks carefully, putting the ones aside that did not fit his pattern.

He showed such diligence for this pursuit, because when he had mastered his goal with the blocks lined vertically, he switched to building horizontally across the mirror, and carefully knocked them down. I marveled at Joshua's attention for the physics of spatial relationships, gravity and motion, and the math skills he practiced while comparing and patterning with the blocks. It's remarkable how children discover and study these things for themselves in a richly provisioned environment, for we could never teach them all there is to know about these wonders in the world.

Engage with Children in Intellectual Pursuits

My work with children, even the youngest babies, is the most intellectually stimulating part of my life. As you read the observation stories here, along with descriptive details and the children's perspectives, you will notice that I make reference to my own interests, curiosities, surprises, and delights in what I am seeing. I offer my thoughts by making meaning using the details from what is unfolding, rather than just quick judgments or opinions. I work purposefully to find the moments that capture my heart and mind because I know my interests are what I give attention to and, in turn, communicate to the children who they are in our group. When teachers are intellectually engaged, side by side with the children in their pursuits, we see more clearly their lively minds at work, and respond in ways that enhance their identity as serious thinkers and learners. The following story is one of my favorites from my work with preschool children, as their joy and wonder about the magic of rainbows matched mine.

Catching Rainbows

In our room we have wonderful windows where on sunny mornings the light comes streaming in. Because our program is located in the often gray and rainy northwest of the United States, the sun is a welcomed friend. To celebrate the sunlight, we created a display in a window with prisms, mirrored balls, and hologram mobiles for the children to explore. The children eagerly gravitate toward the spinning lights and rainbows made by these items. They try out all kinds of actions on them to see what will happen.

The children think and care deeply about the magical colors and lights that visit our room. They are intensely curious and have formulated serious theories and questions about where the rainbows come from and why they visit us. As they play with the light and rainbows through chase games and cause-and-effect explorations, they are careful observers of important details. They clearly notice what is different on the rainbow days. A few have made the connection that when the sun is not out, the rainbows are gone. I delight in the theories the children share as together we seek deeper understandings of these amazing phenomena.

"The rainbow makes all of the colors in our room."

"The rainbow comes from the clouds."

"When it rains, the rain goes right through the rainbow."

"Rainbows are colorful air."

"The rainbow comes to visit because it likes us."

The children's theories show what powerful observers they are of the scientific evidence at hand and also offer delightful interpretations from their unique perspectives. I don't interrupt these spontaneous musings for pre-planned academic activities. Nor have I researched an academic lesson about how rainbows are made. I know that embedded in their exuberant explorations are rich opportunities for collaborating, problem solving, hypothesizing, thinking, and learning. I don't want to limit the children's complex intellectual pursuits by focusing on teaching them the 'right' answer.

My priority is that the children's learning includes amazement, joy, magic, and wonder, rather than activities with no context and dry facts without meaning. I want them to 'play' with their ideas about rainbows in their conversations and through meaningful activities. When the rainbows come, I delight with them as they run and jump and chase them around the room. I suggest that the children think and learn like scientists by talking about and drawing their ideas and theories, and then I turn these into displays or books with photos and stories so the children and I can revisit their thinking to go deeper. After extensive exploration and study of their own theories, I offer books with the scientific facts to enhance their discoveries. These are ways children experience meaningful academic learning.

I find that it takes daily practice for me to really see children. But I know that when I closely observe children's pursuits and take their ideas seriously, I see their lively minds at work and how capable they truly are. When I join the children in their excitement about the world, I enrich my own life and work. Ultimately, when children are supported to pursue their interests and passions, they come to believe that their theories and intellectual pursuits have value. They experience themselves as competent thinkers and learners who can make choices about their learning. They learn to collaborate and see other perspectives and work through disagreements. They study something over time and in-depth to learn about it — in other words, they are intellectuals at work!

Reference

Lehn, B. (1999). *What is a scientist?* Minneapolis: Millbrook Press.

Deb Curtis

Deb Curtis has worked as an educator of children and adults for over 30 years. She has co-authored several books with Margie Carter, where she feels grateful to have deepened so many ideas through that process. The ideas in this article were inspired by the 2nd edition of *Designs for Living and Learning*, Redleaf Press.

A Thinking Lens® for Reflective Teaching

Knowing yourself
How am I reacting to this situation and why?
What in my background and values is influencing my response to this situation and why?
What adult perspectives, i.e. standards, health and safety, time, goals are on my mind?

Examining the physical/social/emotional environment
How is the organization and use of the physical space and materials impacting this situation?
In what ways are the routines, adult behaviors and language undermining or strengthening the children's ability to demonstrate their competence?
How could we strengthen relationships here?

Seeking the child's point of view
How do I understand the children's point of view in this situation?
What might the child be trying to accomplish?
What developmental themes, ideas, or theories might the child be exploring?

Finding the details that engage your heart and mind
What details can I make visible to heighten the value of this experience?
Where do I see examples of children's strengths and competencies?
What is touching my heart and engaging my mind here?

Expanding perspectives through collaboration and research
What other perspectives could enhance my understanding of the meaning of this situation, i.e., perspectives of families, co-workers, colleagues?
How might issues of culture, family background, or popular media be influencing this situation?
What theoretical perspectives and child development principles could inform my understandings and actions?

Considering opportunities and possibilities for next steps
What values, philosophy and goals do I want to influence my response?
How can I build on previous experiences of individuals and the group?
Which learning goals could be focused on here?
What action should I take from my teaching repertoire and why?

Used with Permission © 2007 Deb Curtis and Margie Carter,
Learning Together with Young Children (Redleaf Press, 2008)
in collaboration with Ann Pelo

Be the Change You Wish to See in Your Program

by Elizabeth Beavers and Donna Kirkwood

> Cassie was thrilled to walk across the stage to receive her diploma. She had finally completed her bachelor's degree in Early Childhood Education and was excited to move forward with her career. But when she reentered her Head Start classroom the following Monday, she felt the same as she always had. She didn't feel more prepared, more professional, or more qualified to teach her class of three-year-olds than she had before. She needed some guidance, so she set up an appointment with one of her former professors.
>
> In their meeting, Cassie and her professor discussed various career options in Early Childhood Education. Cassie wanted to move up within Head Start, find an administrative position within the field or become a professional trainer, but really feel didn't feel prepared for any of these positions yet. Her professor reminded her that with only a few years' experience, she might have trouble moving up. And if she wanted to lead or train other teachers, she really needed to hone her skills in her own classroom first. Cassie decided to start by critically examining her practices and working to create the best classroom she could, which would help prepare her to be a trainer or an administrator when the time was right.

Cassie has the right idea. One of the most important factors in being an effective teacher is critically reflecting on our practice. To do so, we need to know what best practices look like, and take the time to reflect regularly so that we are continually learning and improving ourselves.

Identifying Best Practices

There are many tools that can be used to assess classroom quality. Several that are highly regarded are the *Early Childhood Environment Rating Scale (ECERS-R)* (Harms, Clifford, & Cryer, 2005), the *Preschool Program Quality Assessment (PQA)* (High-Scope Educational Research Foundation, 2003), and the *Classroom Assessment Scoring System (CLASS)* (Pianta, LaParo, & Harme, 2007). These assessments look at classroom environment, interactions, and program components that are beneficial to children. Each requires training to use the instruments effectively and can be quite costly. However, teachers don't necessarily have to invest in pricey assessments to understand best practices. Library and online research can provide valuable information about best practices that can be incorporated into a checklist for teachers that can be used to assess quality. Websites hosted by organizations including the National Association for the Education of Young Children (www.naeyc.org), Zero to Three (www.zerotothree.

org), and Child Care Aware (www.childcareaware.org) have resources that can be compiled to create a list of expectations for classrooms based on research regarding what is best for children.

> Cassie had copies of several classroom assessments from her college coursework. She began by completing an ECERS-R assessment on her own classroom. Initially, she was surprised to discover that there were several areas where she needed to add materials. (She needed to add more accessories to her block center and make the science center more inviting.) She also learned that she was not allowing the children to talk as much as she had thought. According to the ECERS-R, she needed to ask more open-ended questions and encourage more positive interactions among the children.
>
> Cassie immediately got to work on improving her classroom. She added new cars, animals, and people to her block center. She moved the science center to a more prominent place in her classroom and committed to switching out the materials regularly to maintain the children's interest. Then she asked her director to complete an observation of her classroom using the ECERS-R so they could compare assessments.
>
> Cassie's director noticed the changes Cassie had made, but believed that Cassie still needed some help with her interactions with the children. She located a local training on communicating with preschoolers and suggested that Cassie attend. Cassie got a lot out of the training; as a result, she started communicating with the children on their level (bending down or sitting in a low chair so that they were eye to eye), asked the children more questions and gave the children time to respond. In turn, the children began asking more questions of their own and listening to each other more intently. When her director did a follow-up observation, she was pleased to see how much more the children were communicating with Cassie and with each other.

Reflection

In addition to knowing exactly what best practices look like, teachers need time to try new methods, reflect on their teaching practice, and explore new ideas. In the busy preschool classroom, teachers need time to consider what is working and what is not. This practice can empower teachers and improve communication and collaboration among staff. When teachers take the time to work together, reflect on their practices and plan for the future, they can solve their own problems, improve their practices in a supportive environment, and better understand the needs of the children and families in their care.

According to the literature, reflection is an "inner dialogue with oneself" (Cambell-Jones & Cambell-Jones, 2002, p. 134) in which an individual examines his or her experiences, beliefs, and perceptions in a way that transforms both thinking and practices (Bell, 2001; Mezirow, 1990; Shulman, 1995; Taggart & Wilson, 2005). Schön (1987) believes that experimentation plays a significant role; teachers should be encouraged to think about their teaching in new ways and generate creative solutions.

Teachers who reflect build new skill sets and become more effective teachers (Marzano, 2012; Zeichner & Liston, 1996). When teachers become reflective practitioners, they move beyond mere knowledge and presence in the classroom to a place where they continually integrate information and modify their skills. Through self-reflection, teachers become aware of how they can truly make an impact in the quality of interactions and meaningful experiences they provide to children.

> Wendy, one of Cassie's colleagues, asked her what she was doing to make her classroom run so much more smoothly, and asked her to complete an assessment in her classroom, too. Wendy was really pleased with how well she did on the assessment, but also found a few areas where improvements were needed. Cassie noticed that Wendy spent a lot of time disciplining her students for running in the room. They worked together to rearrange the learning centers so that all centers could be supervised, were separated by physical barriers, allowed sufficient space for several activities to go on at one time, and minimized traffic patterns that interfered with the children's play. They also separated the quieter centers (reading, math, and science) from the louder centers (blocks and dramatic play). As a result of the furniture rearrangement, the running stopped, the children played more independently in the centers, and Wendy was able to spend more time interacting with them rather than disciplining them.
>
> Using the ECERS-R, Cassie and Wendy were able to objectively assess their classrooms and make the improvements needed. They realized that as they began the process of evaluation, reflection, and improvement, their classrooms started to run more smoothly. Cassie and Wendy realized that this was something that they needed to do on a regular basis and decided to meet once a week to reflect on their classrooms and work together to solve problems.
>
> After a few weeks, their director approached Cassie and Wendy about mentoring some of the other teachers in the program who had noticed the positive changes in their classrooms. Cassie and Wendy started by training the teachers on how to use the ECERS-R and then set up weekly small group reflection meetings, so teachers who wanted to participate could attend the meeting that fit their schedules best.

Mentoring

Critical reflection is a learned skill that is fine-tuned through experiences in which we analyze our beliefs, expectations, and assumptions (Mezirow, 1990). Directors, teachers, or other facilitators can model reflection and support teachers until they internalize the process and can do it independently. This might include the facilitator asking directed, open-ended questions and supporting problem solving and conflict resolution by examining experiences from different perspectives. For instance, if a teacher mentions that the children in her class consistently fight over a favorite toy, the facilitator might ask, "Why do you think this continues to happen?" then "What do you think you could do to prevent this from happening again?" The facilitator might offer specific guidance or allow the teachers to brainstorm and try out new ideas before coming back together to reflect and discuss more. By emphasizing a process approach to developing reflective skills, facilitators can help teachers by initially using frequent structured, yet facilitated, dialogue to promote teachers' independent reflection (Marzano, 2012). The goal is for teachers to internalize the process of reflecting.

> Cassie, Wendy, and their coworkers enjoyed meeting together to discuss teaching practices and planned improvements. By inviting each other to observe in their classrooms, they developed a level of trust they hadn't experienced before. Sometimes they asked their director for help in making needed changes. Their director kept notes and planned professional development based on teachers' individual and group needs.
>
> By the end of the year, most of the teachers were attending the weekly reflection meetings. While no classroom was perfect (that wasn't the goal), when things weren't going well, the teachers knew where to look for
>
> *continued*

answers and had a supportive group to help them reflect and plan. This system worked so well that the director built reflection time into the schedule for everyone the following year. And Cassie was invited to a Head Start program nearby to train their teachers on classroom assessment and reflection. Her career was evolving just as her classroom was.

Summary

Reflection is a skill that must be nurtured and developed. When partnered with very specific guidelines and expectations, reflection can help teachers to improve their practices and provide better care for children. And as Cassie found, engaging in reflection of her own practices served as a catalyst to change for her coworkers, a change in the program's commitment to professional development for staff, and to her creating an opportunity to explore a teacher training role with her coworkers and local early childhood educators.

References

Bell, M. (2001). Supported reflective practice: A programme of peer observation and feedback for academic teaching development. *The International Journal for Academic Development*, 6(1), 29–39.

Cambell-Jones, B., & Cambell-Jones, F. (2002). Educating African-American children: Credibility at the crossroads. *Educational Horizons*, 80(3), 133–139.

Harms, T., Clifford, M., & Cryer, D. (2005). *Early childhood environment rating scale* (Revised edition). New York: Teachers College Press.

HighScope Educational Research Foundation (2003). *Preschool program quality assessment* (2nd edition). Ypsilanti, MI: HighScope Press.

Ideas for Teachers

Implementing Best Practices:

- Enhance your knowledge of best practices.
- Consider classroom experiences from the children's perspective.
- Don't be afraid to try new things.

Participating in Reflection:

- Be open to the process.
- Trust your instincts and the advice of coworkers.
- Be mindful of different perspectives.
- Remember that the goal is to provide meaningful experiences for children.

Pianta, R. C., LaParo, K. M., & Harme, B. K. (2007). *Classroom assessment scoring system*. New York: Paul H. Brookes.

Marzano (2012). *Becoming a reflective teacher*. Bloomington, IN: Marzano Research Laboratory.

Merizow, J., and Associates (1990). *Fostering critical reflection in adulthood*. San Francisco: Jossey-Bass.

Schön, D. A. (1987). *Educating the reflective practitioner: Toward a new design for teaching and learning in the professions*. San Francisco: Jossey-Bass.

Shulman, L. S. (1995). "Knowledge and teaching: Foundations of the new reform." In A. C. Ornstein, & L. S. Behar (eds.), *Contemporary issues in curriculum* (pp. 10–18). New York: Allyn and Bacon.

Taggart, G. L., & Wilson, A. P. (2005). *Promoting reflective thinking in teachers* (2nd edition). Thousand Oaks, CA: Corwin Press.

Zeichner, K. M., & Liston, D. P. (1996). *Reflective teaching*. New Jersey: Lawrence Erlbaum.

Web Resources

Child Care Aware: www.childcareaware.org

Classroom Assessment Scoring System (CLASS): www.teachstone.org/about-the-class/

Environmental Rating Scales: http://ers.fpg.unc.edu

HighScope: www.highscope.org

National Association for the Education of Young Children: www.naeyc.org

Zero to Three: www.zerotothree.org

Dr. Elizabeth Beavers

Dr. Elizabeth Beavers has over 20 years of experience teaching and working with school systems, preschools, and Head Starts in the fields of early childhood and special education. She has served as a classroom teacher, a program coordinator, a consultant, trainer, and teacher educator. Elizabeth is presently an Assistant Professor at the University of Houston–Clear Lake. Her areas of expertise include teacher education (critical and reflective thinking) and instructional/intervention pedagogy in early childhood/early childhood special education.

Donna Kirkwood

Donna Kirkwood has a PhD in Child Development from Texas Woman's University and is currently an Assistant Professor of Early Childhood Education at the University of Houston–Clear Lake. Her research interests are high-quality environments for young children, developmentally appropriate curriculum, and critical thinking and reflection.

Ideas for Administrators

Articulating Best Practices:

- Provide access to published tools such as *ECERS-R* (Harms, Clifford, & Cryer, 2005), *PQA* (HighScope Educational Research Foundation, 2003), or *CLASS* (Pianta, LaParo, & Harme, 2007) for teachers who want to assess their own practices.

- Provide feedback and encouragement through the assessment and change process.

- Provide support as teachers make improvements in their classrooms.

Encouraging Reflection:

- Provide adequate time and space.

- Create a sense of trust and community.

- Provide appropriate guidance and step back whenever possible.

- Celebrate successes and expect setbacks.

- Remember to reflect on your own practices.